QUESTION TIME

Also by Mark Mason

The Importance of Being Trivial
Walk the Lines
Move Along Please
Mail Obsession

QUESTION TIME

A Journey Round Britain's Quizzes

MARK MASON

WEIDENFELD & NICOLSON

First published in Great Britain in 2017
by Weidenfeld & Nicolson

1 3 5 7 9 10 8 6 4 2

A CIP catalogue record for this book
is available from the British Library.

ISBN 978 1474604598

Typeset at The Spartan Press Ltd,
Lymington, Hants

Printed and bound by the CPI Group (UK) Ltd,
Croydon, CR0 4YY

Weidenfeld & Nicolson

The Orion Publishing Group Ltd
Carmelite House
50 Victoria Embankment
London, EC4Y 0DZ
An Hachette UK Company
www.orionbooks.co.uk

MIX
Paper from
responsible sources
FSC
www.fsc.org   FSC® C104740

INTRODUCTION

· · · · · · ·

'Rachel Uchitel, thirty-four. Kalika Moquin, twenty-seven. Jaimee Grubbs, twenty-four.'

Even as Marcus started on the names, I sensed this was going to be a really good question.

'Cori Rist, thirty-one. Mindy Lawton, thirty-four. Theresa Rogers, forty.'

I also sensed, watching him seated at the bar, microphone in hand, that the answer would require a team effort. A germ of an idea was sprouting in my brain, but I needed someone to nourish it.

'Joslyn James, thirty-nine. Jamie Jungers, twenty-six. These, and no doubt many others – what links them?'

Our team huddled together. The germ had been planted by two factors. 'They sound American,' I said. 'Those names – Cori, Mindy, Jaimee. The women have to be American.' Nods of agreement from the other four heads. 'And the ages – they're all in their twenties and thirties, apart from the forty-year-old. No one older than that. Could they be models?'

Again, the thinking met with approval. 'Adult film stars, perhaps?' replied Martin. 'Some of the names sound made up.' But this wouldn't be enough of a link for a question. Not in one of Marcus Berkmann's quizzes: he's better than that.

We ummed and ahhed for a while. Then inspiration struck. 'How about affairs?' I said. 'Could they all have had an affair with the same man?'

Laura slapped the table. 'Tiger Woods. I bet they're all women Tiger Woods slept with.'

And at that we sat back, safe in the knowledge we'd bagged it. That's one of the hallmarks of a great question: you know when you've got the right answer. As soon as Laura said the golfer's name, we remembered the press reports from the previous few months, the names emerging day by day, the impression gradually building that Woods had slept with the entire female population of the planet. Although as Laura was very keen to point out, this impression was – to her certain knowledge – false.

That was in a north London pub called the Prince of Wales in 2010. Today, in my home in Suffolk, I reflect on the question, mentally noting its 'you're sure when you've got it' quality. I am about to embark on a tour of Britain's quizzes – from pubs to radio studios, hotels to museums – and working out what makes the perfect question will be a crucial element of my journey. Come to think of it, the 'teamwork' aspect is a key one too. I'd got halfway to the answer, but it took Laura to complete the job. This, I have found over many years' experience of quizzing, is often the way. Different types of brain and different databases of knowledge will combine to achieve a task that would defeat any single participant. Trivia is a sociable enough substance at any time – the sheer joy of sharing the fact, for instance, that Frank Sinatra was buried with a bottle of Jack Daniel's in his pocket – but put it in a quiz and its bonding qualities are legion.

Another wonderful thing about quizzes is the scope they offer for breathing new life into a subject you thought you knew. I was once presented with the question: 'This 1962 film was named after one of its main characters. It has, at the latest count, spawned twenty-one sequels, though the character in question hasn't appeared in any of them. Which film?' We talked and thought and thought and talked, but despite our toil my teammates and I couldn't work it out. When the questionmaster revealed the answer,[1] our heads hit the table. What was

---

1 *Doctor No.*

particularly annoying was that in listing famous long-running movie franchises we had, of course, mentioned James Bond. But somehow our minds hadn't spotted the twist – that the film is named after the villain rather than the hero – and we'd moved on. As Q was always saying to 007: 'Pay attention.'

You can even learn things when you're the one *setting* a quiz. This happened with a round I did at the Prince of Wales. It was a 'linked' round, in other words one where the answers somehow relate to each other, meaning that even if you can't get a question first time round you might be able to work it out when the link has become clear. This round started with: 'Which type of food is sometimes made in Shanghai from deer placenta and in Mexico from cow stomach?' The second question was: 'The last line of dialogue in *The Italian Job* is "Hang on a minute, lads, I got a great idea." But Michael Caine then adds another short word – in fact he adds it twice. Which word?' Question three: 'The Scottish football team Inverness Caledonian Thistle are often known by which two-syllable nickname?' The answers were 'soup', 'er' and 'Cally' – yes, the link was that all ten answers ran together to make 'supercalifragilisticexpialidocious'. The 'tic' part, for instance, was taken care of with a question about Carolyn Davidson, the graphic design student who in 1971 received $35 for designing Nike's now legendary 'tick' logo.[2] The penultimate syllable was easy – 'what is a female deer called?' – but the best I could come up with for the final sound was a question about the rhyme scheme in 'Groove Is in the Heart' ('not vicious, or malicious, just lovely and delicious'). As my friend Chris handed in his team's answers he said he'd thought I was going to ask: 'What name do skiers use for a straight, as opposed to swerving, downhill run?' Until that night I'd never heard of the *schuss*. After that night I'm never going to forget it.

Patterns are important too. I've known this ever since my

---

2 In 1983 the company's boss added to her remuneration with a diamond and gold ring, together with an undisclosed number of Nike shares.

first non-fiction book, which examined why trivia fascinates us so much.[3] An interview with a Cambridge professor revealed that some of us (predominantly men, though plenty of women as well) have 'systemising' brains – that is, we love order, logic and patterns. So when someone tells us about the choir on Tina Turner's 'We Don't Need Another Hero' including a young Lawrence Dallaglio, we remember that the choir on the *Mr Bean* theme tune included a young Chuka Umunna. And patterns can be useful to quizzers. In 2014, during the Tower of London's display of ceramic poppies, one for every British soldier killed during the First World War, the person setting the Sunday night pub quiz in my village asked how many poppies there were in total. The answer – 888,246 – lodged itself in my memory. How could it not be? All those eights, then the count of two-four-six: the pattern was beautiful, even if the events it denoted were not.

Similarly, sequences can be an inspiration when you're setting questions. A while ago I learned about Richard Drax, the Conservative MP for South Dorset. The surname rang a bell, I looked him up, and sure enough he is indeed related to Reginald Drax, the friend of Ian Fleming: the Bond author named Hugo Drax, the villain in *Moonraker*, after him. Within seconds a question had formed in my mind: what links a Conservative MP called Richard, a cricket commentator called Henry and a cab driver in Bath called Dave? The cricket commentator is Henry Blofeld, whose father Thomas (another friend of Fleming) gave his name to the famous Bond villain, while Dave Scaramanga is the grandson of George Scaramanga, the school colleague whose surname Fleming used in *The Man with the Golden Gun*. There's also the architect Erno Goldfinger, but although Fleming borrowed his name the two weren't friends. In fact, Fleming hated Goldfinger's brutalist buildings. Erno threatened to sue, but decided against it when Fleming said he would rename the character 'Goldprick'.

---

3 *The Importance of Being Trivial*. All good bookshops, and quite a few ropey ones too.

A good quiz is revealing of human nature. For a start, it gives the lie to that old chestnut about male competitiveness. The number of times I've heard women sitting there before a quiz saying: 'Now we don't want you blokes taking this seriously – it's just for fun, right?' And then three questions in they're gritting their teeth and muttering: 'We *have* to win this.' There's also the sheer test of character that is the 50-50 question. There are only two possible answers – you have to choose one, simple as that. That's 'simple' as in 'gut-wrenching nightmare which starts with you being almost sure it's A, then beginning to doubt yourself by thinking it could be B, then doubting your doubts, then doubting your doubts about your doubts, and so on in a game where your own psyche bluffs you into a sobbing, snivelling wreck'. The classic case is: 'Does the Queen face to the left or right on coins?' Whichever one you plump for, the other option then comes sneaking up on you like a neurological con man. Someone in your team will inevitably mention stamps, asking which way the monarch faces on those. Is it the same on both, you wonder, or are coins different? (If the team includes a husband and wife they may as well start consulting divorce lawyers now.) In the end you plump for left, only to discover that it's right. By which I mean left is wrong – she *faces* to the right.[4] It's particularly annoying because you handle coins day in, day out: how can the answer never have lodged itself in your brain? Incredible the things that escape our notice. Another question I failed on was: 'Its official title was "Blood Swept Lands and Seas of Red". How was it more popularly known?' The answer: those poppies at the Tower of London we were discussing only two paragraphs ago.

The places the great god Quiz will lead me into are bound to be many and varied. Quizzes for big business are now big business – I'm looking forward to seeing how a corporate evening turns out. Rather more competitively than a quiz in a village

---

4 Since Charles II monarchs have alternated – if one is left, the next will be right. But they always face left on stamps.

pub, I'd guess (then again, perhaps not). There's also the history of media quiz programmes to explore. I'll mine *Private Eye*'s 'Dumb Britain' column (Anne Robinson: 'In politics, what is the current occupation of David Blunkett?' Contestant: 'Blind.'). And I'll ask just what was going through the mind of *Bullseye* host Jim Bowen as he delivered the question: 'In which state of the United States was President Kennedy assassinated, in Texas?'

Of course, above and beyond all this, there's the trivia I'll discover simply by being on the road in the first place. The history and facts of the places I travel to and through, the stories that Britain seems to generate as if for fun. Perhaps I'll land in Woking, with a chance to visit the grave of Eadweard Muybridge, the man who in 1878 rigged up a series of cameras whose shutters were triggered by threads set off by a passing horse: the resulting photos settled the centuries-old debate over whether all four of the animal's feet are ever off the ground simultaneously.[5] Or I could venture to Winsford in Cheshire, home to the salt mine that keeps Britain's roads safe in winter – it owns the largest underground digger in the world, each scoop bagging a nifty 20 tons of salt. Then again there might be a trip to Dundee, whose two football stadiums (those of Dundee and Dundee United) are the closest together of any two British grounds. Centre spot to centre spot is just 300 yards.

Once you add in the facts I'll learn from the quizzes themselves, this is a project that should prove the old saying about travel broadening the mind. Who knows what you might discover as you sit there hunched over your answer sheet, pencil poised and brain cells humming? That hurricanes with male names kill fewer people than those with female names, because people treat them more seriously and so take better precautions? That the NFL abandoned their traditional Roman numerals for Superbowl 50, fearing that Americans would think 'L' stood for 'loser'? That Lord Kitchener disliked telling the Cabinet his war

---

5　They are, but when they're gathered under its body rather than when the legs are extended. This is why paintings from before that time look so unnatural.

plans because they'd all tell their wives, apart from Lloyd George 'who would tell someone else's wife'.

We shall see. All we know for now is that the microphone has been tapped, the host has cleared his throat, and round one is about to start. It's question time.

ONE

· · · · · · ·

The *Titanic* sank on 15 April 1912. Which two other
boats had famously sunk 15 days before?

It's on nights like this that the pub feels even more womb-
like than usual. We're a few short, dark days into the year,
and as I exit the Tube station at the bottom of Highgate Hill a
spiteful wind whips the litter into cartwheels. Ahead of me is
the climb to the Prince of Wales, which sits at the top of the
very steep hill. The next Tube station along would give me a
shorter, much flatter walk, but I always prefer doing it this way
because the exercise invigorates my brain cells for the quiz that
lies ahead. Ten minutes later I've reached the most villagey part
of Highgate, where the pub backs onto a Georgian square. Being
of an age with the other buildings it's on the small side, and if, as
happens almost every Tuesday, a few dozen people turn up for
the quiz then things can get rather snug.

Heading round to the left of the bar I find my team in its
traditional place, underneath the portrait of erstwhile local
boy John Betjeman. Toby and his wife Louise are sitting with
Martin. Toby is an actor and voiceover artist: portlier at 50 than
he once was (though who am I to talk), he does a fine line
in beards of various lengths and arrangements (the equivalent
options on the top half of his head no longer being available).
This month's effort is quite modest – everything gone but the
sideburns. Louise makes props for movies (*Spectre* and *Star*

Wars are among her latest projects), while Martin has just resigned from his job at a photographic stock agency. I only learned this by reading his two-line biog in the Boxing Day quiz of the national newspaper for which Marcus writes a weekly column.

Marcus had the idea of getting a few of us who regularly act as quizmaster here to contribute a round of questions each, and indeed it is this that's under discussion as I join the table. We pick out our highlights. All of us, for instance, liked: 'The *Titanic* sank on 15 April 1912. Which two other boats had famously sunk fifteen days before?' (Oxford and Cambridge in the Boat Race.) I had a soft spot for: 'In 1970 which English band replaced twelve letters of their name with a single dot?' (Tyrannosaurus Rex, by becoming T. Rex.) Having served a stretch in the Royal Shakespeare Company, Toby had no trouble with: 'Which TV drama, which ran for three series between 1991 and 1993, got its title from Shakespeare's sonnet eighteen, the one that begins "Shall I compare thee to a summer's day"?' (*The Darling Buds of May.*) Modesty prevents me from saying this in the pub, but I was rather chuffed with my own question: 'Where would you find a stock character from the Italian theatre form known as *commedia dell'arte*, a Spanish dance, a famous astronomer, the central character in *The Barber of Seville*, and an Arabic word meaning "in the name of Allah"?' One of those seems daunting at first, but as you gradually recall the character Scaramouche, or perhaps the fandango, or realise that the astronomer could be Galileo, it dawns on you that the answer is 'the lyrics to "Bohemian Rhapsody" by Queen'. The final two components, of course, are Figaro and Bismillah.

Martin's round in the Boxing Day quiz was a linked one. The answers formed pairs: for example, 'chalk' ('the Needles off the Isle of Wight are made of which kind of sedimentary rock?') and 'the Cheesegrater' ('how is the building by Richard Rogers at one-two-two Leadenhall Street in the City of London informally known?'). The thing about a linked round is that the questions in themselves might not be that entertaining: the fun is in spotting the connection. Though in this case I did learn that only one US President has appeared on a coin in his lifetime (Calvin Coolidge), and that the jerrycan was invented by the Nazis – hence its name, when you think about it, though it was originally called the 'Wehrmachtskanister'.[1]

As it happens, Martin is the quizmaster tonight as well, so after a while he stands up from our table, takes the two steps to the side of the bar reserved for said person and picks up the microphone. He reminds us all that the 9 p.m. start time is approaching, so he would be obliged if someone from each team could bring up the pound-per-person entry fee and collect an answer sheet. Soon we're off and running. The three remaining members of our team do moderately well in the first round, which is also linked. Our certainty about a couple of answers – the first character ever to speak in *EastEnders* (Dirty Den) and the chairman of the inquiry into JFK's assassination (Earl Warren) – gives us the theme of 'animal homes'. This inspires guesses on some of the other questions, such as the four-letter acronym by which a water tower in Hampshire, used for training submariners in emergency escape methods, is known. Remembering our badger terminology, we try 'SETT'. And we are right. It stands for 'Submarine Escape Training Tower'.

But despite mid-table respectability after round one, we're soon heading down the table. Against mostly larger teams (maximum size at the Prince of Wales is six) we're doomed. Not that I mind. Apart from anything else I'm sitting with friends having a few pints: if you want to understand the attraction of pub quizzes, never underestimate the importance of the first word. Winning is never the main reason for doing this: I'd much rather lose and learn something interesting than triumph with facts I already know. That is indeed the ethos of this whole project, so it feels good to be starting off on the right foot here

---

1 The national newspaper in question, by the way, is the *Independent*. Within only three months of our quiz appearing, the paper's print version will have ceased publication. Nice work, chaps.

in my regular venue, my spiritual quizzing home, my trivia base camp.

As the evening progresses I learn that the vinyl recordings of greetings and music on both Voyager spacecraft launched in the 1970s needed to be played, by any alien beings lucky enough to intercept them, not at any of the well-known speeds of 78 or 45 or 33⅓ rpm, but 16⅔ rpm. My favourite discovery, however, is the Diomede Islands. These lie in the Bering Strait, the short stretch of water separating the eastern bit of Siberia from the western bit of Alaska. This part of the world has always fascinated me. My childhood was played out against the global background of US–Soviet hostility, with the two empires billed respectively as 'the East' and 'the West'. Of course on a two-dimensional map this is exactly what they are. It was only much later, looking at the region on a globe, that I realised these two supposed opposites almost touch each other. The older I've grown, and the more I've come to believe that a lot of life's 'opposing pairs' are actually the same thing in different disguises, the more I've thought about those few miles of very cold water. Tonight Martin leads me to a new fact about it. Big Diomede (owned by Russia) and Little Diomede (owned by the United States) are only 2.5 miles apart – but because the International Date Line runs between them, they have a time difference of 21 hours. As Big D is starting its Friday, Little D is only three hours into Thursday. Indeed they're sometimes known as Tomorrow Island (Big) and Yesterday Isle (Little). I can't help seeing them as two brothers separated by one of those Perspex screens that divide prisoners from their visitors.

Another joy of a quiz you know you're not going to win is that you can sit back and watch the tussle to see who does. Tonight it goes all the way to the wire: two teams achieve scores of 74 out of a possible 80 (very impressive), so a tiebreaker is needed. Being a well-run quiz, the Prince of Wales has a tradition of properly thought out tiebreakers – in other words, one where the answer is a number you can't possibly know, so you have to make an educated guess. There's no point asking something where the answer is 'Paris' – if both teams know it, or indeed don't know it, the tie remains unbroken. Tonight Martin has a corker: 'What is the total number of words in *Ulysses* by James Joyce?'

One team thinks there are 130,000 words, the other 345,000, meaning they win because the correct answer is 264,834. It'll only net them a pound or so more per person, as the prizes are the entry fees split between the first three teams in a ratio of 3:2:1. But still, a winner has been identified, and this is what matters. Especially to them.

The Joyce question was actually the second tiebreaker of the evening. The Prince of Wales always uses one in the 'beer round', the mini-set of questions (five or six rather than the usual ten) that comes halfway through the evening. It doesn't count towards the quiz itself, but the winners earn themselves a round of drinks. This means that even if overall you're bombing, you've still got something to aim for, something with which you can all the more comprehensively drown your sorrows. Because there are fewer questions (and often they're quite easy), it's very common for several teams to get them all right, so the tiebreaker is always asked up front. Tonight Martin, clearly a fan of word-counts, asked how many there were on the front page of yesterday's *Guardian*. The answer was 1146. It's only now, as the evening draws to an end, that I wonder how Martin knew this.

'I counted them,' he says, calmly and matter-of-factly. Martin, like Toby, has a history in the performing arts, and indeed before he went into the more conventional work from which he has just resigned he used to comprise one half of a comedy duo called the Rubber Bishops. But you would never guess this from his conversational style. While the rest of us are noisily swapping stories and facts and questions and jokes, Martin will sit quietly, observing the general hubbub without feeling any need to rush into it. Only when the rest of us have shut up does he utter a pithy one-liner that brilliantly caps us all.

'Yes, obviously,' I reply, 'but how? Did you copy and paste

them from the web version into a Word document, then use the word-count function?'

'No. I just counted them. In the paper. With my finger.' It would seem that Martin isn't overly bothered about returning to the job market any time soon.

Even though the quiz itself is over, there is still the Snowball to be done. This, as its name implies, is a fund that rolls over from week to week, its coffers replenished by the sale of raffle tickets at a pound a go. If your ticket is drawn you go up and are given the choice of three envelopes, each of which contains a question. If you answer it correctly, you win £1000. If not, a second person gets a go for £500, then a third for £250. If none of the questions are answered correctly – and needless to say, with sums like this on offer, they're always difficult – it all starts again the following week. There is usually so much in the kitty that even if someone wins the grand, there'll still be another thousand (or something pretty near it) available next time.

Normally the Snowball is run by Chris, or if he's away then Marcus, but as neither of them are here tonight the duty has been delegated to Patrick. You'll recognise Patrick if you ever come to the quiz: a barrister of several decades' standing, he's the only regular who wears a suit. The pint glass full of raffle tickets is produced, and a number is drawn: 498. I have 492. OK, in a draw this size you're never going to be *that* far away, but despite the fact I've been coming to this quiz several times a year for the best part of a decade, I have never been called up for the Snowball. Not once. Just about every other regular or semi-regular I know has been chosen, some of them many times. But me – not a sniff. Statistically speaking this is so improbable I am considering penning a short monograph on the subject.

Bitterness aside, I watch as tonight's chosen contender selects his envelope (all the questions are equally easy, or rather difficult), then listen as Patrick delivers the question: 'In 1982, Keith Harris and Orville the Duck had a UK Top Ten hit with "Orville's Song".' Inevitably, from several points around the pub come falsetto renditions of the line 'I wish I could fly'. Then

Patrick continues: 'The song was written by which one-time winner of the TV talent show *Opportunity Knocks*?'

A perfect silence descends. It's a well-observed tradition that, with a thousand quid at stake, anyone who happens to know the answer keeps it to themselves, or at worst scribbles it on a piece of paper to show their teammates. You don't want to be the person who ruins everything with a misjudged 'whisper'. As it happens, no one does know the identity of the songwriter in question, so it's left to Patrick to reveal the name: Bobby Crush. I smile to myself, wondering what might have happened if my partner Jo had been here. As a young child she adored Bobby Crush, and when he looked up from his piano and gave one of his trademark smiles to the camera, her parents would tell Jo he was looking straight at her. Of course, she believed completely that this was how television worked, and was thrilled to think that her hero could see her.[2] If she had come along tonight, and her ticket had been drawn, and she had been faced with that question, would it have come back to her that Crush got his big break by winning *Opportunity Knocks*? Would she have thought 'he's as good a guess as any' and offered the name as her answer? Would she, in accepting her cheque for £1000, have had to rein in her usual sentiment of 'just shut up with your *bloody* facts will you, Mark?', and accept that sometimes trivia can actually have a purpose? Who knows? All I am certain of, reading up on the topic later, is that (a) Bobby Crush was not a stage name (he was born Robert Nicholas Crush) and (b) Orville was named after one of the Wright brothers. The joke is obvious when you think about the puppet's flightlessness, but somehow it had always eluded me.

The evening's other two Snowballs also defeat their challengers. We learn that as well as the Fibonacci numbers, the sequence where each number is added to the previous one to produce the next one (1, 2, 3, 5, 8, 13, 21, 34 and so on), there is

---

2 Message to today's kids: this was what it was like for us. Remember that as you flick between YouTube, Minecraft and Instagram on your iPhone.

a similar sequence but starting with the 2 *before* the 1 (hence 2, 1, 3, 4, 7, 11, 18 . . .) called the Lucas numbers. And that Public Image Ltd, John Lydon's band after he left the Sex Pistols, took their name from *The Public Image*, a 1968 novel by Muriel Spark. Given that the author owed her surname to husband Sidney Spark, which if shortened to 'Sid Spark' would make a great name for a punk, the connection is perhaps more appropriate than one might think.

There we go then. The opening quiz of the project is at an end. I say my farewells, but only for a week, as next Tuesday I'll be back here to take a turn on the quizmaster's stool. It's a lucky quirk of the London bus network that route 271 runs from Highgate to Finsbury Square, just round the corner from Liverpool Street station, departure point of my trains to Suffolk. At this time on a Tuesday night there are so few passengers it might as well be a private taxi. As usual, when we pass through Islington I notice the mailbox rental shop whose window banner proclaims: 'Prestigeous London Mailing Address'. Surely if you're *really* prestigious you can spell 'prestigious'? But then sometimes mistakes are endearing. A friend of mine once attended a quiz where the host asked: 'Which desert was named after a famous female opera singer?' Assuming he meant Peach Melba, came the cries, he might care to add another 's' to the enquiry.

* * *

Back at home, I set about planning the project's next moves. There's Highgate on Tuesday, obviously, but also a friend has told me about a forthcoming quiz in one of London's most famous buildings. He'll be attending, and after checking with the organiser he confirms that it's OK for me to go along too. What's more, one of Martin's questions has reminded me of a city I haven't visited for years, and when some initial digging reveals that it's crawling with quizzes, I mark it down as my first long-haul trip.

So there are those three events to look forward to. Sadly

something that won't be happening is 'Stewpot's Music Quiz Tour'. This was to have been a series of evenings at which legendary BBC radio DJ Ed 'Stewpot' Stewart would host music quizzes in venues around the country. Unfortunately, less than a week ago Ed took the needle off the vinyl for the last time and headed to the big presenter's chair in the sky. The organisers of the tour have left the website in place, so it can act 'as a tribute to the great entertainer and broadcaster'. Accordingly I am able to read, as one of 'Ten Facts You May Not Know About Stewpot', that he once played a request on his show for the Queen Mother. She was a great fan, it seems, and so for the old girl's 80th birthday her daughter Margaret wrote in to ask if her favourite record could be played. What do you think that song was? Something by Perry Como? Bit of Nat King Cole? No, she wanted 'Car 67' by Driver 67, a 1978 novelty record in which a West Midlands minicab controller asks one of his drivers to make a pick-up from a certain address, only to learn that the passenger is the driver's ex-girlfriend. The Queen Mother liked the tune because it was 'a touching story about real human life'.

Another result of my web-hopping is that I'm reminded how common internet quizzes have become. As with most things in cyberspace their quality varies enormously, and they're not really what the project is supposed to be about (the aim is to tour Britain, not sit at home in front of a computer), but for the hell of it I decide to test myself on just the one. It has been put together by the TV channel Dave, who say that the 'intellectual honour' of the nation depends on visitors to their website achieving a high score. Who am I to let them down? So I click on 'start'. The thing about an online quiz is that it has to be multi-choice: despite advances in artificial intelligence, a computer still can't mark individually entered responses. There are differences in spellings, issues like Holland also being called the Netherlands, a whole host of reasons why some disembodied intelligence is just not as trustworthy as a bloke with a pencil sitting at a bar going 'yeah, they can have half a point for that'. But, of course, this also means that online quiz scores tend to exaggerate your intelligence. With four answers to choose from each time (as is the case here), someone who didn't know a single one of the answers could expect to get 5 out of 20 simply by guessing.

Needless to say, this doesn't stop me taking my score of 18 out of 20 as evidence of extreme genius. Only a couple of my answers are out-and-out stabs in the dark. I am afforded the chance to show that I know the capital of Australia (Canberra – built precisely because Sydney and Melbourne were incapable of agreeing which of them should get the nod), and the location of Leeds Castle (Kent). The old chestnut about which man-made landmark can be seen from space is easily negotiated: the answer is 'none'. Definitions of 'space' vary, but most experts use Theodore von Karman's '100 kilometres from Earth' (where the atmosphere becomes too thin to support aeronautical flight), and at that distance you're not going to make out a wall, not even the famous one in China. Another question concerns Del Boy's vehicle in *Only Fools and Horses*. I remember reading that it isn't actually a Robin Reliant, and I'm right: it's a Reliant Regal Supervan. But of course what really delights me about the quiz is not what I know but what I don't know. The official language of Brazil is Portuguese rather than Brazilian. One of the early European explorers of what we now call America rejoiced in the name Juan Ponce de León. And the record for the most UK Christmas number ones is held by... the Beatles. How had this escaped my attention? I know *loads* of Beatles trivia. George Harrison wrote 'Here Comes the Sun' in Eric Clapton's garden... John Lennon used to introduce himself as 'John Lemon'... 'She Loves You' is two versions stitched together (listen to the edit after 'I think it's only fair' – you'll wonder how you ever missed it)... and yet I didn't know that their count of four festive chart-toppers (three in a row from 1963–65) remains unbeaten. Yet another achievement by the Fabs, as the band are known to their most ardent followers.

Can I count myself among that grouping? Clearly not.

* * *

The following Tuesday rolls around, and the Prince of Wales bar stool beckons. It's a relatively quiet night, with only the nine teams – good from my point of view, as it makes the marking easier. Marcus is here this week. He asks how the project is going, and soon we're discussing 'topics on which we've set the most questions'. One of mine is the Apollo moon landings – they're in there again tonight, with 'how many men had walked on the moon before Pete Conrad walked on the moon?' (You'll discover the answer shortly.) Marcus says his are probably James Bond and *Dad's Army*. 'They've both been around continuously since the nineteen-sixties,' he explains, 'and they both represent a particular sort of Britishness.' You could say the same about Marcus – in his mid-fifties he's still rereading the P. G. Wodehouse novels he fell in love with as a boy. The Britishness point helps explain why the American version of *Dad's Army* never got any further than its pilot episode. And it's a big part of the attraction of quizzing. Questions often take you to treasured parts of our national identity, the shared back-story that binds us all together. That's what makes quizzes so nice. Forgive the word – I know 'nice' is horrible – but it's the only word that works. It captures the fun of a quiz, its generosity of spirit, its desire to dwell on the interesting things in life rather than the horrible ones. This is true of Marcus himself, actually, which is why I like him so much. He has the air of someone so familiar with this world's vicissitudes that their barbs no longer bother him (thirty years as a freelance writer does that to a man). Don't get me wrong, his spleen still gets vented from time to time: I witnessed one argument in which Marcus stated his position on Led Zeppelin with astonishing firmness. (He did so by inserting a third word into the middle of their name, a word beginning with 'F'.) But by and large, calmness and benevolence reign. Especially when he's drunk. Marcus is the happiest drunk I know. At the end of an evening, when speech has deserted him completely, he communicates entirely by smiles.

Tonight his team are adopting the name 'Newly Minted Murray', in honour of Britain's tennis hero becoming a father. The news-based pun is one of several possible naming options at a quiz. Another is a play on the word 'quiz'. One team here at Highgate always call themselves 'Qwysiwyg' (taken from the internet acronym for 'what you see is what you get'), and tonight they are joined by 'Agatha Quiztie'. Younger teams have been known to choose 'Quizteam Aguilera'.

My first question is the equivalent of 'one off the mark', the deliberately generous run you give to weaker batsmen in friendly cricket matches. ' "I didn't hit him, but it came close. For reasons best known to himself, he came on unwilling to talk." That was said by somebody who died in January 2016 about somebody else who died in January 2016. Who are those two people?'

The deaths of Terry Wogan and David Bowie are fresh enough in everyone's memory for this to count as a gentle opener. After that things get trickier, though not always as tricky as they might first appear. Question seven is about Ingvar Kamprad, who grew up on a farm called Elmtaryd near the village of Agunnaryd in Sweden. I ask what he founded in 1943. Even those who don't already know will soon realise what happens if you put the first letters of his forename and surname next to those of the farm and the village. Other questions are multi-choice. 'Which of these three celebrities,' for instance, 'did not choose the *Mona Lisa* as their *Desert Island Discs* luxury? Arthur Scargill, Murray Walker, Cilla Black.'[3]

Then there's the question about the Perth Agreement. This, everyone is informed, came into effect on 26 March 2015, immediately affecting a boy called Tane and a girl called Senna. Then on 2 May 2015 it affected somebody else. To what does the Perth Agreement relate? Only two teams get it: the succession to the British throne. It was the protocol (negotiated in the Australian city by Commonwealth leaders) that allowed females

---

3 Murray Walker. He wanted a hammock.

to take their place in line without having to wait for younger brothers. So Princess Charlotte (born on 2 May 2015) won't be bumped down the queue by any male siblings she acquires. To have given her name might have made it too obvious. Tane and Senna, on the other hand, are sufficiently unknown. In fact that was one of the attractions of writing the question – the chance to let people know that the daughter of the Duke of Gloucester gave her kids names you might normally hear bellowed outside an Aldi in Southend. After the quiz is over someone will pay me the ultimate compliment, saying their favourite questions were the ones – like this – that they didn't know.

Neuroscientists will tell you that the human brain uses two sorts of intelligence: 'crystallised' and 'fluid'. Crystallised intelligence is, put bluntly, the stuff you know – capital cities, dates of battles, who was in *Ghostbusters*, that sort of thing. Fluid intelligence, on the other hand, is the ability to work things out, to use information and process it. A good quiz should test both. Simpler questions will require crystallised intelligence: tonight, for example, I ask who has scored more goals in the history of the English Premier League than anyone else. It's a fair bet that most teams will contain at least one football fan, and that the correct answer (Alan Shearer) will be within their reach. But other enquiries are there to check your brain's fluidity. 'Noel Edmonds,' runs the fourth question in round two, 'damaged Elton John's garden, and Nick Mason of Pink Floyd damaged Jeremy Clarkson's garden, in the same way. How?' You're very unlikely to have seen the two television programmes, several years apart, in which I heard those anecdotes. But you should be able to have a stab at it. What do we know about Noel Edmonds, what do we know about Nick Mason, how might the two overlap? True enough, six of the nine teams work it out – 'by landing their helicopter on it'. Mason maintains that he did Clarkson a favour: the two grooves he left in the croquet lawn should make the game all the easier.

As ever when presenting a quiz I take great care to avoid reading out the answers by mistake. You'd think this was a pretty basic error to avoid, but speak to anyone who's hosted more than a handful of quizzes and you'll find they've all done it. My face-reddener came here at the Prince of Wales, with a question that ran: 'About which performer did the cartoonist Bob Thaves once say: "She had to do everything her partner had to do, except backwards and in high heels?" ' Going on to give a little background information about the question (often a nice thing to do – it reassures everyone you know your stuff), I added that some people attribute the quote to Ginger Rogers hersel... ah. There was a short silence as everyone worked out what I'd done, then the laughter started. What amazed me was that some teams still went on to get the question wrong.

At least I'm in good company. As we mentioned a while back, Jim Bowen gave away the answer to that JFK question on *Bullseye*. In fact, that was one of the programme's more subtle mistakes. It dates from the era of shaky sets, minuscule production budgets and inept planning, a time when British TV was only entertaining if it went wrong. For one episode the 'S' in the illuminated 'BULLSEYE' sign at the back of the studio audience wouldn't light up. No problem, thought the floor manager, we'll get that big fat bloke to sit in front of it, and put him on a couple of phone directories. This only made the problem all the more obvious. Another time a wheelchair-bound contestant, whose partner had already answered their questions correctly, only needed a score of ten on the dartboard to win the star prize. Suddenly the producer screamed in Jim Bowen's earpiece: 'Stop him throwing! It's the three-piece suite! What will he want a three-piece suite for, him in a wheelchair? Give us a minute to line the other prize up.' Bowen stalled by saying there'd been a technical problem, then asked the player to throw again. Sure enough he got the score with his first dart, allowing Bowen to cue the video clip which revealed the prize. It was a skiing holiday.

Tonight's excitement centres on the two tiebreakers. The one at the end of the beer round concerns the world record, set recently by a 14-year-old American, for the quickest time to solve a standard Rubik's Cube. Marcus's team guess 6.39 seconds, the team next to them – a couple of lads in their early twenties who have laughed off their lowly ranking in the quiz proper, meaning I'm really cheering for them in the beer round – guess 6.7 seconds. Sadly the answer is 4.9 seconds, so the lads don't even get any free booze. They also laugh this off, which makes me like them all the more. Marcus's team then repeat their triumph in the tiebreaker at the end of the quiz, which is needed to decide who will creep into the money – a whopping £8 – by coming third. We return to *Guinness World Records*, and ask 'To how many decimal places did Rajveer Meena memorise and recite pi in his record-breaking feat of March 2015?' Now That the Life is Gone (an unnecessarily morose team name, I feel) guess 24,701, Newly Minted Murray guess 70,000. Or rather they don't guess it, they know it – one of them clearly read the news report at the time, as I did. Seventy thousand places it is. Obviously Rajveer felt like stopping at a round number.

Marcus, fresh from this triumph, comes up to oversee the Snowball. Obeying tradition I manage to avoid being chosen, and none of the people who are can answer their questions, so the £1000 rolls over yet again. Tonight's punters are left with nothing more than their drinks and the facts they've learned from my questions. That even though the standing long jump hasn't been an Olympic event since 1912, for instance, it is still used by the Brazilian police as an entry test (2.14 metres for men, 1.66 metres for women). That Noel Gallagher has only ever read one novel (*On the Road* by Jack Kerouac). That red appears on more of the world's 192 national flags than any other colour. There was also a 50-50 question: 'The Queen and Prince Philip – one prefers a bath in the morning, the other prefers a shower. Which way round is it?'[4]

The final round was a linked one, the answers (or parts thereof) forming the phrase 'to be or not to be, that is the question'. This was where Pete Conrad came in – he was the

---

4 Queen bath, Philip shower.

third man to walk on the moon, so there were *two* before him.
'That' was dealt with by Take That, who were the solution to
a question designed to entertain rather than tax – in other
words one where the answer becomes clear very quickly but
the information it contains is interesting: 'The members of
which pop group had the following experiences in the years
between 1996 and 2005? One attended South Trafford College
to study for A-levels. One considered drowning himself in the
River Thames but settled in the end for working as a DJ. One
buried his deceased iguana Nirvana under a pile of leaves while
singing "Smells Like Teen Spirit". One was dismayed to see dolls
of himself being given away for free in his local Toys R Us.
One signed an eighty-million-pound record deal with EMI and
became one of the best-selling British solo artists of all time.'
The members were (in order) Jason, Howard, Mark, Gary and
– of course – Robbie. The question paints an even more vivid
picture because of the reversal in fortunes since 2005. That's
showbiz, folks.

* * *

It's hard to imagine a building less like the Prince of Wales as
a host for the next quiz. I'm heading there in the dark of an
early Wednesday evening, mentally noting some of the differences. The pub has just the one bar – this place has nine, plus 19
restaurants. The pub has no staircases (at least none the punters
can use) – this place has 100. The pub has never had its own
rifle range – this place has, and what's more it survived until just
a few months ago. The venue also has over a thousand rooms,
three miles of corridors, its own gym and its own hair salon.
The current building dates from the 1840s, though there's been a
structure with the same name on this site since the Middle Ages.
Tonight's venue is the Palace of Westminster.

I am here for the annual Parliamentary Press Gallery quiz.
The policeman at St Stephen's Entrance directs me down the
long ramp leading to the scanning room, where the security

staff handle the usual 'coins in the tray' routine with a friendliness their counterparts at several major airports would do well to imitate. Having been issued with a pass I head for Central Lobby, where I'm to meet Patrick Kidd, who writes about politics for *The Times*. This means heading through the vast expanse of Westminster Hall, the oldest surviving bit of the Palace, dating back even further than the Middle Ages – it was built in 1097. There's a lot of guff talked about 'our island story' by tiresome people who favour the words 'majesty', 'splendour' and 'redolent', and normally you want to get as far away from them as quickly as possible in case you nod off. But it's simply impossible to stand in Westminster Hall without feeling awed by the sheer amount of history that's happened here. Several monarchs and assorted members of the great and good have lain in state here, the exact spots marked by brass plaques set into the stone floor. Strange to think as you pass over the Queen Mother's that one of the Household Cavalry officers standing guard over her coffin was the future pop star James Blunt.

In one corner of the Hall is the entrance to St Mary Undercroft, the chapel where Emily Davison, the suffragette who would one day die by throwing herself under the King's horse at the Derby, gained some earlier publicity for the cause. On the night of 2 April 1911 she hid in a tiny room off the chapel, not coming out until the next morning. That had been the night of the census, and so Davison was able to record her place of residence as the House of Commons. This at a time when as a woman she couldn't stand for Parliament, or even vote. By 1959 the rules had changed, and one of the women elected that year was Margaret Thatcher. To bring the tale full circle, in 2013 St Mary Undercroft was where Thatcher's body spent its last night before her funeral.

At the far end of the hall I climb the stone steps and notice another brass plaque, this one marking the spot where Charles I stood as he was sentenced to death at his trial here in 1649. The start of proceedings had produced a memorable bit of drama, when the Solicitor General John Cook stood to read the

indictment. Charles, sitting immediately to Cook's left, decided
he wanted to speak, so tapped the lawyer on the shoulder with
his cane. When Cook ignored him, he tapped again and got
to his feet. But still Cook continued to speak, at which point
Charles hit him on the shoulder so hard that the silver tip of his
cane broke off and dropped to the floor. Charles, still not managing to get it into his head that his days of kingly supremacy
were over, waited for someone to pick the tip up. No one did. He
was forced to bend down and do the job himself.

I reach Central Lobby, Parliament's main meeting point
that sits halfway between the two Houses. If all the doors are
open you can look one way and see the green of the Commons
benches, then turn 180 degrees to make out the red of the Lords.[5]
The lobby's wow factor suffers slightly tonight, partly because at
least two of the several dozen lightbulbs in its huge chandelier
have blown, but mainly because a large section of its ornately
tiled floor is cordoned off with some far from ornate wooden
barriers.

'What's going on here?' I ask Patrick when he arrives. You
tend to feel confident asking Patrick things. He studied classics
at university, but in addition to his political duties he also writes
The Times's diary column, meaning that as well as knowing his
Pliny the Elder he generally knows who got voted off *Strictly
Come Dancing* the previous week.

'They're redoing the tiles,' he says, 'making sure they keep
the pattern the same. In fact down there...' – he points to St
Stephen's Hall, the chamber through which I've just walked after
leaving Westminster Hall – 'there was a spot where the pattern
didn't quite match. So they fixed it. Someone in the House of
Lords was outraged, saying the mismatch had been deliberate,
to mark the exact spot where Spencer Perceval was assassinated.'
Knowing that he's speaking to a fellow trivialist, Patrick doesn't
bother explaining that Perceval remains the only British PM to

---

5 Outside, at the respective ends of the building and for the same reason, Westminster
  Bridge is painted green and Lambeth Bridge red.

have suffered that fate. 'The noble Lord asked for the error to be reinstated, only to be told that it had never been a Perceval memorial in the first place, it had just been some workmen getting it wrong when they repaired the tiles after they were damaged during the Second World War.'

We head down to the corridor from which you can step out onto the House of Commons terrace. This overlooks the Thames and is technically, therefore, part of Britain's coastline: the Ordnance Survey includes rivers up to the point where they stop being tidal and change from salt water to fresh water. On this river that doesn't happen until Teddington Lock, well to the west of here. This is the modern opinion – back in 1869 it was thought to be Blackfriars Bridge, at least by the people who built Blackfriars Bridge. That's why the engravings on one side are of freshwater birds, those on the other of seabirds. But instead of heading outside Patrick and I turn left, and make our way up to the Press Gallery bar. This sits immediately behind the Press Gallery itself, which is above the business end of the Commons chamber, directly overlooking the Prime Minister and the Leader of the Opposition as they trade pleasantries.

On the wall of the bar is a large wooden plaque, recording the Gallery's past chairmen. In 1965 it was the BBC's Conrad Voss Bark, with whom you would surely have been ill-advised to argue. Imagine how old I feel when I see another friend, Chris Hope, who writes for the *Telegraph* and is the same age as me, and he tells me that a couple of years ago *he* was the chairman. I first met Chris 20 years ago. We'd both been employed to research a book, and in those days research meant libraries. We arranged to meet in Leicester Square (there's a very good reference library just off it), and Chris turned up wearing a boater. It wasn't a serious fashion statement – Chris is from the north-west, he simply doesn't have the genes for something like that – but I still maintain he must be the only Liverpool FC fan in history to have worn such a hat.

'I like to think the Press Gallery is the last incarnation of Fleet Street,' he says, indicating the corridor off which the various newspapers' offices can be found. 'Now that the papers are scattered all over London, this is the one remaining place where we're all still gathered together.' The corridor is known as the Burma Road.

The noise level in the bar increases as tonight's teams gather – there are a record 21. Amid the crush Patrick introduces me to Matt Chorley, who despite being a colleague from *The Times* will not be joining their team, as he is tonight's quizmaster. Very good at it he is too: in his early thirties and with an innate charm, he nonetheless brings out a stiletto-like wit to deal with the hecklers you're bound to get in a crowd like this. 'Cheap joke!' yell the *Sunday Express* team in reply to one of his barbs about them. 'Cheap paper,' responds Matt. It's no surprise when Patrick whispers to me that Matt used to perform stand-up comedy. You can tell from the way he's comfortable with the mike, holding it at the bottom, letting it droop away slightly as each laugh takes hold. He has that 'go on, I dare you' look – he'd be disappointed if he *didn't* get heckled.

The quiz takes place in the restaurant, which opens out from the bar. Matt kicks off with a few words about each team. The first-ever team representing Jeremy Corbyn's Labour Party, for instance: 'For them it's not about winning but about seizing control of the committee which decides who gets to write down the answers.' After this he explains that there will be seven rounds, none of which are on politics. Understandable – the last thing a bunch of politicos want at the end of the day is some homework. Nonetheless I can't help remembering some of the political trivia I've worked into questions over the years. MPs' coathangers still having ribbons from which Honourable Members can suspend their swords. Three Labour Prime Ministers having had the first name James, none of whom were Jim Callaghan (he was Leonard James Callaghan – the three were James Ramsay MacDonald, James Harold Wilson and James Gordon Brown). Plus my favourite political question, one of those you can't know but where the fun is in the guessing: 'The broadcaster Michael Cockerell has interviewed every British

Prime Minister from Harold Macmillan to David Cameron.
Which was the only one Cockerell saw using their fingers to
count with?'[6]

The next sentence out of Matt's mouth has me emitting a tiny
involuntary shudder. Thankfully he doesn't notice, because I
don't want to turn up and be rude about the man's quiz to his
face, but it's the only possible reaction to: 'You can play your
joker on any round you like.' Ah, that cursed beast, the joker. It
is to a decent quiz what the mosquito is to a garden party. The
evening's excitement and tension should arise from scores that
mount up naturally, not genetically engineered ones that depend
on whether someone else's definition of 'geography' matches
yours. Taking a complete punt on the possibility of doubling
your result in one arbitrarily chosen round is like one team in a
football match suddenly deciding that their next goal will count
as two. People who occasionally organise quizzes include the
joker simply because every other quiz they've ever been to has
included a joker. One day the country will wake up and realise
its collective madness. A bright new future will dawn where
quizzing is rational, and birds will sing and... OK, Mark. As
you say, no need to be rude.

There's laughter as Matt announces that ITN have asked if
their team can be called 'Quizlamic State'. Wordplay is only to
be expected from this crowd – whatever you say about British
journalism, its headlines have always been top drawer. The
Sun on George Michael's public convenience 'indiscretion', for
example: 'Zip Me Up Before You Go-Go.' Sadly, however, team
names aren't used at the Press Gallery quiz, as in such a fiercely
competitive environment everyone wants to know exactly who
they're beating and being beaten by. So 'ITN' it is.

Round one is 'Pot Luck', so it's slightly worrying that among
the teams playing their joker is the one from Number 10

6 Tony Blair.

Downing Street.[7] I know the Chinese phrase that translates as
'wind-water' (feng shui), but not the Kent town which has been
home to both Pocahontas and Gemma Arterton (Gravesend).
The actress who appeared in *The Glums*, *Carry on Nurse* and
EastEnders also defeats me: I would have joined several teams
in their choice of Barbara Windsor, but in fact it's June Whit-
field. It's interesting to watch the teams' faces when, despite
the 'no politics' rule, they're asked for the identity of the first
divorced US President. *The Times*, for one, are floundering.
Curious – I'd have put my life on Patrick knowing this. To
avoid any possible accusations of cheating, I look away when
he catches my eye. Don't want anyone imagining I mouthed the
word 'Reagan' at him. Until Trump's election, Ronnie was the
first and only. Which when you think about what Bill Clinton
got up to is a surprise.

Round two is science and nature. One of the questions
reminds me of my son: 'There are about three hundred in a
baby's body, but only two hundred and six in an adult's – what
are they?' Barney and I have been reading about it recently, and
I assume it's obvious, but the puzzled expressions around the
room indicate otherwise. Goes to show: sometimes you only
know it if you know it. (In this case it's 'bones'.) Discoveries in
this round include the number of astronauts currently on the
International Space Station (six). Not knowing the answer is
pretty unforgivable, as it's only a few days since the Brit Tim
Peake became one of them. Yet another example of how a story
can receive huge publicity without you picking up one of its key
details. What I had noted, however, is that because time runs at
a different speed in space (see the Theory of Relativity), Peake
will age slightly less during his time on the ISS than if he was on
Earth. A difference of 0.005 seconds, to be exact.

Marking is done by teams swapping papers with their

---

7 Look at their front door the next time you see it on the news – the zero is at an angle. This
is of course a modern high-security door, but the digit was made deliberately wonky in
tribute to the one on the original door.

neighbours, so there are the usual trades of 'we'll give you a half for this if you give us a half for that'. After the first couple of rounds Number 10 edge into a half-point lead over the Treasury and the *Daily Mail*. Their joker obviously helped, but still, a lead is what you'd expect from the people who send the Prime Minister to PMQs every week armed with a folder full of facts and figures. It's known as the 'plastic fantastic'.

But the team are threatened with embarrassment in the next round, which is on sitcoms. Matt asks: 'David Cameron name-checked which sitcom ten times in the 2015 Tory manifesto launch?' After a few seconds he adds: 'There's some chin-stroking on the Number Ten table.' I must confess I'm struggling too: how can I not remember the sitting Prime Minister kicking off his general election campaign with multiple mentions of a light-hearted TV programme? Only when Matt reveals the answers do I realise Cameron wasn't referring to a sitcom itself – it was just that he repeatedly used the phrase 'the good life'. (His operatives got there in the end this evening.) Other lessons include Captain Darling's first name in *Blackadder* (Kevin), the number of episodes that were made of *Friends* (236),[8] and the town in which *Open All Hours* was set (Doncaster). Ronnie Barker makes another appearance in question nine: 'For how long was Norman Stanley Fletcher sentenced to prison?' The judge's speech from the *Porridge* credits still plays instantly in your head after all this time ('... presumably accepts imprison-ment in the same *cas*-ual manner ...'), but when it comes to the actual figure those horrible quiz doubts begin to creep in. It was five years – wasn't it? You can see why people used to bottle it when the money got big on *Who Wants to Be a Millionaire?* (As it happens Fletch *did* get five years.) Meanwhile another question – 'who lived on Oildrum Lane?' – prompts happy memories of *Steptoe and Son*, and therefore of Elton John: his middle name (official – he used a deed poll to say goodbye

---

8 Impressive when you consider that for the final two seasons the stars were on $1 million per episode each. At the beginning they'd struggled by on just $22,500.

to Reginald Kenneth Dwight) is Hercules, in honour of the Steptoes' horse.

The theme of the next round is the delightfully childish 'Balls'. The first question – 'who were the finalists in the 2015 League Cup final?' – elicits an enquiry from one person of 'how many teams are you looking for?' It's a very good job for that person that everyone else is concentrating on their own answers, otherwise this lack of familiarity with even the most basic details of football would have caused a great deal of ribbing. Other variations on the theme include 'who is former TV presenter Johnny Ball's son-in-law?' (Fatboy Slim), and 'what is the first line of "Great Balls of Fire"? ("you shake my nerves and you rattle my brain")'. But the best lesson of the round is that the avocado derives its name from the Aztec word for 'testicle'.

And on that note, dinner is served. Plates of jerk chicken waft by, their aroma causing me to regret my decision of a large dinner earlier in the evening. This was taken on the 'always line your stomach before drinking with journalists' principle, so the least I can do now is reap the benefit by having another pint of Guinness. Patrick is on the same, and as I hand him his glass we fall to talking about the logo it bears, the famous harp. It faces to the right, and the firm's copyright on that is the reason the harp on Irish passports faces to the left. The logo also includes the date 1759, the year Guinness was founded. Fairly well known, but not quite as integral to their image as 1664 is to that of Kronenbourg. I once paid for a pint of the lager with a £20 note, and when the barman handed me my change he said: 'There you go, sixteen pounds sixty-three.' Could they not have reduced the price by a penny, just for instances like this?

To keep things quizzical even as everyone eats, Matt has produced a picture round. We might differ on jokers, but he and I agree on picture rounds. They're great for any quiz at which food is going to be served, for the simple reason that they're un-Googleable. Those of lesser moral fibre have been known to use loo breaks during a dinner as cover for looking up answers.

People who also display lesser intellectual fibre will look up *all* the answers, thereby making their cheating absurdly obvious. I once set a round where you had to match 20 celebrities to the years in which they'd turned on the Oxford Street Christmas lights. A couple of teams scored 20 out of 20. At least try and be a *bit* subtle about it – get four or five wrong for credibility's sake.

Tonight's round is in the style adopted by the *Independent*'s weekly quiz:[9] each set of photos makes up the name of a person, specifically a newly elected MP from the 2015 general election. This isn't seen to break the 'no politics' rule, as the fun is in deciphering Matt's cunning verbal gymnastics. Some whiteboard pens followed by a goldfish represent Marcus Fysh. A finger curled against a thumb, Animal from the Muppets and the front page of *Le Monde* lead to Flick Drummond. My favourite is the set showing a toilet, a wave and a set of Allen keys: Lucy Allan. Another memory of Barney: he once heard a reference to Allen keys just after someone had mentioned Alan Titchmarsh, and so deduced that the former had been invented by the latter.

Once the plates are cleared away, it's on with a round about food. We learn that Alfred Hitchcock had a fear of apples – blood was 'jolly' by comparison, he said – and that celeriac is also known as knob celery (Matt knows his audience's level of humour). Also that 200 degrees Celsius turns out to be Gas Mark 6. I'm always more irritated than a normal person should be about the line in Queen's 'Don't Stop Me Now': 'Two hundred degrees, that's why they call me Mr Fahrenheit'. OK, 'Celsius' would have ruined the rhyme with 'speed of light', but 200 degrees Fahrenheit isn't even boiling point. Couldn't Freddie have made it 300?

We're about to head into the penultimate round, and a check of the scores reveals that Patrick and his colleagues have performed a vertigo-inducing surge up the table, and are now

9 The regular one, the quiz that saw the paper through its glory years, not the Boxing Day one by those idiots from the Prince of Wales.

level at the top with Number 10. Both teams have a nail-bitingly precise 47½ points, and tense looks are being exchanged. When Matt announces that the next round is on London, I avoid Patrick's eye even more assiduously than before – one of my books was on the city. When question seven comes around I'm looking away not to prevent accusations of cheating, but because I'm ashamed: even though my book was themed around the Tube network, I don't know which station has the most escalators. (Turns out it's Waterloo, with 23.) I needn't worry, though – *The Times* score one point more than Number 10 in this round, putting them into an outright lead.

Last place, on the other hand, is occupied by the Scottish National Party, who with their 21½ points aren't even halfway to matching the title contenders. The cheer that accompanies this announcement crystallises something that's been bubbling away in my subconscious all evening: how much I dislike all-male groups. This room doesn't fit the category literally – there's a pretty even split between the genders. But the women who report on politics, like the ones who practise it, tend (in my experience) to have a very male side to their character. They need to, in order to survive. Or probably they're like that anyway, to want to work here in the first place. And so the overall atmosphere is the same as you find on a stag weekend or in a cricket dressing room: aggressive, alpha, constantly probing for points of weakness. It's a pack thing – apart from Patrick and Chris I know several other people here tonight, and have had perfectly friendly, civilised chats with them. But put more than a certain number of them together and a victim has to be found, albeit only a temporary one, the role passing from person to person as the banter takes its course. That's all it is: banter. But the undercurrent's there too, and it always gives me a feeling of unease. Of course, I'm sure I'd feel differently if I was any good at it.

And so to the final round. Thankfully *The Times* and Number 10 have both played their jokers already, so the scoreboard is safe from artificial last-minute shenanigans – this will be a straight fight between the two teams, *mano a mano*, power and glory just moments away for whichever team can summon nerve, courage and the name of the 1990s TV show featuring Inspector Raymond Fowler and Constable Maggie Habib. (The round is titled 'Cops and Robbers'.) Slightly unnerving to see a room full of journalism's finest *quite* so pleased with themselves for knowing the subtitle of the seventh *Police Academy* film, but there you go. The question 'who was Sherlock Holmes's landlady?' has me Googling: Matt obviously means Mrs Hudson, but did she actually own the building or was she just a housekeeper? Matt, as you would expect from someone who works for the paper of record, is right. The only person who could afford to own a house on that section of Baker Street these days would be a Russian oligarch.

The final question of the evening asks which band started which song with a sample of the 'everybody be cool, this is a robbery' speech from *Pulp Fiction*. Matt has clearly left this to last so as not to sully the evening too early with the swear words contained in the rest of the quote.[10] Watch closely and you'll see that Amanda Plummer delivers slightly different versions of the speech in the two versions of the robbery that bookend the movie. Matt Paper-of-Record is careful to read out the one used by the Fun Lovin' Criminals (for it is they) on 'Scooby Snacks'. The TV show, should you be wondering, was *The Thin Blue Line*, and the Police Academy film was *Mission to Moscow*. Number 10 and *The Times* eyeball each other as marking progresses, trying to guess from each other's reactions which of them got these and the other answers right. Eventually all the sheets are handed in, arithmetic is performed on the whiteboard (now turned away from the room so that only Matt can see it), and the final placings are announced. More cheers as the SNP retain ownership of the wooden spoon, then we're heading up

---

10 Including the one beginning 'mother–', the one Prince abbreviated to 'MF'. This regularly tops broadcasting authorities' surveys of the most offensive words, outstripping even the 'c'-word.

through the places. The *Sun* and the Treasury lie nearer the bottom than they'd like, the Lib Dems and the Politics Home website are middling, while the *Daily Telegraph*, the *Daily Mail* and the Huffington Post are all just outside the money. The Press Association, says Matt, are in third place. Second belongs to a team on 60 points, with the winners on 62½. Those winners are … *The Times*. Patrick and his colleagues didn't just hold off Number 10's challenge, they actually extended their lead. The press have spoken truth to power.

Everyone indulges in post-mortems and congratulations and recriminations, but mainly they indulge in more drink. It would seem rude not to join them, so I sit with Patrick and his teammates, congratulating them on their success and admiring the trophy now adorning their table. It's a hefty bit of Perspex bearing the Press Gallery's logo of two crossed quills underneath Parliament's portcullis. It was Charles Barry who made the portcullis the instantly recognisable symbol it is today: he put it everywhere he could in his designs for the current building, which replaced the one that burned down in 1834. It's even cast into the metal of Big Ben itself.

Eventually it's time to leave, and I find myself walking across New Palace Yard with Rob Hutton, who reports on politics for Bloomberg News. Looking up, we see that the Elizabeth Tower (as Big Ben's home has been called since the Queen's Diamond Jubilee) is bathed in moonlight. It makes me catch my breath.

'It's beautiful, isn't it?' I say, the words leaving my mouth before my brain knows what's happening. I worry that seasoned old politico Rob will think me a hick.

'I know,' he replies. 'It still impresses me every day. And I've worked here for over a decade.'

We talk about Big Ben, how hardly anyone knows that you're allowed to go on a tour of it (or at least you will be able to once its renovations are complete – book through your MP, and choose the 11 a.m. rather than the 2 p.m. tour to maximise your bongs). How the light at the top is known as the Ayrton Light in honour of Acton Smee Ayrton, the minister in charge when it was installed in 1885 so that Queen Victoria could see from Buckingham Palace whether Parliament was sitting after dark. How listeners to the 9 p.m. BBC News in 1949 were horrified when the bulletin started without the famous clangs. The reason, Auntie Beeb announced in a later bulletin, was that Big Ben was running four minutes slow. Had someone accidentally knocked over the famous old pennies that regulate the clock's mechanism?

No. A swarm of starlings had gathered on the minute hand.

TWO

· · · · · · ·

Which is the only country in the world whose flag is neither rectangular nor square?

It is very pleasing for someone who's writing a book about quizzes to read halfway through a train journey that the station they're heading to is the only one in the world to be named after a novel. It also adds a bit of intellectual heft to proceedings when I remember that this journey is the very one cited by Bertrand Russell in his book about relativity theory. 'If you want to travel from King's Cross to Edinburgh,' writes Russell, 'you know that you will find King's Cross where it has always been . . . and that Waverley Station in Edinburgh will not have walked up to the Castle. You therefore say and think that you have travelled to Edinburgh, not that Edinburgh has travelled to you, though the latter statement would be just as accurate.' Russell's explanation is as close as I've ever got to understanding Einstein's mindbender, but let's park the details for now and concentrate on quizzes. Tonight the Scottish capital will provide not just one but two.

As we saw earlier, Edinburgh came to mind as a possible destination when Martin mentioned it in one of his questions. Specifically: 'Who sits with a book in his hand and his deerhound Maida by his side in Princes Street Gardens opposite the Jenners department store?' Sir Walter Scott, of course, author of the book after which his home city's train station is named.

The attraction of coming here – apart from the fact that I love Edinburgh and haven't been for a long time – is that it'll offer the chance to see how quizzes are done in a different country. And yes, even before you reach the writer's monument, two minutes' walk from the station, the flags and the accents leave you in no doubt you're in Scotland not England, the country that only a couple of years ago came close to voting for independence. Not for nothing is the official animal of this land the unicorn: it was chosen in the 1300s because it's the enemy of the lion, adopted by the English a century before. But equally, Edinburgh feels like a great international city. Glasgow is bigger, and great in its own way, but it's defiantly Scottish. This place is like London and Paris and New York: you can feel at home here wherever you're from. World cities are above nationhood. Edinburgh has more in common with London than it does with Stirling, London more with Edinburgh than with Norwich.

We're into spring now, and there's a freshness to the breeze wafting along Princes Street as I reach the Scott Monument. Much of the turf surrounding it has been ploughed up, obviously as part of some maintenance project to improve the gardens, but for now it has left the place looking a mess. You can't help agreeing with Charles Dickens: 'I am sorry to report the Scott Monument a failure. It is like the spire of a Gothic church taken off and stuck in the ground.' Dickens had more luck over in Edinburgh's Old Town, when in 1841 he went on a walk to kill time before a lecture. In the churchyard of Canongate Kirk he found the grave of Ebenezer Scroggie. Dickens not only misread the name, he also misread the inscription 'mealman' (Scroggie was a successful corn merchant) as 'meanman'. Out of order, thought the writer, to tarnish the poor guy's reputation: it must have 'shrivelled' his soul to carry 'such a terrible thing to eternity'. And so was born one of Dickens's most famous characters.[1] A little further along

---

1 Someone else inspired by the city was Tintin creator Hergé (real name Georges Remi – the pseudonym is the French pronunciation of his reversed initials). Meticulous about details, he sent a researcher to Edinburgh to sketch the Scottish police uniforms that feature in *The Black Island*.

are two benches that remind us what a lottery life is: one com-
memorates a man 'who loved life in Edinburgh' but died at 46,
the other the managing director of a nearby firm whose *working*
life was 61 years.

At the far end of Princes Street I reach the grand red cliff-face
that is the front of the Caledonian Hotel, my home for tonight.
The hotel opened in 1903 to serve the railway station that used
to stand alongside. Since then it has hosted Mikhail Gorbachev
(he had to leave suddenly when Soviet leader Yuri Andropov
died), Nelson Mandela (who as a teetotaller was persuaded to
try some local whisky – 'I'm going to the conference,' he said,
'I hope I'm not too aggressive') and Tony Blair. Paul O'Grady,
who is certainly not a teetotaller, was in residence at the same
time and returned from a long night out in full Lily Savage garb
(minus the high heels, which he was carrying – 'the carpet pile's
so deep'). Stumbling a little too close to the Prime Minister's
room for comfort, Lily was politely but firmly led away by Blair's
protection officers.

This, needless to say, was during the festival. Most of my
Edinburgh visits have been for the same reason, when I made
radio programmes for the BBC. Shortly after acquiring my first
mobile phone I found myself using it in a taxi here. 'Sorry,' I
said to the driver, having quickly ended the call, 'I've become a
cliché, haven't I? The English meejah type on his phone in the
back of a cab.'

'Don't worry, pal,' he replied, 'this month pays for the rest of
my year.' But Edinburgh in March is a delightfully different pros-
pect, so there's plenty of room in the lobby for me to notice the
tartan trousers worn by Malcolm, who has ruled this expanse of
marble for over 20 years. I ask if it's a special tartan.

'The hotel's own.' It was designed by Kinloch and Anderson,
kiltmakers to the Queen. Malcolm points out two lines that run
close together. 'They're to symbolise the train tracks.'

Dumping my bag in my room, I descend the staircase that
Roy Rogers led his horse up when he stayed here (hay was
provided), and set out for a wander round the New Town. A

woman standing in a disused shop doorway on Princes Street serenades the world with a version of 'Don't Go Breaking My Heart', complete with dancing and outstretched hands, one of which grasps a can of lager. I cut through to the parallel George Street, where two young women walk along discussing prayer methods.

'I'll start by talking to God,' says one, uncertainly, 'but then suddenly I'm talking to everyone else.'

'Yeah, that's fine,' comes the reply from her more assured friend. 'You can do it that way.'

This part of town is summed up by the restaurant offering grilled asparagus with shaved Manchego cheese. I can't help but think of Victoria Park to the north: it contains a statue of Edward VII, who always had to be served an even number of asparagus stalks because an odd number would bring bad luck. Not far from the park is the final resting home of *Britannia*, the now decommissioned yacht of Edward's great-granddaughter. I can't see it from here, but gazing down the hill towards the expanse of water it lies on I note a flock of curiously clean chimney pots. They look like new white pawns in a grubby old chess set.

Past the Assembly Rooms – strange to see the pavement free of discarded flyers and networking comedians – then I'm tempted down some steps to a half-basement café. Copies of the *Scottish Independent Coffee Guide* lie around, and sure enough this place features. Apparently it 'focuses on espresso from the Synesso machine and three Mythos grinders... bi-weekly guest coffees – sourced from Europe to Australia – provide plenty of choice and the chance to sample some of the newest roasts around'. Clearly, then, I have to order a cup of tea. Equally clearly it comes in a cup with one of those stupid little handles that a doll couldn't get its finger through. At a nearby table a hipster talks to his friend: 'I'm just trying to think of a way to get value out of this relationship... That's the thing – he *makes* meetings happen.' What would Mackintosh of Borlum have thought? He was the 18th-century Scottish nobleman who coined the phrase 'you'll have had your tea'. It's come to be seen as an Edinburgh excuse for not offering guests a drink, but as with Charles Dickens and the gravestone the charge of meanness is a mistake: Mackintosh actually disliked the slurping sound made by drinkers.

At the end of George Street lies St Andrew Square, dominated by a statue of Viscount Melville, the last person to be impeached in Britain (some money had gone missing at the Admiralty – Melville got off, but never held public office again). The base of the column on which Melville stands is currently surrounded by lifesize stick figures. They're a public art installation, but remind me of the drawings in the Sherlock Holmes story 'The Adventure of the Dancing Men'. Fitting then, because local boy Arthur Conan Doyle based the detective on Joseph Bell, a lecturer at Edinburgh University's medical school. Bell taught his students to study patients closely before making a diagnosis, and would demonstrate the skill by working out the details of complete strangers' private lives.

On the far side of the square, in the Harvey Nicks nail bar, a woman has her left hand buffed while drinking champagne with her right. Walking back down to Princes Street I pass Meuse Lane, where number 11 was home in the 1700s to Hugo Arnot: after neighbours complained about him constantly summoning his servants with rings of a bell he started doing it with gunshots. A left turn past Waverley station brings the trip's first climb, to the collection of classically inspired structures atop Calton Hill which earned Edinburgh the nickname 'the Athens of the north'. The moniker's at its most literal with the National Monument, started in 1826 as a copy of the Greek Parthenon, abandoned part-finished in 1829. Still looks good, though, today inspiring a tourist to photograph his girlfriend with her arms outstretched between two of its columns. The Nelson Monument pays tribute to Horatio. Essentially another tall column, it makes itself different by getting thinner towards the top so as to resemble a telescope. Every Trafalgar Day it flies signal flags spelling out Nelson's famous 'England expects that every man will do his duty' message (perhaps the Union's got more of a future than we assume). Forming a 762-kilogram cherry on the cake is the time ball right at the top: just before one o'clock every day it rises, then falls to denote the hour.[2] This accompanies the firing of the One O'Clock Gun over at the castle, a back-up for foggy days when sailors couldn't see the ball. With an exquisite attention to detail, the authorities who started the tradition in 1861 also produced a map to take account of the speed of sound, with concentric circles each representing one second to show exactly when you would hear the gun at any point across the city.

My bench-habit is indulged yet again on the way down, where I pass one in memory of William Meikle Forsyth, 'son of Mary Meikle and Andrew George Forsyth'. This Scottish tradition of giving the mother's maiden name as a middle name helps explain the Arsenal goalkeeping legend that is Bob Primrose Wilson. Then it's over North Bridge into the Old Town. I pass the university, where the renowned professor Dugald Stewart was so beloved that one student spoke of there being 'eloquence in his very spitting'. Round in the Grassmarket the many pubs are starting to fill with drinkers now that the working day is over. One, the Maggie Dickson, takes its name from the woman who in 1724 was hanged in the Grassmarket for murdering her illegitimate baby. The cart taking her body away for burial jolted, causing her to wake up: the hangman hadn't done his job properly. Scottish law decreed that she couldn't be tried again for the same crime, so she was allowed to go free. (The sentence of hanging was later amended to include the words 'until dead'.) A few doors down is the Last Drop, from which a stag party of a dozen Yorkshiremen emerge. It is clear that proceedings did not start recently. One of the group berates his colleagues for refusing to stay in the pub. 'You're fuckin' cowards, 'in't ya? You shit yerselves, din't ya? Come back and fight 'em. Come on.'

---

2 Originally installed in 1853 so that ships in the Firth of Forth could set their clocks, the ball was brought back into service in 2009. Must be under repair at the moment – tomorrow I will watch and wait in vain.

Despite the message, his delivery is calm and utterly deadpan. His friends ignore him, and the whole scene is played so straight that you begin to doubt it's being played at all. Even as they disappear to another pub I'm not *entirely* sure he's joking.

Time to head for the quiz now. It's in No. 8 Lister Square, a bar whose address requires minimal research. The square is in an up-and-coming part of town, the sort whose marketing literature makes extensive use of the term 'new build'. As well as the offices, retail/leisure units and affordable housing (the phrase which tries to hide but actually highlights the fact that everything else is unaffordable housing), there is a gym favoured by young professionals. It comes as a shock after a couple of blocks of building-site nothingness to see the occupants of seven treadmills suddenly appearing on my left. I almost jump back to get out of their way, before remembering that they won't in fact be breaking through the plate-glass window and running me down: this is the whole point of treadmills. Like the gym, No. 8 Lister Square itself has floor-to-ceiling windows, though thankfully its occupants are behaving less frenetically. The nearest they get to exercise is at the pool table. A very good pool table it is too, one of those big American jobs: it fits well with the bar's exposed brickwork/mismatched armchairs/sepia photos feel. One of the photos shows a rugby team from the Scotland–Wales match of 1903. It's captioned 'Scotch team'. You wouldn't get away with that now.

Setting up his laptop at the far end of the bar is Goose, or as his parents christened him 28 years ago, Andrew Wildgoose. My research on the Edinburgh quizzing scene has elicited several mentions of his quizzes, including his novel method of solving tiebreaks: best paper plane wins it. The purist in me might recoil at this, but the 'don't take anything too seriously' side likes it. Goose's quizzes seem universally popular, and when I find his Twitter feed the issue is settled. One of its facts concerns the medical condition in which bright lights induce uncontrollable sneezing. The scientist who researched it deliberately chose the name Autosomal-dominant Compelling Helio-Ophthalmic Outburst Syndrome: 'ACHOO'.

The act of Goose standing up to greet me takes a while – he's well over six feet tall, with a physique that must seriously intimidate his opponents on the rugby field, but which is tonight clad in an Aerosmith T-shirt, knee-length shorts and trainers. Having started quizmastering to make a bit of money at university, he now does it as a full-time living. The current weekly count is 18 – clearly he can't host them all himself, so he has assistants who share the workload. For both tonight's events, though, Goose himself is in the chair.

'I've decided to go with Leonardo di Caprio as the team name theme tonight,' he says, in tribute to the actor who won his first-ever Oscar a couple of days ago. 'There's a prize for the best name.' Given that the prize is a large box of Milk Tray, there will be envious looks – though no argument – when it's won by Two Can Fit On That Door. Goose has also used di Caprio as the theme for tonight's first round. 'It'll be a good timeless round,' he explains. 'One I can use again in the future. That's why I tend to avoid topical questions based on the news.'

His goal is to make sure everyone has a good night out. 'I always aim for a five-three-two ratio in each round. Five answers most people should get, three that are more difficult and two that are a real challenge.' Using an Excel spreadsheet for marking means that not only does the computer keep running totals, it also reveals how easy or difficult a question has been over its lifetime, going back many quizzes. This helps with future planning. Such analytical precision is very professional, but is stopped from becoming nerdish by Goose's obvious affability. At both tonight's venues he'll be in constant conversation with the bar staff and regular team members, and because he controls the background music as well as the quiz from his laptop he almost assumes the aura of a DJ. I'd wager that in ten years' time Goose will have made a lot of money from running his own business, or probably businesses. I don't know what any of them will be, but they'll depend on being good with people.

'Bad luck, guys,' he says to a team of twenty-somethings who come up to get their answer sheets,[3] 'no football questions tonight.' They're from a company that runs fantasy football leagues, and as such know every stat there is to know about the game. I tell Goose about Ray Spiller, the professional football statistician who bet £100 at 66 to 1 on a player scoring five goals in a match that season. Andy Cole achieved the feat one Saturday against Ipswich, but when Ray rang the bookies on Monday morning they said there was still doubt about the last goal – it had come off the defender and might be an own goal. 'Whose verdict do you use?' asked Ray. 'The Premier League's,' came the reply. 'OK,' said Ray, 'I'll wait.' He then put the phone down, because what he knew – and the bookies didn't – was that the person the Premier League consulted about own goals was... Ray Spiller. Would you believe it, five minutes later his phone rang. It was the Premier League, explaining that they needed a ruling on Andy Cole's last goal because some punter had got a bet on. Ray gave his considered opinion. Another five minutes and the phone goes again. It's the bookies, congratulating him on his win.

After a quick reminder of the rules – including 'illegible handwriting will not be marked' – we're off and running. I wonder if the ten questions about di Caprio will include the derivation of his surname (it's from *capra*, meaning 'goat'). They don't, but when I ask Goose about it he mentions that di Caprio's agent initially wanted him to change his surname as he felt it was 'too ethnic'. This exchange is backed by the music that Goose plays between questions: the normal songs he's been playing the rest of the evening, that is, rather than specially written 'quiz' music, but still it's something that's new to me. At first it seems strange, but soon I realise that it fits the venue – it would seem strange if a bar like this lacked music for too long. Goose keeps it at a level that allows teams to confer: in fact it actually aids that

---

3 With every set of sheets, Goose hands out a flyer for his company, dominated by a logo of the bird that shares his name – it's drawn so the neck forms a question mark.

conferring, making it harder for others to overhear. I like this – a subtle refinement on things as I've known them hitherto. Like all animals, the quiz undergoes Darwinian evolution so it can survive in new habitats.

Question six begins: 'di Caprio has starred in two films with Kate Winslet...' A girl on a nearby table makes excited 'I know the answer' signals to her teammates. 'One is *Titanic*,' continues Goose. The girl looks deflated. Did she seriously think that was going to be one of the questions? Goose, of course, is looking for the other movie.[4]

The end of the first round is where the team name prize gets awarded, so there's a double celebration for Two Can Fit On That Door, who find themselves in the joint lead on nine points. But Goose reminds everyone that the situation isn't straightforward: 'Don't forget, they've got nine players. And as the regulars know, you're allowed to go over the "maximum" team size of six, but for every extra player one point will be deducted from your final score.' This should add a bit of spice to the evening.

Round two is 'Food and Drink'. The question about which Italian dessert uses cream, mascarpone, coffee, chocolate, marsala and sponge fingers is clearly from the first category in Goose's 5:3:2 ratio. I ask him if he knows what 'tiramisu' means. He doesn't, and is delighted to learn that it's 'pick me up'. In return, the other questions teach me that Nando's was founded in South Africa (by Fer*nando* Duarte), and that the average British cow produces 37 pints of milk a day. Round three, being a music round, offers no lessons – instead it offers huge frustration as you try to carry on playing the song in your mind until you reach the chorus while Goose is already onto the next song. You don't know whether to put your fingers in your ears and sacrifice one you might not know for one you definitely do, or give yourself a chance with the second one and hope you can pick up where you left off with the first one when there's silence again. Incredible, the classics that refuse to yield their title: tonight, despite fevered

---

4 *Revolutionary Road.*

humming, I fail on Dusty Springfield's 'Take Another Little Piece of My Heart'. Mind you, the pain of this is soon replaced by the agony of seeing a young woman's face remain totally blank at Kate Bush's 'Wuthering Heights'. Between rounds I ask her if it was even vaguely familiar. 'No,' she says, 'never heard it before in my life.' If Chris being chairman of the Parliamentary Press Gallery made me feel old, I now see the grave yawning.

Two Can Fit maintain their lead as we head into the next (and penultimate) round, but only by three points, which with their handicap means it's no lead at all. They'd better be good on geography, and in particular the only country in the world with a non-rectangular/square flag (Nepal – it's a triangle on top of another triangle), the capital of Canada (Ottawa) and the country in which you'd arrive if you dug directly through the centre of the earth from Madrid (New Zealand). Goose tells me that such pairings – diametrically opposed points on the globe – are known as 'antipodes', from the Greek for 'opposite the feet'. Until now I'd thought the word was just slang for Australia and New Zealand, but that's only because those countries are Britain's antipodal points. Or rather the sea to the south-east of New Zealand is. As Goose has shown, if you want to hit land there you need to tunnel from continental Europe.

Two Can Fit only score six on this round, but that's one more than their rivals, so they're into the lead for real. Last up it's General Knowledge. I know that the city which featured on the original Monopoly board was Atlantic City, and don't know (but feel satisfied at working out – always the sign of a good question) that the man who said 'We made the buttons on the screen look so good you'll want to lick them' was Steve Jobs. His dislike of real buttons – or 'koumpounophobia' – even extended to his clothing: hence all those roll-neck tops. Two Can Fit notch an impressive eight, and so close out their victory. Thirty pounds to spend behind the bar is theirs.

Before the applause has died away Goose is packing up ready for a dash to tonight's second venue, a bar called Lebowski's. 'You'll like it,' he explains, as we hail a cab. 'It's named after the film, and they specialise in White Russians. They do twenty-seven different types.'

A glance at the menu when we arrive reveals the Original, the Dude (as drunk by said character – 50/50 milk and cream instead of just cream), the Little Larry (add white chocolate liqueur) and so on. Each is accompanied by a quote from the film: 'you're entering a world of pain', 'gimme the marker, Dude, I'm marking it eight', 'people forget that the brain is the biggest erogenous zone' ... As if that wasn't enough, the movie itself plays on a constant loop (sound down), the screen surrounded by an ornate gold frame. *The Big Lebowski* doesn't get much bigger than this.

The quiz is much busier than the one at No. 8 Lister Square – 20 teams instead of six, much more of a buzz, a big night out. Goose opens with the Leonardo di Caprio round again, and also reuses him as the team name theme, though here the prize for best name is a more modest packet of Haribos. After round one the quiz differs from the evening's first. In Geography, for instance, we're asked which US state comes second to California in terms of most national parks. California has nine, the runner-up with eight is ... Alaska. While he does the marking Goose plays 'Mr Blue Sky' by ELO. The task is clearly pretty demanding at such a packed quiz, so I refrain from bothering him with the information that Jeff Lynne wrote it after locking himself away in a chalet in Switzerland – after two weeks of bad weather he'd produced nothing, but then out came the sun and the song was born. I also keep to myself the wording of the spoken phrase at the end. Because it's heavily disguised, most people assume it's one of those sinister messages you have to play backwards: actually it refers to the song's position at the end of that side of the album, and says 'please turn me over'.

By the time we're into the next round (Music), Goose's girlfriend Kathleen has arrived. I unofficially team up with her and whichever member of staff happens to be serving at our section of the bar. We know that Randy Newman's 'If I Didn't Have You' was used in *Monsters Inc*. It won him an Oscar, his first after 15 unsuccessful nominations.[5] Newman's acceptance speech began: 'I don't want your pity.' This leads to us swapping Academy Awards trivia, such as Oscar Hammerstein II – the only Oscar ever to win an Oscar. Our conversation means we occasionally talk over a question. Not a problem for us, as we're not actually playing, but this is normally, in my book, the worst offence you can commit. I don't want to become humourless about all this, so let's keep things in perspective and say that the punishment for talking over a question should merely be... oh, I don't know... death. People have to get the message. They might not be bothered about trying to win, but their teammates are. And surely one of the most basic tactical errors you can make if you're trying to work out the answer to a question is not knowing what that question is in the first place. I wouldn't mind if these people gave up completely, stopped taking part in the quiz, sat there and read a book. But no, they talk all over the question then say: 'Eh? What was that?' As though it was someone else's fault they hadn't heard.

The final two rounds – Animals and General Knowledge – are perfect illustrations of Goose's difficulty ratio. There are the easy ones, such as which type of dog the Queen keeps: pedants would remind us some of them aren't corgis, they're the corgi–dachshund cross known as a 'dorgi' – whatever, all of Her Majesty's dogs are fitted with little booties to protect their paws from the Buckingham Palace gravel. There are the middling ones, such as the minimum age for getting married in the UK without parental consent (18). And there are the hard ones, such as which animal is the emblem of the US Republican Party. Hard for me, that is: one of the guys behind the bar is American, so knows it's the elephant. This dates from a political cartoon of the 19th century. The Democrats use the donkey – in 1828 their presidential candidate Andrew Jackson, labelled a 'jackass' by

---

5 Not actually the record – the composer Victor Young was nominated 21 times before finally winning. His victory came at the 1957 Awards, though was slightly marred by the fact he'd died four months previously.

an opponent, neutralised the insult by adopting the animal on his own posters. It worked: he eventually made it to the White House.

We can tell from Goose's concentration levels as he marks that a close finish is in the offing, and sure enough the final results see Quiz Me If You Can winning with 37 points, ahead of one team on 36 and no fewer than five on 35. Goose has been watching his drinking until now, but the first pint he shares with us at the bar disappears in record time. Over a few successors, we discuss the need for vigilance when hosting a quiz, and the related issue of cheating. Goose mentioned smartphones during the quiz – but only the once. 'I tell them to let me know if they spot anyone using their phones, but it doesn't happen that much. Almost everyone who comes to a quiz is coming for the right reason.'

This is my experience too. It's not as though anyone's playing for big money. In fact a lot of the time the aim is to get rid of money, as the quiz is a fundraiser for a school, a sports team or whatever, and anyone who cheats at something like that really should get out less. By and large, people would see the cubicle-bound consultation of their iPhone as a loss of self-respect rather than a gain in points.

'I heard a radio phone-in about quizzes the other week,' I tell Goose. 'There was a guy who runs them for ex-pats in the United Arab Emirates. He always starts by reminding everyone it's a test of their brain power, not the speed of their internet connection.'[6]

But of course you do get the occasional wrong'un, such as those 'twenty out of twenty' buffoons I mentioned. The problem was around even before phones got smart: the Super Furry Animals' 2001 album *Rings Around the World* had the working title 'Text Messaging is Destroying the Pub Quiz as We Know It'. How to counter these fiends? Someone once proposed

---

6 Another caller had been to a quiz which asked: 'What's the UK's biggest carnivore?' 'Ooh, I know this one!' said his wife. 'It's Notting Hill.'

saying that whichever team came second would be the winner, although that would surely wipe out a lot of perfectly innocent victors and only make the cheats more subtle in their subterfuge. Another approach is that of a quiz which came up in the initial Edinburgh research: 'They found a cheating team and so just stopped reading out their scores.'

'You could do that,' says Goose. 'Usually I change their scores and make them come third or fourth, whichever is the highest non-prize position. I love seeing them leave, thinking they should have won. Another thing you can do, if you know they're cheating and they've got full marks on a round, is to announce their score and ask them to wave at everyone. Once the other teams know who they are they'll watch them like hawks. It's often the way they react that confirms it – you find that some teams go on the offensive and get angry at the accusation of cheating. They're the ones who are cheating.'

Goose's favourite incident happened in a music round. 'A girl was using Shazam, the app where you play a song down the phone and it identifies it for you. You have to be directly in front of the speakers, and also while it's analysing the sound there's a blue rotating icon, so it was completely obvious what she was up to. I had a long mike lead, and I crept up behind her, getting closer and closer. Her teammates realised and tried to alert her, but still she didn't realise. In the end I was right behind her, and said down the mic "phone cheating is disallowed". She was scrambling to put her phone away, and her team were laughing. In the end they were the ones who were harshest on her.'

* * *

The haggis is a help. It's part of the Caledonian's cooked breakfast, tucked cosily between the bacon and the tomatoes, all of them joining forces to coax me, step by delicate step, out of the rather fragile state into which those post-quiz pints with Goose have delivered me. There was no singing, no silliness, certainly no unpleasantness. And I can remember every one of the steps

I took from Lebowski's back to the hotel. It's just I'm glad those steps were downhill, that's all.

The corollary of that, mind you, is that today must start with a climb. Having explored the New Town yesterday, I'm going to spend my remaining time in Edinburgh having a look round the Old Town. And in particular the stretch of it known as the Royal Mile. As you'd expect from its name, this road is exactly one mile and 107 yards long. Its westerly end is marked by the castle that looks down on the city from its rocky vantage point. Between me and that castle are the Princes Street Gardens, occupying the valley left by the glacier that moved from west to east during the last Ice Age. Apt in a way, as the pace I achieve in scaling them this morning is rather glacial itself. Not that my frequent stops are just to recover – a beaming sun in a Saltire-blue sky makes for ever more stunning views the higher I get.

The best view of all comes when I reach the top, the castle's wide-open forecourt, or 'esplanade' as it styles itself, a continent-ally poncy touch well out of line with the building's forbidding appearance. And indeed forbidding history. The Black Dinner of 1440, for instance. Nine-year-old King James II was having dinner with his 16-year-old guest the Earl of Douglas, and the Earl's younger brother. Suddenly Sir William Crichton, keeper of the castle, entered carrying a silver serving dish. The dish bore the head of a black bull, dripping blood. Crichton placed it in front of the Earl and his brother, a sign that a death sentence had been passed on them by the Scottish lords. James protested, saying that he forbade the execution to be carried out. But Crichton explained that even a king's authority wasn't enough for that: the two boys were tied with ropes and taken outside. James had to watch through the window as they were beheaded.

There were still bad relations between Scottish noblemen in 1587: James VI tried to end the feud by making the lords walk down the Royal Mile holding hands. Meanwhile over at Borthwick Castle (south-east of Edinburgh) those in charge gave their English prisoners a choice between starving to death in the dungeon or earning their freedom. Obviously you'd pick the second option, at which point you'd be led to the top of one of the castle's 110-foot-high twin towers and told you could go free if you jumped the 12 feet to the other tower. Difficult enough in itself, but you had to do it with your hands tied behind your back. A comfortable position for Herol Graham, the British boxer of the 1980s, who challenged journalists at his weigh-ins to hit him while his hands were thus restricted (no one ever could) – but even he would have struggled with the second condition: you had to perform the jump from a standing start. Even a Brazilian police officer (says he, remembering his question at the Prince of Wales) couldn't manage that.

The esplanade has a few tourists milling around, but only a few. If any are Canadian they should feel at home – James VI (he of the hand-holding) decreed that this bit of the castle was part of Nova Scotia – 'New Scotland' – so that the baronets he was granting said land to could receive their title without the trouble of crossing the Atlantic. If they're American they should look out for the Stars and Stripes scratched into one of the castle's doors by an early compatriot, who was held prisoner here. And if they're Russian they can remember Mikhail Gorbachev's visit here, on the trip where he had to leg it from the Caledonian. Above the fireplace in the castle's Great Hall is a small grate known as the 'Laird's lug' (ear), through which monarchs used to eavesdrop on their visitors. The KGB asked if it could be bricked up. The request was denied.

By now the sunshine and tranquillity have all but rescued me from my hangover, though I'm still glad the Royal Mile is all downhill. And I'm not exactly keen on exploring one of the first buildings on the right: the Scotch Whisky Experience. Instead I turn to the camera obscura opposite, and think of Alan Bennett coming here in 1983 with Alan Bates, when they had a day off from filming. Their guide, 'a genteel Morningside lady', trained the mirror on some scaffolding. 'I often wonder,' she mused in the darkened room, 'if one were to catch them . . . well, unawares. I mean,' she added hastily, 'taking a little *rest*.' That fraitfully refained streak in Edinburgh's character always puts you in mind of *The Prime of Miss Jean Brodie* (even if we now know, after the Prince of Wales quiz, that another of its author's novels inspired the name of a post-punk band). In the film version the school desks had to be made higher to disguise the fact that the girls were played by women, one of them a 20-year-old mother. The actresses were asked not to eat in the studio cafeteria while wearing their school uniforms, as alcohol was on sale. Things are more relaxed now, of course. As Barbara Cartland put it when asked by a journalist whether class barriers had broken down: 'Of course they have – otherwise I wouldn't be sitting here talking to someone like you.'

All the way along the Royal Mile, narrow alleys branch off to either side. One of the first is Lady Stair's Close, which leads into a small square containing the Writers' Museum. Very edifying it is to read about Walter Scott, Robert Burns and Robert Louis Stevenson, but my attention is really grabbed by the tour guide outside explaining Edinburgh's sanitary history to her group. The Princes Street Gardens used to be the North Loch, apparently, a bland name for what amounted to a huge lake of poo. At points it could support the weight of a human being, though at others it was used for witch trials. In the usual fashion, a floater (a person, not . . . you know) was deemed a witch, but if you drowned you were innocent. In 1770 a woman was convicted of witchcraft because she'd tempted a man into marriage by wearing false teeth.

Back over the Royal Mile to Brodie's Close, where the room now housing the Deacon's House Café was once the workshop of William Brodie, the 18th-century cabinetmaker who gave Robert Louis Stevenson the idea for *The Strange Case of Dr Jekyll and Mr Hyde*. His story is also told in drawings on the café's walls. By day Brodie was a respected tradesman, so much so that he earned the title Deacon (president) of the Incorporation of Wrights. Lockwrights, that is – part of making a cabinet is, of course, fitting its locks. What shouldn't be a part of the process is keeping a copy of the lock's key, breaking into your client's house at night and nicking all his stuff. Brodie copied other keys too, like those of the bank that fell victim to his first criminal caper in 1768. That netted him £800, enough to support the average family for several years. In Brodie's case it supported two mistresses and a gambling habit, so he was soon up to his nocturnal shenanigans again. They lasted for 20 years, his conventional life continuing during the day. As well as building cabinets he also designed Edinburgh's gallows. And when one of his burglaries went disastrously wrong in 1788 and he was caught, he ended up dangling from those gallows himself.

It's spooky to sit here, sipping a coffee in the room where so many crimes were planned. You suspect Brodie would be proud that the logo on the café's menu is a masked burglar seen through a keyhole. The code for the toilet door, my receipt announces, is 1894.

'Is that because it's the year Robert Louis Stevenson died?' I ask. None of the staff seem to know, and at least one gives the impression of not being entirely sure who Robert Louis Stevenson was (welcome to Britain, folks), but surely this was the owner's thinking. Alexei Sayle once witnessed his editor at the publisher Faber and Faber punch in the code 1713 to get through a door. 'Of course it's perfectly simple to remember,' said the editor. 'Treaty of Utrecht.'

A quick detour off the Royal Mile onto the George IV Bridge takes me to another café, the Elephant House, famed as the place where J. Rowling wrote some of the first Harry Potter novel in the days before she found her 'K'. Initials were seen as preferable to 'Joanne' (so hiding the author's gender from readers), but Rowling had no middle name and 'J' on its own didn't sound right. So the second letter was added in tribute to her grandmother Kathleen. Inventions can become real, however: when Rowling appeared at the Leveson Inquiry into press freedom she gave her name as 'Joanne Kathleen Rowling'. Her one-time provider of office space is doing well from the connection – even in the few moments I'm standing there two other people come along to read the plaque, and one of them enters the café. The plaque reminds us that Ian Rankin and Alexander McCall Smith have also patronised the establishment.

Back on the Royal Mile (by now called the High Street) I reach St Giles' Cathedral, which on the day in 1707 when the Act of Union was signed between Scotland and England used its bells to ring out 'Why Should I Be So Sad on My Wedding Day?' A few decades previously, when Oliver Cromwell arrived on the High Street after his victory over the Scots in the Battle of Dunbar, most of the crowd commented on the size of his nose. There's a more welcoming atmosphere in the cathedral today, where a minister is reciting a psalm. 'He makes peace in your borders, he fills you with the finest of the wheat.' Only four people occupy the chairs that take the place of pews these days, while a quiet stream of tourists shuffle round the edges, looking at the tablets and plaques on the walls. 'He sends out his command to the Earth. His word runs swiftly...' As ever the church carries on, even though hardly anyone's listening.

A few yards further on, mind you, the church has finally given up the Holy Ghost. The Tron Kirk – where in 1697 a student called Thomas Aikenhead said he wished he was in hell 'so I could warm myself', and so became the last person executed in Scotland for blasphemy – ceased religious trading in 1952. It now houses a small market selling vintage clothes, craft jewellery and the like. Leafing through some Beatles CDs I find there's even one of the band's press conferences. Fully justified, of course – and while we're at it can someone please issue José Mourinho's?

Over the road is Anchor Close, where William Smellie, having somehow survived his inevitable experiences in the school playground, founded the printing house which in 1771 produced the first edition of the *Encyclopedia Britannica*. Despite costing £12 it sold 3000 copies, assisted by the promise of 'unvarnished portrayals of the unmentionable parts of the human body'. Three of these copperplate engravings depicted childbirth with a level of detail so shocking that some readers tore them out. The encyclopedia came in three volumes, the first covering A to B, the second C to L, the last M to Z (do we suspect Mr Smellie was getting tired?) His printing works have gone, but there's a wonderful old stone building at the corner of Anchor Close and the High Street. Depressingly it is now a 'Customer Hub' for Edinburgh City Council.

This part of the city is knee-deep in kilt shops, several of which advertise '5 yard' and '8 yard' versions of the garment. Popping into a shop to investigate, I'm greeted by a Spanish girl who tells me it refers to the amount of material used. 'Eight yards?' I reply. 'That's twenty-four feet. Can you really use that much cloth in a kilt?' Her English isn't fantastic, and she certainly shows no sign of comprehension when I mention the length is the same as that of two full-size snooker tables. All she can do is hold up an 8-yarder from one of the displays and repeat her initial statement. Oh well. One of the Royal Mile's other kilt shops is run by an Indian man in a turban, though as I can't see his legs from the street I don't know whether he's modelling the merchandise.

Quick break for another coffee, and a read through my research notes. One of my favourite Edinburgh stories relates to local hero John Napier, the 16th-century inventor of logarithms. Such work demands absolute peace, so Napier was pretty unhappy about the cockerels in his backyard. Equally, he was clever enough to think of a solution: soaking their grain in brandy. The people at the table next to me – a man and a woman in their fifties, another woman nearer to 70, all wearing verging-on-alternative clothes, the scruffy sort that denote wealth rather than its opposite – are discussing some sort of arts funding application. 'Christina would *love* to get her teeth into this,' says the older lady. 'She is an *absolute* gem.'

At the end of the Royal Mile is the Scottish Parliament. The new one, that is, rather than the 'Creeping Parliament' of 1571, held nearby, which got its name because members had to crawl on hands and knees to avoid the bullets raining down on them from the castle, fired by supporters of Mary, Queen of Scots. The modern Queen of Scots, Elizabeth II, has her Edinburgh residence right opposite the modern Parliament building. You might think this would create a certain tension, but actually there's just a feeling of 'gift shops in it together'. Holyroodhouse's offers everything from tea sets and tankards commemorating Elizabeth's status as Britain's longest-reigning monarch to *Peppa Pig Meets the Queen*. Next to the Scottish Parliament's shop is a display of items and documents concerning the country's political history, including the last volume of proceedings from the old parliament before the 1707 Act of Union with England. The handwritten page ends mid-sentence – 'suchlike another clause in these terms that...' – possibly, they say, because the clerk worried he wasn't going to get paid.

You do wonder how much people – or perhaps how many people – worry about national identity. As I leave the Parliament building the security guards are discussing a planned trip to a pub holding a Turkish night. And institutions find ways of adapting. Back at the train station I look up at the Balmoral hotel, and reflect that it used to be called the North British, 'North Britain' being an old term for Scotland. Something that hasn't changed is the hotel's policy of keeping its huge clock three minutes fast, to help people catch their trains.

Boarding mine, I can't help feeling chuffed with the trip to Edinburgh. It's reassured me that the pub quiz has a long and healthy future ahead of it. Sometimes I worry about it being an old man's game, a tradition that'll die out when Marcus and Toby and I hand in our final answer sheets. And when you do hear about younger people at quizzes it can make you despair: I know of one where a 20-something, confronted with a multiple choice question offering Abraham Lincoln, Benjamin Disraeli, Robert Peel and Mahatma Gandhi, went for Lincoln because 'he's the only one I've heard of'. But last night showed that the next generation *are* up for a quiz. They are young and thrusting and vigorous, and by rights should be spending every waking moment on their next internet start-up. Yet there they were, pints in hand, doing a quiz. As with all the best traditions, there was reinvention involved. You don't want to keep everything the same for its own sake – that way lies morris dancing. So these people were answering questions on Leonardo di Caprio, and Goose was doing his marking on an Excel spreadsheet.

But still: they were keeping the flame alive.

THREE

· · · · · · ·

The smallest crab in the world is named after
a vegetable, because it's similar in size to
that vegetable. Which one?

'Paul Sweedlepipe,' begins Tim Smith, Steve Wright's sidekick
on Radio 2. 'Chevy Slyme. Conkey Chickweed. Nicodemus
Boffin. What links them?'

Wright hasn't got a clue, and asks for the list to be repeated. It
doesn't do him any good – inspiration still won't appear.

'They are all,' says Smith, 'characters in novels by Charles
Dickens.'

Nice of him to turn what could have been just another 'factoid'
(the bits of trivia with which Wright spices his programmes) into
an actual question. It's one of several guises in which quizzes
have appeared recently. There was the email from Ian Woolley of
Quiz Britain, a national database listing forthcoming events. He
has been helping with my research, and heard about a wedding
quiz – guests at the reception will be treated to a quiz about
the bride and groom. Intriguing, but not worth me going along
to, as the project's aim is to discover trivia of general interest.
Then there's the urinal in a London pub that conducts surveys
based on which pressure pad a gentleman directs his aim at.
The question, displayed on a head-height screen, was whether
a drugs-cheat sports star should be allowed to compete again
(left pad for yes, right for no) – but surely this could be adapted

to allow actual quizzing? Most trivia machines offer four possible answers, so you'd only need to double the number of pads. It would certainly counter the 'John Wayne' problem for any celebrities at the urinal: the star once advised a young Michael Caine against wearing suede shoes, because men could be so amazed at finding a star next to them that they'd turn to look. Wayne knew this because it had happened to him.

Then there are newspapers. Specifically the *Independent*, which the Prince of Wales has killed off with its Boxing Day quiz. Marcus doesn't seem to hold this against us (probably because the quiz was his idea in the first place), and uses his final column to list some recent Snowball questions. My favourite is: 'During the making of the film *Beat the Devil* in 1953, Humphrey Bogart was involved in a car accident and lost several teeth, which compromised his recorded dialogue. Who was brought in to overdub his lines?'[1] Elsewhere in the paper there is the final version of the *Independent*'s own quiz. Here we're asked: 'Which major UK retail outlet has the same name as Odysseus's dog in Greek mythology?' Copious brain-ferreting produces nothing, so I'm forced to turn the page upside down for the answer: Argos.

Also, of course, there are real-life quizzes themselves. One is the Sunday night affair in my Suffolk village's pub. It's been ages since I went, largely because on that day of the week, after a large lunch or dinner, a decent amount of wine and a young child making his presence painfully obvious, by the 9 p.m. start time I'm either asleep or well on the way. But the project can't pass by without at least one visit, so by careful Rioja rationing I manage to get there. Gareth is in the chair. When he's competing rather than compèring, his stock one-liner is 'One either way?'. He shouts it whenever an answer is numerical, even (especially) if it's something like '99 Red Balloons' or '*Fahrenheit 451*'. Funny. The first time. Tonight, however, with Gareth asking rather than answering the questions, we are safe. We learn that the Exocet

---

1   A very young Peter Sellers.

missile took its name from the French for 'flying fish', and that a 'baldrick' was a belt, worn over one shoulder, in which you carried a sword. There's potential controversy when Gareth asks: 'The centre circle on a football pitch is used at kick-off, restarts, and for which other aspect of the game?' My team knows he means the penalty shoot-out – all players except the penalty-taker and the two goalkeepers have to remain inside the circle – but others shout 'what about the minute's silence?' Nice try, but not actually part of the game.

Then there's the latest trip to Highgate, where Patrick is our host. Question six elicits one of those wonderful moments of teamwork, an answer which neither Martin nor Toby nor I would have got on our own but which quails before our combined powers. Patrick wants to know which word replaces both of the blanks in: 'Some men are born mediocre, some men achieve mediocrity, and some men have mediocrity thrust upon them. With BLANK BLANK it had been all three.'

'It has to be someone whose first name is the same as their surname,' I say. Then inspiration strikes. 'What about . . . argh, the guy in *Lolita* . . . what's his name?' Then it comes to me. 'Humbert Humbert.'

'Good call,' says Martin, writing it down.

'Hang on,' says Toby. '*Lolita* is in the first person. Humbert Humbert narrates it. He wouldn't be saying that about himself, would he?'

Fair point. But we're in motion now, seeking the answer like a pack of sharks. 'It has to be another character with a similar name,' I say.

Martin slaps the table. 'Major Major. *Catch-22*.'

Of course. Now that he says it the quote comes back to us. We congratulate each other, bathing in the glow of our collective brilliance. This is very much how it must have felt, I imagine, for the members of the Brazilian football team in the 1970 World Cup.

A healthy smattering of instinct and knowledge on the other questions puts us one off the lead after the first round.

(Difference between a mural and a fresco? Former painted on dry plaster, latter on wet. Which bank has recently closed its personal banking service to its approximately 4000 customers? Bank of England.) Sadly, however, this is to be the high point of our evening, as from then on we tank massively. To the question 'in which building would you find Britain's largest pipe organ?', we instinctively write 'the Royal Albert Hall'. Then the words 'Liverpool Cathedral' pop up from my subconscious. Is it that instead? Toby and Martin dissuade me from changing our answer, on the grounds that you should always go with your first thought. The answer is Liverpool Cathedral.

But my worst moment comes in the beer round, which Patrick prefaces with an announcement that he's sometimes criticised for not asking enough questions about popular culture. The fourth question refers to *Emmerdale* ('whatever that is,' says Patrick), but we're also alert to the fact that the hidden link between the answers will probably also be of a populist nature. It's incredible what overthinking can do to your mind. Possibilities shoot this way and that, overlapping to produce yet more possibilities, which you then cross-reference and back-reference and side-reference until your synapses are fried and you barely know your own name.

'It can't be that,' I say, referring to the theory which has been bubbling up since question three, namely that the first names of the people in the answers are the first names of the Jackson Five.

'Why not?' asks Toby.

'Because the only answer we're sure of is this...' – I point to 'Michael Caine' – '... and there was no Michael Jack—'

In fairness to them, Toby and Martin do let me stay for the rest of the evening.

* * *

My final quiz before the next field trip takes place in a town near me in Suffolk. Sunday nights being something of a fallow patch for restaurants, the owners of one here recently hit upon the wheeze of getting me to run a combined quiz/dinner. Having hosted events for my son's school/the local cricket team/etc., my quizmastering abilities have something of a reputation locally, but despite this the restaurant sold out and people had a good time. So they've asked me back. Tonight's event has the added twist that it's being included in an attempt by a group called PubAid to set a record for the world's biggest quiz. Over a thousand establishments from all over the country are running evenings simultaneously, the aim being to raise money for charity. (In the end the amount will reach six figures.)

The guidelines laid down by *Guinness World Records* don't require us to use exactly the same questions as everyone else – in fact only the first one has to be the same. This is: 'Who was the first black person to receive an Oscar for Best Actor or Actress?' (Sidney Poitier, 1964, *Lilies of the Field*.) After that we're free to use as many or as few of the supplied questions as we want. Anyone who has ever fished in the sea of quizzes available on the internet will know how prepared I am to be unimpressed. More often than not questions are inaccurate, parochial, arcane, ambiguously phrased or all of the above. But PubAid's selection is pretty good. I'm tempted by: 'In which year did Lloyd George try to nationalise Britain's pubs?' – 1915, apparently – though a better question would have been: 'What, in 1915, did Lloyd George try to nationalise?' Add in a couple more clues and if someone knows the history of the government desperately trying to keep First World War munitions workers off the sauce they'd stand a good chance.[2]

As it is, there are two questions I actually use. 'The name of which famous pop group is also the Aramaic word for father?' is tricky. You could make it easier by adding '... though that's not why the four members of the group settled on the name'. Yes, Agnetha, Bjorn, Benny and Anni-Frid chose 'Abba' for less

---

2 Lloyd George also hassled George V into locking up Buckingham Palace's wine cellars to set a good example. The King ended up annoyed that while he spent the war on the wagon, the workers continued getting drunk whenever they wanted.

learned reasons. The other question is: 'Which world-famous landmark is located on the southern slope of Mount Lee?' Again, difficult, but it's one of those whose value lies in the cries of 'oh, of *course*' when you read out the answer. I didn't know the name Mount Lee, even though I do happen to know a bit about the landmark. An actress called Peg Entwistle committed suicide by jumping off it in 1932, for example. And it was originally longer than it is now – the letters 'L-A-N-D' appeared at the end. Yes, it's the 'Hollywood' sign, originally put in place to advertise a real-estate development. Peg's final journey was from the top of the H.

Unlike the Prince of Wales, the restaurant has a wireless mike, meaning I can wander among the tables. This is fun, as it lets you give a running commentary on people's answers. One of the questions is: 'Of which city did Ernest Hemingway write: "If you are lucky enough to have lived in x as a young man, then wherever you go for the rest of your life, it stays with you, for x is a moveable feast"?' As I move away from two tables, one of which has put Barcelona and the other Paris, I say: 'I've just seen two answers, one of which was right, the other wrong.' It's fun watching the two tables eyeing each other, trying to read levels of confidence. And indeed eyeing me as I read their answers: the mind games require a poker face. What's astonishing is that at every quiz there's at least one team who cover up their sheet as I approach. 'I don't know why you're doing that,' I'll announce. 'I *know* the answers, remember.'

Hemingway's moveable feast was Paris, by the way. Round one also reveals the century in which smoking was banned in the chamber of the House of Commons (17th), before round two offers up the only letter of the alphabet not to appear in the name of any US state (Q) and the celebrity whose nickname arose at his birth in 1974 when his sister learned that he was to be called Edward (Bear Grylls). By this point the starters have been eaten, so to give teams some peace over their main course without letting the quiz element fade completely, they are supplied with a picture round. It features cropped photos of

11 celebrities, whose first initials can be rearranged to spell the name of the restaurant. Always a delicate task, setting this sort of round. I obviously know who the celebrities are, so have to guard against making it too difficult as I set to work with Photoshop. Still, you'd be surprised how many people are recognisable from just a tiny fraction of their image. George Best's beard, for instance – never been another one like it.

Tonight's picture round produces one of my favourite-ever wrong answers. The image in question has deliberately been left uncropped to show the whole face – the face of a statue. The answer is Horatio Nelson, my thinking being that people might doubt themselves because he isn't wearing an eyepatch. Nelson never did: yes, he was blinded in his right eye during a battle, but there was no external damage. It's thought the eyepatch misconception arose when 19th-century portrait painters added one to convey his blindness. Either way, his statue in Trafalgar Square certainly doesn't have one.

Even given the room for self-doubt, however, it's hard to see how one team thought it was a statue of Evel Knievel.

* * *

One day in 1941, Winston Churchill had a meeting at 10 Downing Street with Charles de Gaulle. The Frenchman was never his favourite person, and Churchill informed his private secretary that he would not shake de Gaulle's hand or speak to him in his native language. The conversation would be conducted through an interpreter – Colville himself. True to his word, Churchill simply indicated a chair when de Gaulle entered, then sat down and began: 'General de Gaulle, I have asked you to come here this afternoon...'

'*Mon Général*,' said Colville, '*je vous ai invité...*'

Churchill glared at his secretary. 'I didn't call him "*Mon Général*",' he said. 'And I didn't say I'd invited him.'

That is one of several hundred, possibly several thousand, stories with which I could have started this section. Winston

Churchill isn't just the greatest Briton ever (BBC poll, 2002), he's also the most quoted, the most anecdotalised and – crucially for this book – the most trivialised Briton ever. That's trivialised as in 'there's lots of trivia about him', not 'his achievements have been derided'. Who could do that, after all? In fact the trivia about Churchill only adds to his glory. It makes him more loveable, more human, rounds out the picture. It also provides fuel for quizzes. Never in the field of human quizzing has one man given rise to so many questions. Which was his favourite brand of champagne? (Pol Roger – he always filled his own glass and those of his neighbours at lunch, then passed the bottle along, but only to the left because passing to the right was bad luck.) In his 'We shall never surrender' speech, Churchill said that the British would fight on the beaches and which four other places? (Landing grounds, fields, streets, hills. When he sat down to cheers from the Commons, he turned to a colleague and muttered: 'And we'll fight them with the butt ends of broken beer bottles, because that's bloody well all we've got!') Churchill said that dogs look up to us and cats look down on us – but which animals, in his opinion, treat us as an equal? (Pigs. He kept them at Chartwell, his house in Kent, but not to eat: he believed no animal could be slaughtered if you had wished it good morning.)

Even now, over half a century after his death, Churchill gets everywhere. Anyone who ever had anything to do with him is guaranteed a mention in the obituary columns. John Mitchell, for instance, the navigator of Churchill's private plane. His death at the age of 97 in February 2016 brought tales of how the aircraft was named *Ascalon* (after the lance with which St George killed the dragon), and how Winston once insisted on landing it himself, 'only for his stomach to get in the way of the control column with near-disastrous consequences'. There seems to be a link from Churchill to just about everything and everyone. He shared a chauffeur with Elvis Presley: when the star discovered that Gerald Peters used to drive the great leader he christened him 'Sir Gerald'. One of Winston's granddaughters, Arabella, was a co-founder of the Glastonbury festival. (She later lived in a squat and married a juggler called Haggis McLeod.) As I write this chapter European Union leaders are having a summit, a word we owe to Churchill. When the Cold War began its freeze in 1950, Churchill called for 'a parley at the summit' between Western leaders and Stalin. He used the word again in May 1953, which happened to coincide with Edmund Hillary's attempt on Everest, and the name stuck. Also in the news is an app launched by ex-US Defense Secretary Donald Rumsfeld, which allows you to play Churchill's fiendishly difficult version of the card game Solitaire. And then there is the Archbishop of Canterbury. Justin Welby's father, it turns out, wasn't his father after all: real paternity lay with Anthony Montague Browne, the last-ever private secretary to ... Winston Churchill.

Wherever you go in Britain you're reminded of the man. Staying at the Swan Hotel in Southwold, I notice the framed page from their visitors' book of June 1940, when Churchill was visiting that part of the Suffolk coast to review sea defences: unlike every other guest he omitted the ditto marks underneath 'British' in the nationality column – obviously that went without saying. Passing the National Portrait Gallery in London I see they have an exhibition of Churchill photos. There's a shot of him and his wife Clementine in Westminster Hall (through which I passed for the Press Gallery quiz), being presented with Graham Sutherland's portrait of him, a gift from Parliament on Churchill's 80th birthday. They both hated the painting, and after her husband's death Clemmie had it burned. There's also the famous 'Roaring Lion' photograph by Yousuf Karsh, the leader's defiant expression the result of Karsh taking away his cigar.

All of which reminds me of something I've been meaning to get round to for years: visiting Blenheim Palace. I've been to Chartwell, I've been to the Cabinet War Rooms in London, but somehow I've never been to the Oxfordshire stately home in which Winston Churchill entered this world on 30 November 1874. So in a tribute to the man, the legend, the root of all those questions, I decide that the next quiz will tie in with a trip to

Blenheim. Initially the plan is to visit the quiz nearest to the palace itself. It seems the White House pub in Bladon, the neighbouring village, whose churchyard is home to Winston's grave, has one every week, but further enquiries reveal this has recently ceased. Actually that's not such a bad thing, because staring at the map has put me in mind of the city just down the road from Blenheim – Oxford. How can I not visit Oxford if I'm looking to learn stuff? That's that, then: a trip to Blenheim Palace, followed by a quiz in Oxford, followed by a mooch around the university city itself.

It could almost be what Tony Blair was thinking of when he coined the phrase 'education, education, education'.

* * *

The appointed day – a Sunday during what other universities call 'summer term' but which in Oxford is known as 'Trinity term' (it includes Trinity Sunday) – dawns bright and warm. As I trundle my car along Blenheim's drive, pausing every few yards to let someone else in the queue ahead pay at the little booth, there's plenty of time to see why Churchill was so in love with the place.

'This great house,' he wrote, 'is one of the precious limbs which join us to our famous past ... I am proud to have been born at Blenheim.'

It's a proper palace, the only home in England to hold the title other than those occupied by royals or bishops. What makes Blenheim all the more imposing, and Churchill's awareness of his family history all the more understandable, is that it was built for one man: John Churchill, the 1st Duke of Marlborough, whose victory at the Battle of Blenheim in 1704 earned him this building as a reward. He's there to remind us of the fact, atop his 134-foot column way off to the right, overlooking the palace grounds and the elms he had planted in the formation of his victorious troops.

I follow the marshals' instructions and park on the grass, then walk round to the main entrance. In weather like this business is brisk, and some nifty footwork is required to avoid getting trapped in the middle of a group of Chinese tourists. You enter through the East Courtyard, where to add to the gaiety of nations an Indian couple who have just got married here are posing for photos beside their wedding car, a gorgeous Beauford. Its cream panels set the bride's bright pink dress off a treat, while in the background the couple's more elderly guests are loaded into an elongated golf cart for the trip from the Orangery (where the service has taken place) to whichever far-flung corner of the estate is hosting the reception. Everyone looking on, including those eating in the Oxfordshire Pantry Café (once Blenheim's dairy), send smiles of good luck, except for – as is traditional at all weddings – one of the elderly female guests, who scowls from the golf cart in disapproval.

Heading across the gravel-strewn Great Court, I climb the steps and enter the main doors. You always look at houses like this and think 'must be a bugger to heat', but Blenheim's huge cast-iron radiators are so fierce they bear warning notices. Overlooking the hall is a beautiful wall-mounted clock by Negretti and Zambra of London, matched on the other side by what looks at first like another clock, but which you then notice has the points of the compass instead of numbers: it's linked to a weather vane. The wind direction at the moment is halfway between ENE and E, and I wonder what this is called. Looking it up I discover that ENE doesn't actually stand for 'east by north-east' – there's no 'by'. The directions between north-east and east run 'north-east by east', 'east-north-east' and 'east by north'. Follow this through and you'll realise that *North by Northwest* isn't a real direction either – the title plays on the film's reference to Northwest Airlines.

I turn to the right and join the visitor-crocodile working its way round the palace. The Churchill exhibition is towards the end: first you enjoy the story of the richer branch of the family, the one with all the Dukes of Marlborough in it. Some visitors, it seems, are unsure of the exact ancestry. 'Winston Churchill,'

says one woman, 'his parents were servants, weren't they?' '*No,*'
says her exasperated husband, 'they *owned* the place.' (Neither of
them is right.) Another man tells his wife that Churchill wasn't a
duke, but had his own big house called Chatsworth. All of this,
in accordance with standard 'Brits in a Stately Home' behaviour
code, is conducted at a whisper. The leader of the Chinese group,
on the other hand (I can't quite shake them off), bellows everything, proving it isn't just Brits who operate a policy of 'if they
can't understand you you they can't hear you'. Most of the Chinese
see the visit as an exercise in photography rather than learning,
with one man capturing everything – his entire journey round
the palace – on a camcorder. His holiday videos will be as long
as his holiday.

Blenheim steers a nice line between 'real family home' –
photos in the Green Drawing Room and the Long Library show
the current Duke (the 12th) and his clan, including one of the
Duke himself asking Bill Clinton for an autograph – and 'the
aristocracy are barking mad': there are gazelle heads on the wall
and a china service the 3rd Duke got from the King of Poland 'in
exchange for a pack of stag hounds'. Sadly I can find no further
details about my favourite Marlborough story, the one involving
the 10th Duke's visit to his daughter in America. Very unusually
he had travelled without his valet, and came down to breakfast
on the first day complaining that there was something wrong
with his toothbrush. 'I can't get it to foam,' he grumbled. Eventually, his daughter deduced the problem: the valet hadn't been
there to apply the toothpaste.

We pass through more rooms. The Red Drawing Room offers
a Van Dyck painting titled *Lady Killigrew with a lady called 'The
Countess of Morton'* (did they not believe her?) and chaperone
sofas which, according to the information panel, gave 'courting
couples just enough privacy'. Really? All that makes one of these
different from a normal chaise longue is a small divider at one
end. It comes up to just above waist level. Did the gooseberry
sit there pretending not to notice as the canoodlers stretched
out beside him? Or did he have the long bit, nodding off so

one of the lovers could sit on the other's lap in the short bit? The Green Writing Room boasts a clock by a Paris maker called Léonard Bourgeois (the only thing in here that is), while the Saloon (still the venue for the family's Christmas lunch) contains a fireplace whose logs catch your attention. Something isn't quite right – lifting one up I find they're made of brick, complete with fake charring.

Piece together the clues in the First State Room and you get a tale of how dynasties fade and fight back. The Marlboroughs' rise started with the victory note (a replica here – the British Library has the original) sent by John Churchill, telling of his victory at Blenheim. Written on the only piece of paper to hand – the bill from a French tavern where he and his troops had stopped – it begins: 'I have not time to say more but beg you will give my Duty to the Queen, and let her know her Army has had a Glorious Victory...' It was given to Colonel Parke, who took eight days to ride back to England and deliver it, first to Churchill's wife (sensible chap), then to Queen Anne at Windsor Castle. On the mantelpiece is this year's Quit Rent, a small flag handed to the monarch each 13 August (the battle's anniversary) as rent for Blenheim – if it wasn't paid the land would revert to the Crown. But by 1895 the Marlboroughs needed the dowry from the 9th Duke's marriage to the American Consuelo Vanderbilt (her portrait hangs over the fireplace) so they could restore the gold leaf on this room's walls and ceiling. Then a century later it was the Duke holding out his pen to Bill Clinton.

Into the Second State Room, whose walls bear huge tapestries depicting the siege of Bouchain, the final campaign which secured victory at Blenheim. Winston Churchill said this showed his ancestor's military genius more clearly than any other battle. (A pity, therefore, that Earl Cadogan's dog, accompanying the troops as a mascot, is for some reason depicted with horse hoofs.) Portrait-over-the-mantelpiece honours go to Louis XIV, the 1st Duke's adversary. 'Why would you have him over your fireplace?' asks the woman next to me. Maybe the Duke was like Henrik Ibsen, who put a portrait of his rival playwright

August Strindberg over his desk because 'I cannot write a line without that madman standing and staring down at me.' Or Hugh Carleton Greene, the BBC Director-General who bought a painting of Mary Whitehouse just so he could throw darts at it.

The Third State Room has a portrait of the 1st Duke that his wife particularly liked, not least because at 17 guineas she considered it good value. Given that that's less than I paid to get in here today, you could say she had a point.[3] Finally, a right turn brings you into the Long Library, which at 180 feet certainly justifies its name. In 1954 Christian Dior used it for a fashion show and during the First World War it was a hospital ward, but the date catching my attention is the one on the statue of Queen Anne as you first enter. Commissioned by the first Duchess as a memorial to the woman who'd given them Blenheim in the first place, its Roman numerals denote 1746 – though the '40' is rendered as 'XXXX' rather than the customary 'XL'. This sort of thing excites sad people. Indeed I've been known to set quiz questions on Roman numerals, such as 'which year uses the most?' (1888 – MDCCCLXXXVIII). Looking up, I notice that the large white spaces on the ceiling bear slogans like 'More saltpeter than black powder', 'More aluminium than lead' and 'Enough to make it explode'. The lettering is modern, and an enquiry to one of the guides reveals that it's the work of Lawrence Weiner, an American conceptualist who accepted the invitation to fill the spaces with art, as no one had got round to doing so in the three centuries since they were left blank for just that purpose. His work always concentrates on words – he was influenced by the graffiti of his New York childhood – though he refuses to explain them, wanting the viewer to make up his own mind. The guide and I agree that the message in the central space – 'More than Enough' – refers to a house of this size being built for only one man.

---

3 A guinea – so called because the coin was made with gold from that part of Africa – was worth a pound and a shilling. Racehorses are still sold in guineas: the seller gets the pound, the auctioneer the shilling.

At the far end of the library is an organ, which with over 2300 pipes is believed to be the largest privately owned one in Britain.[4] Well into its second century, the instrument needs expensive restoration work. The appeal for this is being overseen by a group called 'Friends of the Organ'. You can sponsor a small treble pipe for £25, or a 32-footer for £300. In the meantime the instrument is still just about playable, and by happy accident I'm in time to hear today's guest recitalist blast out some Mendelssohn. A crowd quickly gathers, before realising they like the idea of an organ sonata more than they like the reality, and they disperse just as quickly. One of the few who remain is a weeks-old Chinese baby with its parents (on their own, not part of the Group of Terror). I can't help imagining the 1st Duke returning to survey the scene. His mind would have been blown. Did he ever see a Chinese person? Even Mendelssohn's music was over a century in the future. Yet the baby is taking everything for granted – Lawrence Weiner's words on the ceiling directly above it, the robes worn by the 10th Duke at the coronation of George VI, the sounds emerging from those long metal tubes. At this age the whole world is equally strange, and therefore not strange at all. As the organist continues to play, the baby's eyes close and a peaceful sleep begins.

Retracing my steps, I find the door halfway along the library that leads to the Churchill exhibition. The first thing to grab my attention is a beautiful silver badge engraved 'On His Britannic Majesty's Service ... Colonel The Duke of Marlborough ... He is to be afforded every assistance to reach his destination with the utmost expedition.' This was arranged by Churchill, who started the First World War as First Lord of the Admiralty, as a favour to his cousin, the 9th Duke. Too old for active service, the Duke nevertheless wanted to do his bit, so Churchill had a word with Lord Kitchener and the Duke was appointed a special messenger to the forces. By the end of the war things had changed somewhat: the disasters of Gallipoli and the Dardanelles forced

---

4 Horrific memories of my 'Liverpool Cathedral' mistake in Highgate. That one has 10,268.

Churchill to resign from the government. Instead of spending more time with his family he went to serve in the forces himself. Which is why another item in the cabinet is a piece of shrapnel from a 30lb shell that fell between Churchill and the 9th Duke. It 'might have separated us for ever', reads Winston's engraved message, 'but is now a token of union'. I hope the great man wouldn't feel offended by this, but his military decorations and ribbons, laid out next to the shrapnel, are so numerous and multicoloured that they remind me of nothing so much as a flattened-out Rubik's Cube.

The friendship between the two cousins dated from child-hood, when Churchill and Sunny (as the 9th Duke was known) played a game called 'French and English'. Invented by Winston, it had only two rules: Winston was the General of the English Army, and no promotion was allowed (in other words Winston would always be General of the English Army). The room contains his baby saddle, a small leather seat which was tied to the back of his pony Rob Roy so he could learn to ride. Much of his childhood was spent at Blenheim, his father Randolph and American mother Jennie preferring to gad around London. Winston was looked after by his grandmother Frances and nanny Mrs Everest, or 'Woomany' as he called her. The impish-ness that would endear him to the public began here. His younger brother Jack once remarked: 'Winston is teaching me how to be naughty.' In time Winston would call his own son Randolph. The pattern continued: Randolph's son was Winston (also a Tory MP), and his son is Randolph. He was born on 22 January 1965, just two days before his famous great-grandfather died, meaning some newspapers announced the two events in the same edition. The newest Randolph became a father in 1996... to a daughter. Two more children followed in 1998 and 2003 – both daughters. Would there be a chance for the pat-tern to continue? There would: a son finally appeared in 2007. But Randolph obviously decided the famous tag would be too great a burden in the 21st century, and christened his boy John. Winston's in there as a middle name, though.

Also in this room is a bust of Churchill. The benefactors who paid for it are listed on individual gold plaques, the most impressive being (as it always is in such lists) 'Anonymous'. Making my way through the crush into the second room, I see that it concentrates on Winston's relationship with his wife. He first saw Clementine Hozier at a grand ball. He liked what he saw – too much, in fact, because when his mother introduced them as requested, the famous Churchill eloquence disappeared. Winston was so tongue-tied he couldn't even ask Clemmie to dance, and someone else whisked her away. It was four years before they met again, at a dinner party given by Clemmie's aunt Lady St Helier. Even then things nearly went awry: Churchill was late. Fortunately, the empty chair was the one next to Clemmie, so when he arrived he had a chance to impress her. This time the patter emerged, and the relationship was off and running.[5] By August 1908 Clementine was here at Blenheim for a house party, organised by the 9th Duke so that Winston could propose. A post-breakfast walk to the rose garden was planned. Clemmie waited at the appointed place. No Winston: he had overslept. Only Sunny's hastily improvised 'carriage ride in the park' suggestion stopped her storming back to London. By the time they returned Winston had hauled himself out of bed, and off the pair went for their walk. 'It was a fine day,' recalled Clemmie years later, 'and we had been walking in the rose garden (... no proposal) when Winston said: "There's rather a nice summer house near here. Why not rest in there?" We sat for half an hour and still nothing was said... I looked down at the stone floor and noticed a beetle slowly moving across it and I thought to myself: "If that beetle reaches that crack and Winston hasn't proposed, he's not going to."' Eventually, however, the question was asked. The answer was yes.

The next day Winston took Clemmie to Oxford station so she could return to London and tell her mother the news. When

---

5 One of Winston's previous crushes had been on the actress Ethel Barrymore, great-aunt of *ET* star Drew.

the train pulled in he couldn't bear to be parted from her, so he jumped on as well. This need to be together would continue for the rest of his life. Their pre-marriage nights together at Blenheim, spent of course in separate bedrooms, were such agony that they sent notes to each other, carried along the corridors by staff. One of Clemmie's read: '*Je t'aime passionnément* – I feel less shy in French.' The written word was important throughout their marriage. While apart they penned four letters a day to each other, and even if they were together and Clemmie had something difficult to say she did it in writing: that way Winston could reflect on it without losing his temper. Another ploy to ensure domestic peace was never having breakfast together. They tried it once, said Winston, 'but we had to stop or our marriage would have been wrecked'. The tactics obviously worked – not once did the couple go to bed on an argument. Or, as you put it when you're Winston Churchill: 'Never once have we closed our eyes in slumber with an unappeased difference.'

Talking of the famous eloquence – as I'm reading away, a low growl begins to sound from the next room. At first it's more like earth being moved than a human voice, and I'm reminded of Richard Burton's story from his run as Hamlet at the Old Vic in 1953. Uttering his opening lines one night, he heard an 'extraordinary rumble' coming from the front row. A sideways glimpse revealed Churchill in the front row, performing the part himself. 'I tried everything to shake him off,' said Burton later. 'I sped up, I slowed down, I missed bits out.' But Churchill was determined. 'He was with me to the death – every word.' The Prime Minister even appeared in the actor's dressing room during the interval. 'My Lord Hamlet,' he intoned. 'May I use your lavatory?'

Heading through to the third room I find the source of the growl, a push-button panel that lets you replay some of Churchill's most famous speeches: a jukebox of jaw-jaw, to quote his own term for the thing he preferred to war-war. At school he won a prize for reciting from memory Macaulay's *Lays of Ancient Rome* – all 1200 lines of it, without a single slip. Writing his speeches took just as much effort as delivering them: it's said that for each minute he spoke he put in an hour's preparation. As his friend F. E. Smith said: 'He has devoted the best years of his life to preparing his impromptu speeches.'

One of the books I've consulted in preparation for this trip is *Mr Churchill's Secretary* by Elizabeth Nel, who worked for him from 1941 to 1945. On a silent typewriter, she reveals – Churchill didn't want his train of thought interrupted while he dictated. He also preferred '-ized' to '-ised' (one in the eye for those who think it's an Americanism – the form was used for centuries in England), and called his paper hole-punch a 'Klop', prompting unlikely thoughts of both a Liverpool FC manager and the sitcom *'Allo 'Allo!*. Nel was intimidated at first by Churchill's irritability, but ended up adoring him. The passages where she describes him dictating his speeches are almost as moving as the speeches themselves. He would 'walk up and down the room, his forehead crinkled in thought, the cords of his dressing-gown trailing behind him ... Sometimes he would pause to light his cigar, which with so much concentration was neglected and frequently went out ... Sometimes his voice would become thick with emotion, and occasionally a tear would run down his cheek. As inspiration came to him he would gesture with his hands, just as one knew he would be doing when he delivered his speech, and the sentences would roll out with so much feeling that one died with the soldiers, toiled with the workers, hated the enemy, strained for Victory.'

They don't have Churchill's dressing gown here, but they do have one of his 'siren suits', the all-in-one garment he designed himself for air-raids, so he could put it on quickly over whatever he was wearing. (The same thinking also inspired his specially made zip-up shoes.) This suit is a fetching red number in what looks to be (it's in a glass cabinet) a beautifully soft material.[6] The garments were tailored by Turnbull and Asser of Jermyn

---

6 Shamefully, I can't resist the same petty thought I had standing before an original Elvis costume: 'I'm taller than you.'

Street, and sometimes made their way back there to have cigar burns repaired.

At this point there's more 'Brits in a Stately Home' behaviour. A woman is blocking the exit, but the couple behind her won't say 'excuse me'. Instead they stare at her back, getting visibly irritated when telepathy refuses to work. Eventually she senses their presence, and steps aside with an apology they're too angry to acknowledge. Following them through, I enter the penultimate room. It's a room I've read a lot about over the years, and to find myself standing in it without knowing I was going to comes as a shock. Because this is the room in which, on 30 November 1874, a full two months before the event was expected, Winston Leonard Spencer-Churchill was born. Preparations had been made at his parents' new London home, but the birth was hastened by what Lord Randolph described as a 'rather imprudent and rough drive in a pony carriage'. You'll often read that Churchill was born during a ball, but the letter in which his father describes the carriage ride makes no reference to that. Someone who asked Churchill himself to clear up the confusion later in life got the reply: 'Although present on that occasion I have no clear recollection of the events leading up to it.' But the statesman didn't mind being born in a small room – indeed when Blenheim was about to be opened to the public in 1950 and someone suggested substituting a bigger chamber, Churchill refused: 'You cannot attempt to hoodwink the British people and, if you do, I shall expose you.'

On show are the chair in which Jennie nursed her newborn and one of Winston's baby vests. His premature arrival meant that clothes and a cradle had to be borrowed from the wife of a solicitor in nearby Woodstock. In a small gold frame fixed to the bedstead are some locks of hair tied with a white ribbon. 'Sir Winston Churchill's Curls,' announces a decades-old placard. 'Cut from his head when he was five years old.' Some more recent wording describes them as 'a rich auburn'. Known to the rest of us as 'ginger'. Why the need for such reticence, when they've got Winston Churchill on their team? He'd gone bald by the time he was famous, but if gingers issued more reminders that the greatest-ever Briton was one of theirs, surely the stigma would disappear?

The final room covers Churchill's funeral. I love the fact that his birth and death are put next to each other like this: a reminder of his beloved Shakespeare's 'seven ages of man', in which we end up as we started, old age a 'second childishness' where we lose our teeth and hair. The fact that Churchill lost his so early gave him all the more time to consider the similarities between life's end and its beginning – as he said when a woman told him her baby looked like him: 'Madam, *all* babies look like me.' Another of his lines is written above the door in the 'death' room: 'The journey has been enjoyable and well worth making – once.' He didn't believe in an afterlife, 'only in black velvet – eternal sleep'. His velvet started just after 8 a.m. on 24 January 1965, a date Winston himself had predicted, telling Jock Colville that he would die on the same day as his father. (Lord Randolph exited on 24 January 1895.) His funeral at St Paul's was attended by six monarchs, one of them Britain's – in an unprecedented move the Queen entered the cathedral before Churchill's coffin, and left after it. The locomotive pulling Churchill's funeral train had its three identification discs arranged in a 'V' formation as a tribute to his famous hand gesture.[7] The body was delivered to Hanborough, the nearest station to Bladon. Six red telephone boxes had been installed in the village so that journalists could report on his burial, and the local milkman delivered double amounts the previous morning so he wouldn't disturb the solemnity of the funeral day.

After leaving Blenheim I drive down the road to the church itself, and stand at the grave from which you could originally see the palace.[8] Winston is surrounded by several family members, including his brother John who gloried in the middle name

---

7 Roofs damaged by German bombing raids during the Second World War were often retiled to include a 'V' formation. One in Dagenham added three dots and a dash (Morse code for the letter), while another included a silhouette of Churchill himself.

8 Since Churchill's burial some trees have grown which block the view.

'Strange'. Also there, of course, is Clemmie, who on visiting her husband's grave in 1974 was heard to whisper 'not long now, darling'. (It would actually be another three years before she joined him.) The white horizontal gravestone is agreeably modest (just the couple's names and dates, without even Winston's 'Sir'), and accessible enough for people to leave flowers. Someone has added a handwritten poem, which concludes: 'Fate gave us Winston just in time, To rid the world of Nazi crime.' Even the name of the funeral bells' peal was humble: 'Plain Bob Minor'. In the days that followed thousands queued to pay their respects – an old lady who arrived for the normal Sunday church service was given a police escort lest people think she was trying to jump the queue.

The path used by Bladon dog-walkers as a shortcut through the churchyard goes right past Churchill's grave: I bet he'd have liked that. Ditto the fact that the information leaflets inside the church are available in English and German. And I'm sure he'd want me to record the reminder in the visitors' book that Bladon church isn't all about Churchill: between 'very fitting for a great man' and 'we are honoured to be here in remembrance of such a great man' there is 'we lit a candle for Debbie'.

As I step outside again and take one last look at the grave, I remember the Chinese toddler from a few minutes ago, in the final room at Blenheim. He was there with his grandmother, watching the video of Churchill's funeral. Hearing Big Ben's final bongs of the day (it was silenced at 9.45 a.m. as a mark of respect) the little chap sang along with them, his random notes forming a haphazard harmony. And then when some soldiers were shown marching in step, the toddler stamped around to mimic them.

I bet Churchill would have liked that too.

* * *

It seems only right this evening, here in the city of Oxford, whose university has for a thousand years exemplified the very highest standards of academic rigour, nurturing world-famous thinkers and scientists, people who have won Nobel prizes by the armful and revolutionised just about every area of intellectual endeavour, that I should be sitting in a pub thinking about the rumour that Lionel Messi was named after Lionel Richie.

He wasn't, as it happens, and there's a small part of me that will never get over my disappointment at that. But I take comfort in the fact that it *is* true that Messi's great rival Cristiano Ronaldo was named after Ronald Reagan. Not for political reasons, although Reagan was in the White House at the time: it was because in his previous career the Gipper had been Ronaldo's father's favourite actor. All of this comes to mind because the City Arms is showing tonight's Barcelona match, and as Callum and Oli – the two students who run the quiz – haven't turned up yet, I'm watching proceedings in the Nou Camp.[9] Eventually the pair arrive. I know it's them because one of them stands on a table and plugs a small white box into a power socket above the bar. This is no ordinary quiz, you see – this is a SpeedQuizzing quiz. Which means you take part via your smartphone. Downloading the app only takes a few seconds (certainly now they've installed the wifi booster), then you're ready to go. The exact details of how it works are still eluding me: Callum and Oli have explained briefly by email, but they are in their early twenties and I am in my mid-forties, so it's going to take more than that. For now, I start by asking the obvious question – with everyone using their phones as an integral part of the quiz, how do you stop them cheating?

'We thought that would be a problem too,' replies Oli, the taller of the two, the more conventionally handsome, the clean-shaven one. 'We used to do quizzes the conventional way. But when we started using the app the scores went down, not up.'

'It's *speed* quizzing,' explains Callum (dreadlocks, straggly beard, scarf knotted loosely over a hooded top). 'There isn't time

9 The second-largest football stadium in the world. Top spot goes to the Rungrado 1st of May Stadium in North Korea, though soccer isn't its only attraction. In the late 1990s, for instance, several army generals convicted of an assassination attempt on Kim Jong-Il were executed there. By being burned.

to cheat.' Teams get ten seconds for each question (the quiz-master can start the countdown from his laptop whenever he wants), and the answer is revealed before you move on. There's a bonus point for the team with the quickest right answer. You can also set different types of questions, continues Callum. 'A "poll" question, for example. All the teams answer, and those in the majority get points. Like the other week we asked who would win in a fight between me and Oli.'

'And the result was?'

Callum smiles. 'Me, of course.' For the record, I think he's right. Oli might have the reach, but Callum looks tougher, more streetwise – he'd get the better of Pretty Boy.

It's fairly quiet tonight, with just the seven teams. ('Final term,' says Oli. 'Revision.') We decide the quickest way for me to understand how the quiz works is to just let them get on with it. Oli's in charge of round one – they write alternate rounds, neither telling the other his questions so they can play along themselves. The theme of this round is science and nature, starting with: 'The smallest crab in the world is named after a vegetable, because it's similar in size to that vegetable. Which one?' Oli reads it a couple of times, then presses the button on the laptop (positioned, in true pub quiz style, at the end of the bar) which starts the ten seconds. The left-hand side of the screen lists the team's names, and letters soon start to appear next to them: 'P', 'B', 'M' and so on. As soon as the time is up Oli announces: 'Well done to Quizzard of Ox and Happy Birthday Alex – you're right, it is the pea crab.'

'So that's how it works?' I ask Callum. 'You just put down the initial letter of your answer?'

He nods. 'It's not perfect, obviously. I mean, last week one of my questions was about a mountain, and the answer was Kilimanjaro – I only realised when I was reading it out that if a team thought it was K2 they'd still get it right, despite the fact they'd got it wrong. If you see what I mean.'

The reasoning behind all this doesn't take long to work out. Even if there wasn't the time constraint, making it difficult for teams to type a long answer, there'd still be the problem – as we saw with online quizzes – of whether a computer can mark properly. A question I've used in the past is: ' "But it is to be decided by Indian men." These words were spoken on the fourth of December 1919, somewhere in London. Where, and what was notable about the person saying them?' The answer is they were the first words spoken in the House of Commons by a woman. (Nancy Astor, in a debate about Indian legislative councils.) Imagine the different ways that can be phrased. The human brain can tell instantly whether or not a team has got the right idea – could a computer? And before you say they're getting cleverer all the time, consider the incident, not so long ago, where a computer was asked (as part of one of those 'can computers converse with humans?' contests): 'What is the capital of France?' It answered: 'Paris.' It was then asked: 'Do you know what the capital of France is?' The computer was stumped.

Nevertheless, the system works well enough for an entertaining quiz. As well as alerting me to the pea crab, the first round also reveals that an octopus has three hearts, the largest eye in the animal kingdom belongs to the giant squid (40 centimetres in diameter), and leprosy is also known as Hansen's disease (he was the Norwegian scientist who pioneered research into it). Oh, and there's the collective noun for a group of hedgehogs – a 'prickle'. Serious types would say it's an 'array', but we all need a laugh on a Sunday night, and anyway Oli can override the computer's marking for individual teams if he wants to. There are a couple of picture questions – the system sends the image out to everyone at the same time, in this case images of the planet Jupiter and the bird known as the cassowary, which is like an ostrich or an emu except smaller and with a shorter neck. Meanwhile the fact that 'Bovine Spongiform Encephalopathy is the scientific name for which well-known disease?' even counts as a question makes me feel old. Mad Cow Disease struck Britain in my mid-twenties, but this lot weren't even born.

Round two is 'Humanities', and includes a picture question asking 'if you were in this building, which city would you be in?'

I don't know it, but only because my wander round Oxford isn't happening until tomorrow morning – it's the city's Museum of Natural History.

'We often use "local knowledge" questions,' Oli tells me as Callum continues. 'Like "which Oxford college did Margaret Thatcher attend?"' The answer is Somerville, though later relations between the university and Thatcher weren't always easy, the academics objecting to many of her policies. One, Alan Tyson, hatched a plan to gain revenge. He was a fellow of All Souls, the college which dates from 1438 and enjoys the full name 'the College of the Souls of All Faithful People Deceased in the University of Oxford'. This refers to those killed in the Hundred Years War with France, meaning All Souls has been called 'the noblest war memorial in England'. When Thatcher came to visit during the miners' strike of 1984, Tyson was deputed to show her round the Common Room. The walls were hung with portraits of past fellows, including the eminent economist G. D. H. Cole. Tyson's idea was to show the picture to Thatcher and say: 'This, Prime Minister, is a former fellow, G. D. H. Dole.' With any luck, she would have replied: 'Cole, not Dole.' When it came to the moment, however, Tyson lost his nerve.

The rounds continue, touching on the animal with the longest gestation period (elephant, 22 months), the place known to the Romans as 'Cambria' (Wales) and the substance of which the Kenyan government recently burned a huge quantity (ivory). As well as the main computerised quiz, Oli and Callum have also kept a foot in the lo-tech camp by leaving sheets of Dingbats on every table. These are the teaser puzzles giving visual clues to well-known words and phrases. Tonight's, for instance, include 'amUous' (ambiguous), '01110101100110 Hope Dylan' (bits and bobs) and, appropriately for the setting, a 'o' above 'MD, PhD, BSc' (three degrees below zero). The duo mark these and enter the scores into the computer. I'm hoping for a draw so I can suggest a 'nearest the correct answer' tiebreaker that occurred to me today: 'Winston Churchill's bedroom at Chartwell was always maintained at exactly how many degrees Fahrenheit?'[10] Sadly, there's an outright winner: Lyndon B's Famous Johnson. Quizzard of Ox come second, Quizzly Bears third, and in fourth place, proving that Oxford can still give a hard time to Tory Prime Ministers, is a team called Dodgy Dave's Ice Cream Van. (I'm not sure about the ice cream van reference, but the first two words are a label once applied to David Cameron by Labour backbencher Dennis Skinner.) The most memorable team name here, says Oli, was 'Can We Have the Number of the Blonde Girl Behind the Bar?' I'd love to report a blossoming romance, but she said no.

As the evening winds down I fall into conversation with Rob, a student at New College and a regular at the quiz.

'Which team were you on?' I ask.

'Quizzard of Ox.'

'Ah, bad luck – you must all have been disappointed at not winning.'

'Actually it's just me.'

'You were playing on your own?'

He nods.

'And you came second?'

Another nod. Rob is modest to the point of diffidence. After a while another student joins the conversation. I don't catch his name, but he too is a regular, and he too is self-effacing. Neither of these guys, you imagine, would want to run the quiz, they just like taking part. They remind me of lots of Oxbridge students I've met over the years – state school, far from privileged background, socially awkward, very clever. They give the lie to the myth about the country's two most famous universities being crammed with chinless dunces in old school ties. Not that those types don't exist. At Oxford they're personified by the Bullingdon Club, the upper-class dining group whose restaurant-destroying antics are the stuff of legend. The group was originally a sporting club which visited the Bullingdon point-to-point race. The name

---

10 74.

also lives on in HM Prison Bullingdon, which seems keen to get in on the bad-boy act itself: in 2003 its deputy governor was arrested for possession of cocaine.

Not-Rob tells me about his other quizzing activities. Specifically his attempts to get onto the TV programme that seems quintessentially British, but which was actually copied from a 1950s American show called *College Bowl*. We're talking, of course, about *University Challenge*. 'I was selected for my college's team,' says Not-Rob. 'Twice, actually. But we didn't get through the auditions.' These feature a combination of quiz questions – the sort you'd get on air – and interviews. Not-Rob says he's going to try again, and if the resolve in his voice is anything to go by, I wouldn't bet against him. We mention the recent clip from the programme that went viral, an Oxford student taking a fraction of a second to solve: 'What day of the week will it be one hundred days after Monday?' The answer is Wednesday. 'How did you know that?' said an incredulous Jeremy Paxman. The student (Magdalen, Binnie) was amazed at everyone else's amazement. 'Modular arithmetic,' he replied.

Rob and I then discuss my Oxford research. I'm particularly intrigued by the revelation that the 'high table' – the important one reserved at formal meals for the fellows of a college – really is higher than all the others in the room. By six inches. 'At least six inches,' adds Rob. 'In fact at my college it's more. It's on a platform across the top of the room. They get nicer food as well. Prepared by a different chef.'

Which reminds me of something else in my notes. There is a word that's said to have been coined in Oxford, as an abbreviation for the Latin phrase meaning 'without nobility'. *Sine nobilitate* was shortened, and hey presto we had 'snob'.

* * *

Al Green would approve of the way my Monday morning starts: the early stages of a wander round Oxford take me to the river. The river what, though? Every so often a fact crops up that makes me feel stupid for not knowing it already, and so it is with the river that flows through Oxford.[11] I'd always heard about the Isis, and was also aware that the Thames runs through this part of the world, but somehow my subconscious had decided to keep these two bits of knowledge separate from each other. It turns out that the Isis *is* the Thames, at least from its source in Gloucestershire to a few miles east of here, where it joins the River Thame – hence the ancient name Thame-isis, which became 'Thames'. You could therefore say that the Boat Race is a home fixture for Oxford, so it's all the more shaming that Cambridge have led in the overall tally since 1928. For years the BBC's radio commentary was provided by John Snagge, who sat in a boat behind the teams and so often found it difficult to see who was in the lead. At Dukes Meadows there were two flag-poles, one with a light blue flag for Cambridge, the other with a dark blue one for Oxford, and a man raised the appropriate flag to denote the state of play. For that part of the race, therefore, Snagge watched the flags rather than the boats. Meeting the man in question years later, he said it must have been very difficult to watch the race and operate the flags at the same time. 'Not at all,' replied the man. 'I just used to listen to that John Snagge on the radio.'

There's a decidedly serious air to Oxford this morning, students' faces composed into masks of concentration as they head to the libraries for more revision. It's funny to think that Churchill, who spent much of his childhood down the road, never studied here, or indeed at any university. He regretted it, and spent much of his Army time in India reading to make up for his lack of education: each day he tackled 50 pages of Macaulay's *History of England* and 25 of Gibbon's *Decline and Fall of the Roman Empire*. Another Prime Minister who skipped

---

11 The one I've just walked near, that is – there's also the Cherwell, in which Oxford dons used to bathe naked. One day a female student floated by in a punt, at which point the dons hurriedly covered their genitals. All except Maurice Bowra, who placed a flannel over his head saying: 'I don't know about you, gentlemen, but in Oxford, I, at least, am known by my face.'

university was the Duke of Wellington, though his successes later got him appointed Chancellor of Oxford, in which post he campaigned against the city getting a train station because it would 'encourage the lower orders to move around'.[12] The aforementioned David Cameron, meanwhile, attended Brasenose, the college whose name came from its brass door knocker in the shape of a nose. This was taken to Stamford in Lincolnshire and ended up on the door of a girls' school: in 1890 Brasenose bought the school just to get the knocker back. It now hangs over High Table in the Dining Hall.

The academic air near the Bodleian Library is punctured slightly by the girl I overhear entering with a friend: '... prob'ly the bit with the most citations an' stuff'. 'The Bod' is a reference rather than a lending library, meaning you're not allowed to take books away. Not even if you're Charles I – the library refused him permission to borrow a volume when he was resident in Oxford during the Civil War. And to this day every student enrolling at Oxford has to promise 'not to bring into the Library, or kindle therein, any fire or flame'. I wander out onto 'the High' (so much extra effort, that word 'Street'), and down to Magdalen College, where there's an information board about Magdalen Park. During the Second World War meat supplies ran so low that to stop the deer here being eaten they were officially classified as vegetables.

Back up the High, past Logic Lane (a school of logicians used to operate there), and thence to the main entrance of University College. The only two Bullingdon-ish specimens I'll see all morning are standing here, both well over six feet and both wearing white tie and black tails. The English guy has added a white carnation as an extra touch, though his colleague (Eastern European with an American twang) stays in contention with an Astrakhan collar on his jacket. As if their shoulders-back, pavement-blocking stance isn't enough of an invitation to stare,

---

12 Even when Oxford finally did join the network, you couldn't buy a ticket to anywhere with a racecourse: the authorities didn't want the students gambling.

they're careful to broadcast rather than merely have their conversation. 'That beautiful part,' says Mr Astrakhan, 'where you
had to indicate the lesion in the monkey.'

Over the road there's an early victory in the day's 'best comment on an A-board' competition, because no one will beat
the Rose Tea Room's 'Hello – is it tea you're looking for?' Then
down Alfred Street to take a look at the Bear, Oxford's oldest
pub (1242). It's too early for booze, though it wouldn't have been
for Churchill: 'When I was younger I made it a rule never to
take strong drink before lunch. It is now my rule never to do
so before breakfast.' A tour guide is telling his group about the
mid-20th-century landlord here who complimented male drinkers on their ties – when they leaned closer he'd cut the tie off. To
recompense them he offered a free half-pint of bitter. Another
famous Oxford boozer is the Turf Tavern, where in the early
1950s a student set a new world record for drinking the yard
of ale (2.5 pints). His time was 11 seconds, his name was Bob
Hawke and he went on to become Prime Minister of Australia.
The Turf was also the venue, it is said, for Bill Clinton's famous
meeting with a spliff, the one where he didn't inhale.

This tour guide, by the way, is more conscientious than his
19th-century predecessor, who regularly stopped outside Balliol
College and announced: 'The head of Balliol College is called
the Master. The present Master of Balliol is the celebrated Professor Benjamin Jowett, Regius Professor of Greek. *Those* are
Professor Jowett's study windows and *there...*' (he would grab
a handful of gravel and hurl it at the panes, bringing Jowett to
the window, seething with rage) '*there*, ladies and gentlemen,
is Professor Jowett himself.' Round in Cornmarket Street is the
Crown, whose board relates that 'famous people are known to
have stayed at the inn, including Shakespeare who was a friend
of the vintner, John Davenant, and is said to have been more
than friendly to John's wife.' Carrying on, you reach St Giles, the
wide street forming one of the main routes north out of Oxford,
and home to St John's College. Old boys include Inspector Morse
(forced to leave after a failed love affair affected his academic

work) and Tony Blair. The latter formed a band called Ugly Rumours, the name taken from a graphic on the cover of the Grateful Dead album *From the Mars Hotel*. A sign reminds you that 'in accordance with government legislation all buildings and enclosed spaces in St John's College are non-smoking'. The legislation in question was the Health Act 2006, passed when the Prime Minister was one Tony Blair. He himself gave up cigarettes on his wedding day (orders from Cherie), but didn't object to others smoking even the wackier form of baccy – during his first term as Prime Minister he went round to dinner at Dave Stewart's London house, and was happy for another guest, the film director Robert Altman, to light up a post-prandial joint. Winston Churchill, as we've established, was more a Cuban cigar man: at Chartwell he saved his unfinished ends for one of his gardeners, Mr Kearnes, who broke them up and smoked them in his pipe.

Inspired by Callum's question last night, I make a point of heading for the Museum of Natural History. Like its namesake in London, this place leaves you undecided as to which is more impressive: the exhibits or the building itself. (Its stone pillars and vaulted roof give the same Victorian Gothic feel as the one in the capital.) On the reception desk sits a stuffed fox, its eyes gleaming so brightly you feel nervous about reaching out to touch it. However, a small boy remains unimpressed: 'I want to see the *bear*.' Another boy loves the lifesize model of an iguanodon, but thinks it's a brontosaurus. His mother short-temperedly corrects him in a West Country accent: 'It's a ...' – she peers at the panel – '... a iga-don.' There's the jaw of a sperm whale, displayed vertically: if I jumped I might just about reach the tenth tooth from the top. A cabinet devoted to the dodo mentions the animal's appearance in *Alice's Adventures in Wonderland* by Oxford boy Lewis Carroll, and reveals the sad story of its extinction. The flightless bird (think large pigeon) was pootling happily around Mauritius until Europeans arrived in 1598 and started eating it, as well as allowing their dogs, cats and pigs to destroy its eggs and habitats. A few live ones were brought back to Europe, but fed on the wrong food they became obese.

I wind up my time in Oxford with a final meander through the town centre. It dawns on me that for all Churchill's regret at not going to university, it was the right decision. The best lessons in life are the ones you find yourself – in museums, in books, on the telly, wherever – rather than the ones the education system thinks you should have. Certainly with university: who can know at the age of 18 which subject they love enough to study it for three years? That time of life should be about flowering, developing, changing. Churchill preferred discovering things for himself – look at his experience of painting. He became so good that some of his works (deliberately submitted under the pseudonyms 'Charles Morin' and 'David Winter', so they'd be judged on their merits) were accepted for exhibition by the Royal Academy. He did landscapes rather than portraits, 'because no tree has ever complained about its likeness'. And yet what was his advice to those thinking of taking up the hobby? Did he advocate years of disciplined study at art school? Did he hell. 'Buy a paint box and have a try!' was his advice. 'Audacity is the only ticket!'

FOUR

· · · · · · ·

Which comic strip took its title from the names of a French theologian and an English political philosopher?

June now, and I'm on my way to Northamptonshire County Cricket Club. Not to see bat connect with ball, but pen with paper. The ground is the venue for this year's World Quizzing Championships.

It's all very well splashing around in the shallows of amateur quizzes. They are the territory where I feel most comfortable. I am, after all, the man who temporarily forgot about the existence of Michael Jackson. But just for once I want to swim down to the other end of the pool, witness the world of the serious quizzers, the guys (and occasional girl) who *really* know their stuff. Not for them the breezy, slapdash approach of the Prince of Wales, the potter down to the pub for a laugh and a pint, and if you happen to know Donald Duck's middle name then that's a bonus.[1] These are the people with encyclopedias for brains, the ones who see quizzing as a way of life.

Driving into Northamptonshire on this pleasant Saturday morning, I wonder how much of my research about the county would be known to today's contenders. The answer, surely, is all of it. They'd know which family have lived at Deene Park since

---

1 Fauntleroy.

1514 – the Brudenells, seven of whose males became the Earl of Cardigan. The last Earl led the Charge of the Light Brigade at the Battle of Balaclava in 1854, an incident so famous that the woollen waistcoats worn by the officers came to bear his name. (Just as their woollen headgear took the name of the battle.) The quizzers would know that Silverstone started life as a deserted airfield on which some friends held the Mutton Grand Prix, so-called because one of them ran over and killed a sheep that had wandered onto the track. They'd know that the river Nene gave its name to a Rolls-Royce jet engine, and that Rushden and Diamonds Football Club were formed by the 1992 merger of Rushden Town and Irthlingborough Diamonds. The latter chose their sparkly second word in 1947, a tribute to the Russian team touring Britain at the time. Or so they thought – it was actually Moscow *Dynamo*, but the mistake had been made. Talking of football: the quizzers would know that until 1994 today's venue was also home to Northampton Town FC (they used the address 'Abington Avenue' while the cricket club used 'Wantage Road', which runs along the other side of the field). And that in 1970 Manchester United came here and beat 'the Cobblers' 8–2, George Best scoring a double hat-trick.

Having parked up, I locate the Hevey Suite, named after a building-supplies company, though the first syllable could equally describe what you want to do after looking at the room's yellow and purple carpet. Thankfully the room opens out onto a terrace, beyond which is the relaxing green expanse of the empty cricket field. It's on the terrace that I find Jane Allen and Chris Jones, founders of the British Quiz Association, organisers of today's event. Chris is the one I notice first – he's a great big bear of a man, at least the sort of bear who wears shorts and a polo shirt emblazoned with 'quizzing.co.uk', and whose silver beard is neatly trimmed apart from the goatee segment, which sprouts sumptuously. Jane is in his shadow, but only literally – her enthusiasm for quizzing, combined with a background in PR, has helped the World Championships grow to the extent that this year's (the 14th) has over 2500 entrants around the world.

Jane, I'll learn later, was born on the same day Britain adopted its decimal currency. She 'narrowly avoided being called Penny'.

There are 125 venues spread across 45 countries (Kazakhstan came on board this year) and time differences mean that although as many places as possible will compete at roughly the same time, some venues have turned their papers over already – Australia and Russia, for instance. Hawaii, on the other hand, won't get under way until much later. But everyone's tackling the same questions. 'We have to work hard to make sure they're fair for everybody,' explains Jane. 'The questions can't be about *East-Enders* – they have to reference things that people in Hungary and Singapore and Oman are all going to know about.' To help with this, the question-setters come from several different countries – Estonia to India, Belgium to the USA. 'There are different styles,' Jane adds, 'so we have to work hard to harmonise them. The Belgians always set very long questions, for some reason.'

Once the paper has been agreed, it's translated into the different languages – 14 this year. 'We did once have a blind contestant in Holland, so we got it translated into Dutch and then into Braille.' One of the people taking part at the cricket ground is Croatian, so he has been provided with the questions in his native language. He's happy to answer in English, though. And so later on I will look at a piece of paper on which is printed: '*Temeljen na romanu Irvinea Welsha, u kojem filmu iz 1996, o ovisnicima o heroinu u Edinburghu Ewan McGregor glumi Rentona, a Robert Carlyle Begbieja?*' Written in biro in the answer box is: 'Trainspotting'.

The participants are starting to arrive, and it's clear that many of them know each other from previous events – Jane runs the monthly quizzes that make up the National Quiz Circuit, as well as the 'scene' more generally. The very best quizzers earn their living from it – several appear on the BBC's *Eggheads*, others on ITV's *The Chase*, and plenty took cheques from Chris Tarrant on *Who Wants to Be a Millionaire?* Pat Gibson took the biggest cheque: very sweetly, his million-pound question required him to know that of the four horse races listed, the one which wasn't part of the American Triple Crown was the Arlington Million. But if I hadn't recognised, say, Kevin Ashman from his role on *Eggheads* (fifties, wire-framed glasses, demeanour of a friendly geography teacher), I wouldn't have been able to tell him apart from today's other quizzers. The room boasts an awful lot of clothing from less fashionable parts of the high street (including at least one Van Der Graaf Generator T-shirt), and it's not one of those gatherings where you feel intimidated by everyone else being more attractive than you. Though, as Jane reminds me: 'People accuse quizzers of being nerdy – but between them the people here have won several million pounds' worth of prize money.' Not that they'll be adding to it today: the World Championships are purely for prestige.

Jane and I fall into conversation with Adrian, a middle-aged chap in a red fleece who has journeyed here from Streatham. Today is his first time in the World Championships. 'Of course I'm not expecting to win,' he says. 'Or get anywhere near the top. These are the best of the best – I'm just starting.' Adrian used to compete in crossword competitions. 'But I found I couldn't break into the higher echelons, so I decided to switch to quizzing.'

'That's the beauty of an event like this,' says Jane. 'Anyone can come along and pit themselves against the best of the best. It's like being given the chance to run a hundred metres against Usain Bolt.' It so happens that I've used Bolt in a quiz question: 'what is his top speed, in miles per hour?' The answer is 28, meaning that outside a school he'd be illegal. Perhaps even more incredible is that top marathon runners – who are running for two hours rather than ten seconds – average nearly 13 miles per hour. This means, a friend and I worked out the night before watching the 2012 Olympic marathon in London, that they cover each 100 metres in about 18 seconds. 'I couldn't do *one* burst of a hundred metres in that time,' I said. 'Could I?' Before we knew it Matt and I had measured out a course on the (thankfully very quiet) street outside his house. I *just* about managed the distance in the time. Then Matt had a go. Halfway through his attempt

I thought about calling an ambulance. It would probably have arrived at the finish line before he did.

Chris is checking people's names against the list of those who pre-registered. Thankfully some other participants turn up on the day, because the count had been standing at 111, and on a cricket ground that's seen as unlucky (possibly because the score resembles three stumps with their bails knocked off). Despite it being a shade past 11 a.m. one or two people get straight on the lager, though most stick to tea or coffee, and one chap asks for a glass of milk. Others have no need of the bar, having brought flasks.

One guy is doing last-minute revision from a notebook. The pages are filled with writing so small and dense that he needs a magnifying glass to peruse it. One diagram shows several rectangles drawn inside each other. 'They're pitches and courts,' he tells me, and as I lean closer I see names such as 'basketball' and 'Gaelic football', along with their dimensions. 'I thought it'd be a good way to remember them.' Below are several concentric circles, each representing a different sport's ball.

As people take their seats at the half-dozen large round tables (and several smaller ones out on the terrace), the projector screen scrolls through photos from previous years' championships. The venues around the world differ greatly – Tartu in Estonia uses a historic tiered lecture hall, in Vilnius it's a bookshop,[2] while the Indian contestants in Chennai occupy what seems to be a cinema whose seats have come from old cars.

There's also Boulder, Colorado. 'The Americans have such great placenames, don't they?' I say to Chris.

'I know. A friend of mine once went to Intercourse, Pennsylvania. He only did it so his credit card statement would say "Intercourse".'

The papers for part one are handed out. The covering page explains the rules: there are eight rounds (four in this first part,

---

2 I have to look up which country Vilnius is in before I'm certain (Lithuania). Good job I'm not competing today.

four in the second), and each player's seven best scores will be added to achieve their total. (Their weakest round will only come into play in the event of a tie.) 'Phonetically incorrect answers will be accepted,' says one rule. 'This is a test of your knowledge NOT spelling.' A nice touch, as is the final instruction: 'We hope you find the quiz both challenging and enjoyable. Good luck!' At a little after midday Chris reminds everyone that they have an hour to complete part one, then invites them to begin. There's a communal swishing sound as the pages are turned over, then silence.

The first round is 'Media', the opening question the one about *Trainspotting*, which I could have got even in Croatian. It's soon apparent, however, that this is the 'one off the mark'. The next question I can answer is number ten: '*A Portrait of the Artist as a Young Man* was the first novel of which Irish writer?' (James Joyce.) After that it's 12 (the steps Sylvester Stallone runs up in *Rocky* are in Philadelphia), and then 21 (the 1981 German film about a submarine is *Das Boot*). Surrounding this populism are an awful lot of stinkers. I have no idea, for instance, about the 1973 François Truffaut movie which won the Best Foreign Film Oscar for depicting the backstage goings-on of the film *Je vous présente Paméla* ('Day for Night' – its French title of *La Nuit américaine* is also acceptable). Or the country of which journalist Svetlana Alexievich, winner of the 2015 Nobel Prize for Literature, is a citizen (Belarus). Or the fictional Japanese character, a blind masseur and swordmaster (really?), who was portrayed by actor Shintaro Katsu in 25 movies between 1962 and 1973 (Zatoichi).

Question 13 irritates me: 'Hannibal was helping Clarice catch what serial killer in *The Silence of the Lambs*, whose nickname suggests he plays on an NFL team?' Of course I know it, we all know it – but my memory refuses to dredge up 'Buffalo Bill'. Instead I'm sidetracked (as no serious quizzer would be) into thinking about the 'refrigerator problem'. This is the nickname Jonathan Demme, the film's director, uses for plot inconsistencies, such as the fact there's no way Hannibal could have known the number of the landline he calls Clarice on at the end of the film, just before sauntering off to have 'an old friend for dinner'. That's something you'd only notice, says Demme, once you'd got home from the cinema and were opening the fridge to get something to eat. It's not going to spoil your enjoyment of the film. But as I say, today's participants aren't thinking about that. They're thinking about the only film ever to receive four female acting nominations (*All About Eve*), the comic strip that took its title from the names of a French theologian and an English political philosopher (*Calvin and Hobbes*), and the name of the hook at the lower right corner of vowels in East European languages that denotes nasality (*ogonek*).

Then, as they continue onto the 'World' round, they're thinking about the island in Europe which is the third most populous in the world (Great Britain), the device on the underside of an aircraft wing that measures air temperature from changes in electrical resistance (thermistor), the southernmost province of the Netherlands (Limburg) . . . Compared to my chances on this paper, the cat in hell is a dead cert. So I wander back out onto the terrace, where Jane and Chris are sitting at the far end with their laptops.

'We've had some scores coming in,' says Jane quietly, so as not to disturb the contestants nearby. 'New Zealand, for instance. And Madagascar – we've got twelve people taking part there.' It looks unlikely that any of them will make the leader board, but still, it's wonderful to think that all around the globe, on the same day, thousands of people are all tackling the same questions.

Jane tells me about the British Quiz Association's other activities. 'We verify questions for TV shows – *Pointless*, and the National Lottery quiz *Win Your Wish List*, and *Celebrity Squares* and a load of others. You have to be very careful that answers are accurate and up to date. In sport, for instance, where records are changing all the time. And also that the question is phrased correctly – you can't have any confusion or ambiguity.' A lot of the emails in Jane's inbox at the moment relate to the Quiz

Olympiad. 'It's an event we're organising this autumn in Athens. A whole weekend of quizzes – for individuals, pairs, national teams, quizzes just for fun. We're going to visit the Acropolis as well. It was inspired by the early modern Olympics – they had artistic events as well as sporting ones.' There were medals for painting, music and literature. Even for town planning: the 1936 gold went to Werner March, for his design of the Berlin stadium in which the Olympics were being held. Given Germany's set-up at the time it would have been a brave judge who'd made any other decision, though no such chicanery was needed for the Olympics' founder Baron de Coubertin to win the 1912 poetry gold – he submitted his entry (like Churchill at the Royal Academy) under a pseudonym. The artistic events were finally dropped after the 1948 games. One of the last competitors was Britain's John Copley, whose silver in the engravings and etchings category makes him, at 73, the oldest Olympic medallist ever.

Our chat is interrupted by the sudden appearance of a man in his late thirties. He is sporting fair hair whose waves almost qualify as curls, and a frown.

'Chris,' he says. 'Could you ... please ... be quiet?'

'Sure,' says Chris. 'Sorry.'

'Thank you,' says the man, then returns to his table at the other end of the terrace. His eight words were all polite, but there was no adjustment in facial expression for any of them. Jane (taking care to re-establish our lower volume levels) explains that he is Ian Bayley, a regular on the circuit and the 2011 *Mastermind* champion. Of course at this stage of the proceedings Ian isn't allowed to consult his smartphone, but I am, so within seconds his Wikipedia entry has appeared before my eyes. 'Ian Bayley,' it starts, 'is a British computer scientist and quiz player who, despite his youth when compared with other leading players (he was in his early thirties), won several medals in quizzing, both in singles and as a member of a team.' Later we read that 'in 2010 he won the final of the BBC Radio 4 quiz *Brain of Britain*, scoring more points than the other three contestants put together'. For his *Mastermind* triumph of 2011 ('actually recorded in October 2010') he answered questions on the paintings of the National Gallery. In an earlier tilt at the crown (2009, when he reached the final but came second) his specialities had included *Doctor Who* in the 1970s. Ian also represented both his seats of further education (Imperial College London and Balliol College, Oxford) on *University Challenge*.

By the time I have digested all this and looked up, Ian is on his feet again. But it isn't to reprimand us, or anyone else, for being noisy. Instead he has stepped over the low wall that separates the terrace from the outfield, and is pacing slowly around as he continues to study his paper. The frown is still in place. Although it can only be one of concentration, or possibly annoyance at himself for the answers he doesn't know, it somehow gives Ian the air of one of those professors who are permanently affronted by the rest of the world having the sheer nerve to exist. At one point his prowling takes him near the pods in which waiting batsmen sit during T20 matches. As this is the trendy form of the game, the pods have a space-age design – it's like seeing Lord Reith next to a McLaren F1. Ian gets even more irritated a few minutes later, when a member of the ground staff asks if he'd mind moving for a second so he can adjust the boundary rope. He is probably confused about why this needs doing on a non-match day. Then again the groundsman would probably be confused about why Ian's trying to remember which 1835 Gaetano Donizetti opera is loosely based on a novel by Sir Walter Scott.

Once the hour is up, Chris asks everyone to swap papers with a partner for marking, then begins running through the answers. There's the occasional cry of 'argh!' when someone hears an answer they couldn't quite recall, or '*yes!*' when they hear one they did. At question nine in History – 'What great sporting figure shares his name with a khedive or 'viceroy' (1769–1849), who is considered the father of modern Egypt?' – someone calls out 'You've done it again!' The answer is Muhammad Ali, whose death was announced this morning. (Clearly the Championships have a history of killing people.) I happened to know this answer, but did not know that strictly speaking the Las Vegas strip is in a city called Paradise rather than Las Vegas, or that Adolf Hitler is said once to have applied for a job painting scenery for Bertolt Brecht, or that the only country to produce nuclear weapons then voluntarily dismantle them is South Africa. I also like question 22 in History, not because the answer is interesting (Rollo – the Viking who became the first ruler of Normandy), but because it refers in passing to someone called Charles the Simple.

I happen to be standing near Kevin 'Egghead' Ashman, and see the ticks mounting up on his paper like bees on a honeypot. It's the *breadth* of knowledge that's astonishing. OK, you're not surprised when he knows the name of the weeping Greek mask that represents tragedy (Melpomene), accompanying the laughing Thalia who represents comedy. Or the gas at the core of a star which, when it runs out, leads to the star expanding to form a red supergiant (hydrogen). Or the Chilean archipelago that comprises the islands Melchor, Benjamin, Cuptana and Guamblin (Chonos). But you do blink in wonder when he knows that the US rock band who recorded the 2006 track '45:33' is LCD Soundsystem. I know from reading an interview with Kevin that pop culture is one of the subjects he has to 'swot up on'. Just as impressive as his knowledge is his attention to detail. Glancing across at his paper, being marked by his neighbour, Kevin notices just in time that he has misread question 21 in History. Not surprising – it's a wordy one, starting 'The name "Bloody Sunday" has been given to many tragic events...' – winding its way through '... unarmed demonstrators led by Father Georgy Gapon...' – before finishing at 'In which year did this revolution-sparking event take place?' Kevin realises he's mistakenly put the country, so reaches across and beside 'Russia' adds '1905'. Seconds later his neighbour adds yet another tick. I like the trusting air of this event – everyone could see what had happened, and they know Kevin isn't going to cheat. As Jane was telling me earlier, that's one of the reasons for not having prize money: it keeps everything suitably Corinthian.

Once Chris has completed the answers everyone has a few moments to check they're happy with the score they've been awarded. They then put their papers into – another nice down-to-earth touch – plastic washing-up bowls positioned around the room. After this there's a short break to recharge the mental batteries. I chat to David Stainer, a 38-year-old whose unruffled manner must reassure clients in his day job (tax lawyer in the City of London), but who I have approached for clarification on the 'you've done it again!' comment about Muhammad Ali.

'Lots of people have died just after featuring in the quiz,' he confirms. 'Etta James, for instance.' He adds that the soul singer's real name was Jamesetta Hawkins, an early manager converting the first half into her stage name. David is a serious contender today – his record in past years features more than one Top Ten placing, and he's also toured the TV studios (*Mastermind*, *University Challenge*, a tidy little £64,000 on *Who Wants to Be a Millionaire?*). He met his wife on the student quiz circuit: something tells me their two young sons will fare well with 'what's the fastest animal in the world?'-style enquiries.

David says family life has left him with less time for quizzing. 'But I'd be lying if I said it's just for fun. It's still a pretty serious hobby. I've got an hour commute each way for work every day, so that's time I spend reading, plus another hour once the children have gone to bed.'

'Do you tailor your reading towards your quizzing?'

'I read mainly non-fiction anyway, and yes, I do tend to pick books on subjects I want to learn more about. For instance, I've just read a huge history of baseball. I did the same last year with basketball.' Any subject, he says, can be interesting. 'Apart from classical mythology – I just can't get engaged with that. But anything else, yes. The hardest thing is getting from nought per cent interested to fifty per cent. Once you're past that you've got a basis for all the new stuff you're learning.'

'Any particular areas of expertise?'

'I guess everyone has them to some extent. But what really

makes a champion is avoiding large areas of weakness.' I'm reminded of Kevin's answers just now.

Part two, for which the players have another hour, starts with 30 questions about science. I feel rather chuffed with myself for being able to answer the second – the German scientist (1858–1947) after whom a constant is named and who is considered to have originated the theory of quantum mechanics (Max Planck). But after that it's downhill, rapidly. The only living mammal with a bony shell? No idea. (It turns out to be the armadillo. Not the pangolin, the question-setter has been careful to note – its armour is made of keratin rather than dermal bone. You have been told.) The proper name of the amphibian known as the 'Mexican walking fish'? Dunno. (Axolotl.) The question that does grip me is: 'When written in Roman numerals, which number will come last alphabetically?' The answer is 38 – XXXVIII. I remember the statue at Blenheim with its XXXX rather than XL. This would make the answer 48 rather than 38. But I refrain from mentioning it, because (a) I know it's an exception and (b) I want to get out of here alive.

Question six in Sports is also intriguing: 'Which sport's international hall of fame opened with twenty-one inductees, including two Tarzans – Johnny Weissmuller and Buster Crabbe?' It's swimming. The Lifestyle round (good catch-all title, that) has one of those questions that's easy to answer but imparts an interesting little snippet in the process: 'What pizza-loving quartet ate Domino's in their 1990 movie but have been associated with Pizza Hut pretty much ever since, including in their 2014 movie?'[3] Further down the page is a question whose penultimate word always brightens up a quiz: 'The Hounsfield unit (HU) scale is used to assess human organs in which modality of imaging that was supposedly developed using the profits that accrued to EMI from the sales of Beatles records?' Turns out it's the CT scan (standing for 'computerised tomography'). Godfrey Hounsfield's research for EMI's medical arm was made

---

3 The Teenage Mutant Ninja Turtles.

possible because the Fab Four had made its entertainment section so rich. There is also: 'Described as "soft but very firm" with
notes of lemon, bergamot, blackcurrant and fir cones, Leaders
Number One is a 2015 fragrance inspired by which world
leader?' The very existence of such a scent is reason enough to
laugh at Vladimir Putin – the fact that 'number one' can mean
something else in English only adds to our amusement. (Could
have been worse, Vladimir.)

Other than this, though, there's plenty of 'which city in central
China, home to such literary giants as Sima Xiangru and Yang
Xiong...' and 'in Celtic myth, the supernatural races known as
the Tuatha Dé Danann and Fomorians...' So for much of part
two, as Chris sits on the terrace entering the scores from part
one into his spreadsheet, I gaze at the cricket field. The sport has
furnished us with tons of trivia over the years. Chaminda Vaas,
the only international player with more initials (W.P.U.J.C.) than
letters in his surname. The pavilion at Lord's having its famous
red terracotta only because a stonemasons' strike deprived the
architect of his preferred material. And – always good as a tiebreaker in quizzes – the lowest individual score never to have
been made in Tests: 229. As and when someone achieves that,
the answer will go up to 238. The most common score in Test
cricket, unsurprisingly, is nought, slang for which is 'dismissed
without troubling the scorers'. The late Bill Frindall of *Test Match
Special* hated that phrase: two batsmen getting out in quick succession is a nightmare for the scorers.

Eventually the time for part two is up, and we listen as Chris
reads out the answers. I'm standing near the bar, and with everyone marking someone else's paper there's nothing for the staff to
do. One of them leans across to the guy next to me and, making
sure she's not disturbing him during an answer, whispers: 'That
man over there looks like the one off *The Chase* – it can't really
be him, can it?'

'Yes,' comes the reply. 'Paul Sinha.'

Has she only just realised that this is an event for serious
quizzers? Certainly it has to be the only event this suite has

ever hosted in which a man at one end of the room saying 'Max Horkheimer' causes a man at the other end to say '*Get in!*' I like the way Chris is open to corrections. The answer to one question is 'isobutylene', but when someone who clearly knows what they're on about assures him 'isobutene' is the modern equivalent, Chris allows it. Would that the same philosophy had reigned at a charity quiz I once attended, where the guy in charge insisted – despite objections from several of us – that the longest-serving British Prime Minister of the 20th century was Winston Churchill. Only two things stopped me from giving him the dates to prove that Margaret Thatcher's term was longer than both of Churchill's combined. I didn't want to look a geek, and I knew that every team had put 'Thatcher', so there was no net loss.

By now it's 3 p.m. and time, to quote Richard Griffiths in *Withnail and I*, for a late luncheon. This is a sandwich buffet, and as people pile their plates there's plenty of scope for swapping scores, commiserating with each other about near-miss answers, seeing which questions your friends got wrong and so on. When Kevin Ashman is sitting back at his place, I ask if he's feeling confident.

'I think so, yes,' he says. 'You can never be sure, obviously, with all the players round the world. But I know I've scored higher than Pat [Gibson] and Olav [Bjortomt, defending champion] and Ian [Bayley].'

His manner isn't boastful or arrogant. All day long Kevin has exuded an air of tranquil goodwill, and I'm sure that had he come second, or indeed twentieth, he would have behaved exactly the same. We chat about how much pleasure he gets from quizzing now that it's his profession rather than a hobby. I mention that today has reminded me of Steve Davis being asked once if he'd enjoyed his domination of snooker during the 1980s. 'I didn't really enjoy winning,' Davis said. 'It's more that I was scared of losing.'

Kevin nods. 'Yes. I can certainly relate to that.'

Compare and contrast with the story Jane tells me later in the

day. 'Kevin was on holiday with us in Dieppe, and we were looking out at the sea. My son, who was about six at the time, had
just learned about the first man to swim the Channel [Matthew
Webb, 1875]. He told Kevin about it – of course Kevin knew, but
just smiled and said "really?" Then my son asked: "Who was the
first person to swim it the other way, from France to England?"
And Kevin didn't know. He didn't make any pretence about it
– he cheerfully admitted that he didn't know. The question had
never occurred to him.'

Perhaps the joy of a new question will always trump the joy
of a new answer.[4]

Post-lunch there are a couple more quizzes, but neither
counts towards the World Championships – these are just for
fun. They'll give Chris and Jane time to gather more results
from the other venues, and allow another cerebral run-out for
those who fancy it. First up is a quiz run by the team behind
SpeedQuizzing, the app used by Callum and Oli at the pub in
Oxford. People arrange themselves into teams, each of which is
handed a device the size of a mini iPad on which to submit their
answers. My misgivings about the system aren't removed, but at
least the guy in charge (small, Northern, quick-witted) puts on a
decent show and gets some laughs. The first, he happily admits,
is at his own expense, when the opening question – 'Alcohol is
made up of oxygen, hydrogen and which other element?' – is
answered correctly by all 24 teams. (In other words they all type
'c' for 'carbon'.) Mr SpeedQuizzing suddenly realises this is not
his usual crowd.

Nonetheless we all learn something over the next hour. I learn
that as well as 'Money Money Money' and 'Honey Honey', Abba
had one other song whose title was multiple uses of the same
word ('Ring Ring'). That the decade with the most official James
Bond films was the 1960s. And that the ninth most populous
city in Texas is called Piano. There are further lessons in store
as we move into the other 'just for fun' quiz, a music one. It's

---

4 In this case the answer is Enrique Tirabocchi of Argentina, 1923.

traditional for this to be set by last year's winner, so the questions today are the work of Dave Bill. He's another quizzer with media form, having triumphed on *Only Connect, Pointless* and – most relevantly – Ken Bruce's Radio 2 quiz *Popmaster*. A memory comes back to me that there's a word for someone who, like Dave, has a first name for their surname. As it happens I'm wrong, but my Googling reveals that some people think such characters aren't to be trusted. They back up their theory with the fact that Lee Harvey Oswald had *three* first names, and look what he did. I feel this to be harsh, particularly as Dave has crafted a set of impeccably researched questions for Chris to read out.

It's lovely to learn, for example, that the real first name of Norman Cook (as in Fatboy Slim) is Quentin. In a round themed around 'elements' comes the question: 'Who is the only artist to take a song with the word "silver" in it to the top of the UK charts?' Surely it has to be Jeff Beck, with 'Hi Ho Silver Lining'? Equally juicy is: 'Which 1999 single holds the record for the longest title of a number one record without any repeated letters?' By the time it comes to marking papers, I'm sitting next to David Stainer. (Lots of people have left now – including Kevin Ashman – and there are plenty of spaces around the room.) The Jeff Beck guess is wrong – it's 'Silver Lady' by David Soul. And the 'without repeated letters' record is 'King of My Castle' by Wamdue Project.

David turns to me. 'Fourteen letters,' he says. 'Actually it's the joint record holder, to be accurate. There's also "Uprocking Beats" by Bomfunk MC's.' But he doesn't make a thing of it.

It so happens that 14 is also the number of unrepeated letters in the equivalent record for British placenames. I know this because it was in my last book, and I can't resist mentioning it to David.

'Ah, Bricklehampton,' he says, with the fond look of a football fan remembering a beloved player of yesteryear. 'It's one of my "things" – unusual "number of letters" facts.'

We're soon swapping them. Ones about Tube stations, such

as Pimlico being the only one to share no letters with the word 'badger'. (I once tweeted that: a woman replied that she had lived in Pimlico for 30 years, and this fact had made her more proud of the area than anything else.) Ones about US states, like Alaska being the only one whose name can be typed on a single row of a QWERTY keyboard. Ones about football clubs, too. The grand-daddy, of course, is Hull City, the only team in the top four divisions whose name features no letters you can colour in. But we also mention Bury (shortest name), Swindon Town (only name to share no letters with the word 'mackerel') and, fittingly, Northampton Town (one of only four teams whose name begins and ends with the same letter – the others are Liverpool, Aston Villa and Charlton Athletic).[5]

'And of course you'll know the only team whose name ends with an "r",' I say.

David's face goes blank. 'No – I don't.'

I feel like a club chess player who's just checkmated Kasparov. Not that I was trying to – in fact I'm torn between feeling proud that I knew something David didn't and feeling horrified that I knew something David didn't. But there's no need to worry: his eyes only narrow for a few seconds before the answer comes to him. 'Tottenham Hotspur.'

'Correct. A lot of people forget about them because they think it's "Hotspurs".' I did that fact on a radio programme once. Someone rang in to say: 'They're not the only one – what about Crewe Alexander?'

Finally, as seven o'clock ticks by, it's time for the results of the main event. Or rather the provisional results – with some countries still to submit their scores there's a theoretical chance the current position could change. But if there was a potential champion out there he or she would surely have featured on the radar before now, so the Top Ten are very unlikely to get stormed. Everyone gathers at the end of the room with the

---

5 York City are sometimes allowable, but of late they've tended to yo-yo between league and
   non-league status.

large screen, onto which Chris projects each name as he reads it out, starting with the tenth-place finisher. This is David, on an admirable score of 156. Everyone else applauds, and those nearby offer handshakes. Moving up we encounter a couple of Belgians (including the splendidly named Ronny Swiggers), but the podium finishes are reserved for people who were in this room. I say 'were' because they've all gone home – Pat Gibson (third with 165), Olav Bjortomt (second with 167) and Kevin Ashman, whose confidence that his 171 would make him champion was well placed. It's his fifth title, including a hat-trick from 2004 to 2006.

As the room begins to clear, I find myself looking out at the field again, and thinking about a talk I once attended in a New York bookshop. It was to launch a book about baseball, and as the author spoke I was struck by yet another similarity – there are many – between that sport and cricket: both games throw up more statistics than you could shake a bat at.

'Do you think some people get into baseball,' I asked when it was time for questions, 'because they love facts and figures, rather than the sport itself?' The same was certainly true, I added, of cricket.

The author was smiling and nodding before I'd even finished, as were several members of the audience. Some statistics – and here I'll have to revert to cricket, that being the game I'm familiar with – stick in the mind because they're interesting. Don Bradman's Test average of 99.94, for instance. Not only is it miles ahead of anyone else's, it's also that pesky little 0.06 short of a hundred. And so it always cues up the story of how Bradman was out for a duck in his last-ever innings, having needed only four to make his average the round ton. But there are plenty of stats that aren't interesting. This doesn't mean there aren't people who can remember them. Just pray you don't find yourself sitting next to one of those people at dinner.

You can probably guess where all this is heading. So before we take the next step, let me first say that David and Kevin and several of the other people I've spoken to today are perfectly pleasant souls, and I'd be happy to trade trivia with them over a pint or two. City lawyers like David can't function without people skills, and a truly boring person wouldn't have Kevin's self-awareness on the 'scared about losing versus happy about winning' point. And even when it comes to some of the other participants today, the ones I'd think twice about before accompanying to the pub, I can see where they're coming from. They're coming – I'd wager – from a background where, for whatever reason, they didn't fit in. Didn't get the jokes, didn't make the jokes, didn't find the classroom's centre of gravity or know how to stay there if they did. Something – perhaps nothing as tangible as clothes or looks or hairstyle, perhaps just an indefinable 'differentness' – stopped these people from joining the gang of normality, stopped them being ordinary. Ideally they would have changed that. But as they couldn't, they decided to stand outside the ordinary – literally 'extra-ordinary' – on their own terms. Turn the specialness to their advantage.

If all of that sounds presumptuous, I can only plead that it's rooted in experience. The social currents of my own classroom pushed me to the outside, and for a while I delighted in provoking the process still further. Chance pulled me back in later life, but even now I sometimes look at people who don't fit in and feel an empathy with them, feel I could join the non-joiners.

Either way, one thing from today is certain: these participants, or at least some of them, are quizzing for precisely the opposite reason from me. Their ideal quiz is one that teaches them nothing because they know all the answers. My ideal quiz teaches me loads. Which returns us to the idea I mentioned at the start of the project: what makes the perfect question? We'd already established that teamwork is crucial: Laura's brain combining with mine to realise that all those women had had affairs with Tiger Woods. Now I can add another factor: the perfect question has to teach you something. Today's Teenage Mutant Ninja Turtles question, for instance, taught me that their pizza tastes had changed over the years. OK, in an era when product placement has become a Hollywood norm that's no real surprise, so the lesson is not a great one – but still, you get the idea. Most of the WQC questions have been the 'which city in central China...' variety, and there's no joy of discovery there. Nor is there much joy in a quiz taken as individuals, so today falls down on the 'teamwork' front too.

But still, I'm glad I came. Competition quizzing might not be for me, but it's demonstrated what an incredible bit of kit the human brain is. Kevin's LCD Soundsystem moment was a highlight, particularly to someone like me who can these days struggle to remember whether he's just fed the dog or not. (The dog's anxious looks at his bowl are a clue, though I'm starting to suspect he's realised what's happening and might be trying it on.) I would say that the name 'LCD Soundsystem' will always now make me think of Kevin. But I don't think my memory's up to that.

* * *

Later in the evening, I'm standing looking at Charles Bradlaugh's right index finger. At the moment it's attached to his hand. This isn't always the case. The statue of the 19th-century MP for Northampton is slightly outside the town centre, pointing due west. By which we really do mean pointing – and his out-stretched digit sometimes gets removed by vandals. Scant respect for the man who battled so Members of Parliament could recite an atheist vow when they were sworn in, rather than swearing to God. The fight involved him being locked in the prison cell underneath Big Ben and paying fines for voting in the Com-mons illegally. There were also several by-elections where the voters of Northampton kept asserting their support for him. Eventually Bradlaugh won. But MPs still have to promise to support the monarch. Several make clear their unhappiness at this, like Tony Benn at his 1997 swearing-in: 'As a committed republican, under protest, I take the oath required of me by law...' Whenever Benn, as a Privy Counsellor, had to kiss the

Queen's hand, he put his thumb across it so his lips met his own flesh rather than hers.

I have dinner in the Cordwainer, a pub whose name is the old word for a shoemaker (as opposed to a cobbler, who repaired them). Northampton's association with the trade goes back as far as the Civil War, when the town made over 6000 pairs of shoes and boots for Oliver Cromwell's troops. Charles II didn't forget this – when he got the throne back he ordered the destruction of Northampton's walls and some of its castle. In 1960 Northamptonshire was the obvious choice when the German Klaus Martens sought a UK manufacturer for his boots, and Dr Martens are made in Wollaston to this day. But Northampton caters for more traditional tastes as well. A black pair of Church's Chetwynd brogues were Tony Blair's lucky shoes – he wore them to every Prime Minister's Questions of his decade in Number 10.

My post-meal stroll reveals a town centre that's struggling. Lots of the shopfronts are boarded up, while several bars and restaurants have also gone out of business. Despite it being nine o'clock there aren't many people out yet. Cabs are only now beginning to appear, depositing groups of people displaying their finery and a faint air of menace. Clearly Northampton is one of those towns that get going late, then go with a bang. In the wee small hours, there will be establishments where a man would be well advised to take great care when looking at a woman, lest another man take exception. (You could swap the genders over and that sentence would still apply.) But then the course of true love and all that: the *Northampton Mercury* of 10 April 1802 contained the following notice: 'ELOPEMENT – WHEREAS MARY, the Wife of William Smith, of Irthlingborough, in the County of Northampton, has eloped from her said Husband – Notice is hereby given, That if she does not return to her Husband within seven Days from the Date hereof, she will not be taken in.'

The establishments on Gold Street include Booze City and Bodification (tattoos and piercings), as well as Michael Jones, the jeweller's outside which 71-year-old 'Supergran' Ann Timson foiled a gang of robbers in 2011, armed with just her handbag. She was only able to run up to them 'because that morning I'd put support bandages on both my legs in preparation for my afternoon dance class', but once in place she administered a comprehensive thrashing, allowing the five men to be brought to justice. A woman made the mistake of asking Supergran if she was all right. 'I thought it was a bit patronising,' said Timson later. 'I know I am a pensioner, but there's no need for a stranger to call me "dear".'

I remember the Beatles fan I knew who grew up in North-ampton, and who was in his first job when *Sgt. Pepper* came out. His lunch hour gave him just enough time to buy the record, get it home and listen to the first side, but then before he could listen to the other side he had to return to work. (Another Fabs-head of my acquaintance says that a resignation would have been in order.) Past the Guildhall I go, then turn towards the Royal and Derngate theatre. Its bar is filled with patrons awaiting the second half of a performance by the Proclaimers, but back in 1934 one of the members of the repertory company here was a young Errol Flynn. Given his later reputation it's no surprise to learn that there were 'issues'. He was dismissed for throwing a female stage manager down a stairwell, and legged it from Northampton owing substantial sums for pyjamas, pants and socks supplied by Montague Jeffery, the menswear store just up the road from the theatre. Peering through its windows tonight I see ties and braces and diamond-patterned socks that can't be too different from those supplied to Flynn, much of the merchandise stored in those wooden glass-fronted drawers that always remind you of John Inman.[6]

Time to head home now, but not before having a drink in the Wig and Pen. Their silenced TV screens are showing the BBC News Channel's continuing tributes to Muhammad Ali,

---

6 The inspiration for *Are You Being Served?* was actually Simpsons of Piccadilly, where the show's writer Jeremy Lloyd once worked. These days the building is inhabited by Waterstones, making it Europe's largest bookshop. Total length of shelving: eight miles.

the automated subtitling service as ever getting things *nearly* right. (Favourite mistake ever: 'There will now be a moment's silence for the Queen Mother' coming out as 'There will now be a moment's violence for the Queen Mother'.) I watch clips from the Rumble in the Jungle, the fight where Ali exhausted George Foreman by soaking up his punches for seven rounds, then said to his opponent: 'Man, this is the wrong place to get tired.' It's moving to see the progression of Ali from champion of the world to broken old man, and also to think that his sort of fame, the sort where almost literally everybody on the planet knew your face, has gone forever. Given that I'm on my own it would be embarrassing to raise a glass to the screen, but lifting my pint for one sip I subtly extend my arm a bit further than usual.

And I think of a quiz question I've used several times. 'A sporting poem often recited during a sporting career that lasted from the nineteen-sixties to the nineteen-eighties has the second line "your hand can't hit what your eye can't see". But its first line is much better known. Who wrote it?' That second line is the rejoinder to 'float like a butterfly, sting like a bee'. Given the clues – the dates of the career, the reference to hitting, the fact that Ali was famous for his poems – I'm amazed at how many people are stumped by it.

Today I met several who certainly wouldn't be.

FIVE

· · · · · · ·

In the original version of the Band Aid hit 'Do They
Know It's Christmas?', who sang the opening line
'It's Christmas time, there's no need to be afraid'?

Where next? Inspiration takes a while, though trivia is
bouncing around as usual. I learn that the word 'tom-
foolery' comes from the antics of Thomas Skelton, the jester
at Muncaster Castle in Cumbria. And that Frank Valori, the
contractor who demolished the famous arch outside Euston
station, used some of the stones in the construction of his own
house, Paradise Villa in Bromley. Also that Alexander David
Mungo Murray (born 1956) is both the 9th Earl of Mansfield
and the 8th Earl of Mansfield. The two titles refer to different
Mansfields – respectively the one in Nottinghamshire and the
one in Middlesex. In a move that only the British aristocracy
could have executed, the two titles were created separately then
unified under a single holder in 1843.

But although these facts can be turned into questions for
my own quizzes, they don't suggest a particular *type* of quiz I
can visit. To kickstart my brain I monitor all sorts of quizzes,
including the daily one in *The Times*, which as it happens is set
by Olav Bjortomt, who came second in Northampton. One of
his questions is: 'Lucrezia Borgia's silky hair reputedly inspired
the Bolognese chef Zefirano to invent which ribbon pasta?' This
passes the 'perfect question' test of teaching you something: it

obviously has to be tagliatelle. Then again it might be fettuccine – reading up on the difference teaches me that fettuccine
is associated more with chefs in Rome and Tuscany. Tagliatelle
tends to be wider: indeed at the Bologna Chamber of Commerce
you'll find a glass case containing a solid gold replica of a piece,
demonstrating the official measurements of six millimetres wide
and one millimetre thick.

All this is lovely, but it still doesn't help with my next variety
of quiz. That problem is finally solved by a magazine article
in which Sebastian Faulks relates his youthful appearance on
University Challenge. Faulks and his teammates (Emmanuel
College, Cambridge) prepared by visiting the pub. Instantly, of
course, we're supporting them. Irreverence while representing
an elite university is always to be applauded, as in the story of
John Rush, another Cambridge man, who wanted a 'Blue' (the
award given to those who appear in a sporting contest for the
university) but was no good at sport. In 1964 he volunteered to
box against John Coker, the Oxford heavyweight so fearsome
that no one else would face him. Rush's friends were convinced
he was going to get battered, but at the opening bell he simply
ran towards Coker, head down, and belted him in the groin. The
referee warned Rush that if he did it again he'd be disqualified.
He did, he was, and he got his Blue.

No physical danger for Faulks on *University Challenge*, but he
faced a Glasgow team who looked 'brainy and sober'. Not that
he cared. 'I was powered up; I was a Ferrari on the grid, roaring
with ethanol-powered confidence. [The deliverers of his etha-
nol had been bitter and barley wine.] ... Bring it on, Bamber.'
Bamber obliged: 'Your starter for ten. What was the military
rank of the gentleman who gave his name to the standard score
in golf before the arrival of the dreaded par?' Faulks was straight
in with the correct answer: 'Colonel.' It takes a moment for the
implication to sink in: yes, I knew about 'Colonel Bogey', and
yes, I knew about a bogey in golf – but I didn't know they were
connected. In the 19th-century, it seems, a level score was known
as bogey, as though you were playing against an imaginary

opponent called Colonel Bogey (his name inspired by the old concept of the 'bogey man'). Then in 1914 the tune was written, taking its first two notes – the 'Hit-ler' in 'Hitler has only got one ball' – from a golfer who used to whistle them instead of shouting 'Fore!' Only later did courses tighten their scoring systems, par becoming the new standard and the old bogey score amounting to one over.

So delightful is this discovery that it temporarily blinds me to the hint in Faulks's article. Eventually, though, I come to my senses: a quiz show. My next trip has to be to a quiz show. Let's see how the broadcasters deal with the beast. God knows why the idea hasn't occurred before. My *University Challenge* conversations in Oxford, all the media gigs performed by the contenders in Northampton, not to mention the quiz shows coming at you every day over the TV and radio airwaves. And only the other week *Mastermind* featured in an exchange I had on Twitter. The last-ever Land Rover Defender, I'd noticed, was rolling off the production line on the same day that Gordon Goody, who used one in the Great Train Robbery, died. 'The curse of *Mastermind*?' replied someone, going on to explain that the robbery had recently featured as a specialist subject (competition for the World Quizzing Championships in the hitman stakes). Needless to say, I had to look up the episode on iPlayer and test myself. Proving that *Mastermind* is becoming obscenely easy, the early questions featured the farm where the robbers hid (Leatherslade) and the game on which their fingerprints were found (Monopoly). The only thing of interest I learned was how to pronounce 'Bridego', the bridge where the robbery took place. It is, at least according to John Humphrys, 'Brid-*ay*-go'. One of the other specialist subjects was the Apollo moon missions, so obviously I had to check that out as well. Did moderately well, learned that during its return to Earth Apollo 10 reached 24,790 miles per hour – still the fastest that mankind has ever travelled.

Mr Apollo scored 13 points with no passes, but Mr Great Train Robbery did even better – 14 and no passes. So I had to watch the general knowledge rounds to see who won. The other two contestants' questions threw up the only English Pope in history (Adrian IV), the radio call 'wilco' being short for 'I will comply', and – as if to prove my point about Winston Churchill's ubiquity – his family's request, when they gave Chartwell to the nation, that there should always be a ginger cat called Jock living there. Then Mr Apollo took the chair. His round, including a question about Ann Frank's diary entries always beginning 'Dear Kitty' (her imaginary friend), took him to a score of 23 and no passes. Mr GTR's, featuring the revelation that the word 'gerrymander' derives from Massachusetts Governor Elbridge Gerry redrawing the state's district boundaries for his own electoral advantage (one of the districts resembled a salamander), involved two passes but still gave him victory with 25. And as ever the handshakes at the end reminded me of one of my own quiz-setting staples – if all four contestants in an episode of *Mastermind* shake hands with each other, how many handshakes will there be? You wouldn't believe how heated the debates get. '*No*,' one team member will growl to the others, 'you've already *counted* that one . . .' The correct answer is six – four people each shaking hands with the other three, divided by two because each shake features two people.

Mastermind owes its existence to the Nazis. Bill Wright, the programme's inventor, had been held prisoner and interrogated by the Germans during the Second World War. The experience gave him the idea for a forbidding, intimidating quiz show where the contestant sits in a spotlight. The 'name, occupation, specialist subject' element mirrored the name, rank and number that were the only three pieces of information prisoners had to give under the Geneva Convention. In the credits of early episodes the presenter Magnus Magnusson was actually listed as 'Interrogator'. At the cuddlier end of the TV quiz scale is the Tory politician Baroness Trumpington, who as a young woman used to supplement her income by winning prizes on game shows, then selling them. Her trick for being picked from the audience was to wear a hat and white gloves, and make the man she was with wear a bow-tie. Meanwhile, over the pond, the show *Jeopardy!* was won in 2011 by Watson, a computer designed for the purpose by IBM.[1] The $1 million prize was donated to charity.

But the quiz show I'd really like to have seen was neither American nor British. It aired in the Soviet Union, in 1957, and was called *Evening of Merry Questions*. By showing ordinary citizens on screen, went the thinking, the show would highlight the successes of the Communist revolution. But one night the host invited viewers to come to the studio, the only 'task' being that they had to dress in a woollen coat and felt boots. Over 500 people stormed the live transmission, waving at the cameras, tearing down the curtain and demanding prizes. Many were drunk. One was carrying a live chicken. The transmission was suspended for 'technical reasons', and the show never returned.

* * *

I'm still mulling over the issue of which quiz show to visit a few days later, when I attend an event held by some of my friends in a London bookshop. They are all 'Elves' on *QI*, the researchers who provide the facts with which Sandi Toksvig and her guests make merry. They've organised a quiz to promote the paperback publication of some of the show's books, such as *1411 QI Facts to Knock You Sideways* and *1339 QI Facts to Make Your Jaw Drop*. The shop, the Holborn branch of Blackwell's, is no slouch in the quiz department itself, ex-manager Gary regularly hosting events as well as tweeting the shop's followers with visual clues to the name of a book or author. My favourite was a Photoshopped image of Ronnie O'Sullivan balancing a pint of lager on his head while playing a shot. (Beatrix Potter.)

In fact the publishing world as a whole is fertile territory

---

1 Named after the company's first CEO, rather than as a nod to HOLMES, the computer database consulted by British police (Home Office Large Major Enquiry System).

for quizzes. Literary festivals often run them, and there's one on Radio 4 called *The Write Stuff*. I've set plenty of book-based questions myself. 'The world's thickest book,' for instance, 'with a spine measuring twelve point six inches, is a collection of every story featuring which fictional detective?' (Miss Marple.) Then there was: 'The first seven words of Edward Bulwer-Lytton's 1830 novel *Paul Clifford* have become famous as a phrase in their own right. So famous, in fact, that since 1982 the English department at San Jose State University have held the annual Bulwer-Lytton Fiction Contest, in which entrants have to write the "opening sentence to the worst of all possible novels". What were those seven words?'[2] And as well as book trivia proving useful as question fodder, there's the stuff that's delightful in its own right. T. E. Lawrence losing the manuscript for his masterpiece *Seven Pillars of Wisdom* at a train station and having to write it again. (To show that fate likes puns, the station was Reading.) One of the soldiers who landed in Normandy on D-Day being a young J. D. Salinger, carrying six chapters of *The Catcher in the Rye* in his backpack. And – most importantly of all – the Norwegian version of the Mr Men book *Mr Bump* having the title *Herr Dumpidump*.

The Elves' quiz isn't book-themed as such, though some of it gives a nod in that direction. The theme of the first round, for example, is that all the answers are titles of novels. We learn that the snack food worn by the Aztecs as jewellery was popcorn, and the time of day for which 'cockshut' was an old English word is twilight (that being the time you locked up your poultry). After this Alex hands over to Dan, which makes for a nice contrast in styles: Alex is a quietly spoken and studious 20-something, while Dan is a few years older and has – God knows how, because he was born in Hong Kong to an Australian father – an American accent which he puts to great use in everything from stand-up comedy to hosting the *QI* podcast *No Such Thing as a Fish*. His round is a 'true or false' one. There are ten statements, so your

---

2 'It was a dark and stormy night.'

chances of getting them all right just by guessing are 1 in 210, or 1 in 1024.[3] We encounter 'Bugs Bunny is a rabbit' (false – he's a hare), 'Doritos were invented at Disneyland' (true) and 'Anne Boleyn was the first woman to play golf' (false – it was Mary Queen of Scots). My favourite statement is 'speed cameras were invented to speed drivers up'. It's true: the Dutch racing driver Maurice Gatsonides wanted a way of monitoring his speed around corners so he could plan the ideal line. The device he came up with, the 'Gatso', was so good that he started supplying it to police forces for precisely the opposite purpose. The yellow-backed cameras you see (hopefully in time) on UK roads today are Gatsos. Maurice was often caught by his own invention, but professed not to mind: 'I love speeding.'

The final round is hosted by James. Originally from Bolton, he brings a Northern single-mindedness to most challenges, and as he's spent longer as an Elf than most of the others (he's nearing 40), he is used to presenting information in unusual ways. So his round tonight is themed entirely on the Pacific island of Nauru. Of course the questions branch out cleverly from that limited brief, as with the one about the island's Presidents having to send their trousers away for dry-cleaning to the capital city of Victoria in Australia, there being no dry-cleaning firm on Nauru itself. (What is that city? Melbourne.) James also asks what the Nauruan language has in common with Malayalam, an Indian language, a quality shared by no other in the world. The answer is that the names of these languages are palindromes. Discussing this afterwards with the members of Marvel-Themed Cheese Strings (other team names include Sandi Toksquiz), I offer 'a man, a plan, a canal – Panama', and receive in return 'a dog, a panic, in a pagoda'.

One of tonight's questions travels in the other direction. I'm testing out a potential new tiebreaker, a fact gleaned from a book I've just read about the *Titanic*: how much would the ship's rivets

---

3 Just as Alec Stewart's chances of making an incorrect call for every coin toss during the five-match Ashes series of 1998–99 were 1 in 32. He managed it.

have weighed if you put them all together? James thinks it's three tons. Anna (fast-thinking, fast-talking) goes for 20 tons, Anne (fast-thinking, fast-talking, though in a Scottish rather than an English accent) goes for 55 tons. The show's originator, the much-decorated TV producer John Lloyd, is also in attendance, and blows everyone else – if you'll forgive the metaphor – out of the water, guessing 1000 tons. The correct answer is a staggering 1200 tons.

It's tempting to make *QI* itself my quiz show – they're currently in the middle of recording the new series – but its appeal lies as much in the banter and jokes that develop from the questions as in the questions themselves. Entertaining viewing though this produces, I'm perhaps better off choosing a more 'traditional' quiz show – that is, one where the stars are the facts you learn rather than the panellists. Calls are made, emails are sent, and a plan (though not a man or a canal) forms.

First, however, there's another journey to make. I'm going to north London again. To somewhere near the Prince of Wales, but not the pub itself. I only wish it was.

* * *

You might have noticed that Chris – not my journalist friend Chris, and not the one from the World Quizzing Championships either, but the one at the Prince of Wales, the guy who, along with Marcus, oversees the Snowball round every week – hasn't actually been present on any of my visits to Highgate. This is because he's been battling cancer. It didn't stop him hosting his traditional 'first quiz of the year' at the pub, which always consists entirely of questions about the previous calendar year, its news and events. As it happens that was the last time I saw Chris. And now comes the news that it's going to remain the last time I saw him.

The funeral is being held at East Finchley Cemetery. As we wait outside the crematorium I chat to Martin, who tells me of a recent trip to see John Soane's memorial in the churchyard of Old St Pancras, behind the station. Its domed roof was the inspiration for the red telephone box.

'The memorial's Grade One listed now,' says Martin. 'One of only two in London that are.'

I pause for a moment to consider whether it's respectful to be doing trivia at Chris's funeral, before realising he would have been offended if we hadn't.

'And the other one is...' I reply, giving myself time to work it out. 'We're obviously excluding Wellington in St Paul's and things like that, where the building is Grade One listed in itself?'

'Obviously,' says Martin. And then, when I confess to being stumped: 'Karl Marx.' Not far from here, in Highgate Cemetery.

'There are only two Grade One listed buildings on the Tube network,' I say. 'The Bank of England – because of its Tube entrance in the south-west corner – and fifty-five Broadway.' This is the huge building over St James's Park station, the headquarters of Transport for London itself. 'Do you know about the Jacob Epstein chisel thing there?' This is the point at which Jo would be muttering 'God help me' and wandering off in search of gin.

Martin doesn't know the story, so I relate the outcry over Epstein's statue for the building. It featured a naked boy whose penis was deemed too prominent for public decency. The sculptor had to climb a ladder and chisel an inch and a half off the offending part. Halfway through this we're joined by Shahab, who responds with the story of Bologna's Piazza Maggiore, where the fountain is watched over by a statue of Neptune. Its sculptor, Giambologna, was similarly forced to reduce his work's manliness, but got the last laugh by arranging Neptune's outstretched left thumb so that anyone standing behind him sees it as an erect penis.

All this and the ceremony hasn't even started yet. In fact it doesn't start until 15 minutes past the appointed time. This is a deliberate move by Marcus and the other organisers, in tribute to Chris's notorious tardiness: he's literally late for his own funeral. There are tributes from different people, reflecting various aspects of Chris's 66 years on the planet: his love of Scotland (for holidays – he was Norf London born and bred), of music (Pink Floyd's 'Great Gig in the Sky' fills the crematorium) and so on. Dave, who used to work with him in the haulage industry,[4] gets in an early mention of quizzing by relating Chris's phone calls to test out new questions. Dave would keep him talking while he fired up Google, then proceed to amaze Chris with his astounding knowledge. But the topic is formally addressed by Marcus, who talks about the man he first met in... well, when? 'Chris and I discussed this more than once. I'd say it was late 1992, and he'd say "No, no, no, no", it was early 1993. Eventually I brought along documentary evidence that it was late 1992 – and he still wouldn't believe me. Christopher John Pollikett was the single most stubborn man I have ever known.'

Marcus talks lovingly of his teammate, how he knew 'an awful lot about an awful lot of things', despite having his weaknesses ('he believed that pop music had come to an end in 1976'). How Chris has left Marcus and another friend Stephen his quiz questions. 'Forty-five thousand of them. A life's work, really. But those questions were written and deployed and maintained with love and unquenchable enthusiasm. And absolute respect for the craft. Because he was really good at it. The best, I think. Even if there were too many questions about Harry Potter and progressive rock and obscure Scottish castles. "No one's heard of that castle," I would say. "Well I've been there," he would say.'

Marcus finishes by announcing that in Chris's memory an annual quiz is going to be instituted, between the Prince of Wales and the Royal Oak, another pub at which Chris regularly took the questioner's mike. The following Tuesday I'll find myself at the first of those two pubs. I'll learn from co-hosts Darrien and Dave that the Tory MP Jacob Rees-Mogg holds the record for the longest word ever in *Hansard* ('floccinaucinihilipilifica-tion'). That in 2008 Nicolas Sarkozy failed to get a voodoo doll

---

4 One of my biggest sorrows about Chris's death is that now he will definitely never write his oft-discussed book about the M6.

in his likeness removed from sale, but that as a result of the court case the doll now has to carry a warning that piercing it with needles 'constitutes an attack on the personal dignity of Mr Sarkozy'. That Adam Ant was the only performer at Live Aid whose single went down in the charts as a result of the concert, and that the only non-Beatles record in the five biggest sellers of the 1960s was 'Tears' by Ken Dodd. A further revelation will be that one of the actors who dubbed Gerry Adams's TV and radio appearances when his voice was banned from news programmes was *The Crying Game* star Stephen Rea.

But the evening's greatest excitement will come after the quiz proper, when the first Snowball question asks which writer was responsible for the 1884 short story 'J. Habakuk Jephson's Statement'. It was based on the true tale of the abandoned ship the *Mary Celeste*, and is responsible for the mistaken belief that the ship's first name was *Marie*. John, whose raffle ticket was the first one drawn, happens to know that the answer is Arthur Conan Doyle. And so he wins £1000. Not bad for 20 seconds' work. It's rare that the top prize goes, and indeed this is the first time I've ever witnessed it. All those times I saw Chris read out the questions without anyone bagging the grand, then on my first visit since he died, it happens.

Stupidly my initial instinct is to look around for Chris so I can tell him. Instead, I console myself by remembering the last time I saw him, sitting at the bar, picking up the mike to start proceedings.

'Evening everyone,' he said, 'good to be here.'

It was a nondescript comment, the sort of thing anyone would have said. But it dawned on the whole pub – and must have dawned on Chris as well – that in his position the words had a special meaning. A few people uttered 'hear, hear', this turned into cheers, then the cheers turned into applause.

It clearly caught Chris unawares. 'Well,' he said, when the noise had died away. 'Bloody hell.'

* * *

It's funny how things can go full circle. The building in front of me inspired the most famous room number in English literature, then that room number re-entered the building as a programme in its own right. It was during the time he spent working here – BBC Broadcasting House in central London – that George Orwell first encountered Room 101. It was a conference room in which he attended many tedious meetings (he was a talks producer for the corporation's Eastern Service). No surprise, then, that the number got the billing it did in *1984*. Half a century later Broadcasting House welcomed *Room 101* back, this time as the title of a radio (and later TV) show in which guests nominate the things they hate.[5]

As I approach the old bit of the building, the curve of Portland stone that's been here since 1932, I glance to the right and see the billion-pound wall of glass that allowed the Beeb to bring its TV and radio operations under one roof. That sent something full circle too – the problems of having the Bakerloo Line as your neighbour. The brown bit of the Tube map runs down the western side of Broadcasting House, so when the radio studios were in the basement you could sometimes hear trains rumbling past during a broadcast. (Engineers had to mark it on their programme reports.) Shifting the studios to higher floors ended that difficulty – but then TV news came along and built *their* studios in the basement of the new wing. The studios had to be mounted on special shock-absorbing springs to prevent Huw Edwards going all shaky on you.

As it happens I need the old reception today, the small one in the 1932 wing, the one with the Eric Gill sculpture of Prospero and Ariel over the door. Gill also designed Gill Sans, the typeface used by Penguin Books and British Rail, and indeed the BBC itself. The man I'm about to meet has told me (when we got sidetracked into the subject in our introductory emails) that 'I use it for all official correspondence if I can – there's something

---

5 We could pedantically point out that in the novel Room 101 contains the thing you *fear*. Of course fear and hate are closely linked – but let's not get too psychotherapeutic.

very clean and satisfying about it.' Attention to detail like this is only to be expected from the producer of Radio 4's three main quiz programmes, *Brain of Britain*, *Round Britain Quiz* and (the one I've come to see recorded today) the music quiz *Counterpoint*. When Paul Bajoria arrives in reception – early fifties, tall, lean, learned-looking – it's from the street rather than the offices: he is based in the Beeb's Salford offices, and has travelled down this afternoon. Some recordings take place up there, some in London.

You can see why Auntie wants to avoid being capital-centric, but her arrangements often evoke Kafka rather than George Orwell. When I worked in this building 20 years ago the 'internal market' had just been introduced, a system which set the cost of borrowing a CD from the BBC's library so high that it was cheaper to go and buy a copy from HMV on Oxford Street. So that's what people did. Paul and I are soon swapping such tales, his relating to the meeting rooms in Salford.

'They're named after famous BBC programmes. The trouble is some of the programmes also have their production offices there. So you're never sure if a sign is pointing you to the meeting room or the office. It'll say "Match of the Day", but if you think you're going to meet the *Match of the Day* production team you're sorely mistaken. It's the same with Woman's Hour and A Question of Sport.' The system also gives rise to some absurd sentences. 'You find yourself saying things like "see you in Teletubbies at three".'

As Paul doesn't have an office at Broadcasting House we retire to a café a few yards down Regent Street.[6] He tells me how he came to be in charge of Radio 4's quiz output, which across the three programmes amounts to 43 half-hour episodes a year. 'The first one I was given was *Round Britain Quiz*, in the late nineties. It had been around since 1947, growing out of something called

---

6 A producer once invited some guests to drinks in his Broadcasting House office, and when things got slightly out of hand and some minor damage occurred he received a letter from management warning that 'under no circumstances are BBC premises to be used for the purpose of entertainment'.

Transatlantic Quiz, which they did for a couple of years after the war. The technology had appeared where you could have one team in London and the other in New York or Washington.' Today's kids, even if they paused for a second from their video calls conducted on smartphones on the bus, will probably never realise just how exciting this must have been at the time. '*Round Britain Quiz* carried on the same idea – for decades the teams really were in different studios dotted around the country. Then for a while they pretended that was happening, when actually they were in the same studio.'

Gradually the other programmes got added to Paul's remit. For a while he also produced a radio version of *Mastermind*. 'Our policy for setting the specialist subject questions on that was always to go to the acknowledged expert in the field. That could be tricky, because some experts like writing long-winded, pedantic, impossibly difficult questions. There was also the case – in the TV version, not mine – where the contestant had chosen Franz Liszt or something, and they went to the professor of musicology at such-and-such university because he was the expert. The professor replied "I'm very happy to set the questions – but you do know I'm the contestant, don't you?"'

I tell Paul the sorry tale of my agent's father. He worked in publishing, and edited the official biography of Winston Churchill written (in several volumes over many years) by Martin Gilbert. It was to Gilbert that the producers of *Mastermind* naturally turned when my agent's father appeared on the programme and selected Churchill as his specialist subject. 'You do know he's my editor, don't you?' said Gilbert. The producers said they did, and it wasn't a problem. Nevertheless, to remove any possible accusations of favours being done, Gilbert came up with the hardest set of questions you could possibly imagine. As my agent puts it, 'they were along the lines of "what colour socks was Churchill wearing on the second day at Yalta?"' His father bombed, achieving one of the lowest scores in the history of the programme, and was pretty shaken up by the whole experience.

'You never set out to do that to anyone,' says Paul. 'Most people who take part in our quizzes are very nice, and you want them to do as well as possible.' He pauses. 'But once in a while there's the odd arrogant one, and I have to admit there is a certain satisfaction when you see someone breeze in, assuming they're going to win, and then they crash and burn.'

This, of course, is one of the key ingredients of a quiz programme. Not crashing and burning necessarily, just the human drama of how the contestants deal with pressure. If – as I think is the case – pub quizzes are a continuation of sport by other means, a method of exercising your competitive instinct, then quiz shows give you that pleasure (you can try and answer the questions yourself) *plus* the fun of watching other people under the cosh. You are both participant and spectator.

What does Paul look for in a question? 'I guess it's one where when you hear the answer, you want to store it away. There's such a massive amount of information out there that it's only reasonable to expect people to remember something if it's memorable. Something that makes you prick up your ears. For instance, if there's a connection, say, someone from the nineteenth century having the same name as someone who's famous now. The classic example of that is Joseph Bazalgette and Peter Bazalgette.' The engineering genius whose revolutionary new sewer network massively improved Londoners' health, and his great-great-grandson who invented the TV show *Big Brother*. (Back to Orwell again.)

This sort of 'linking' question features most heavily in *Round Britain Quiz*. A typical example runs: 'If I swim back to a Nevada city, where I play a board game and I learn to go dancing, what language do I speak?' The answer is Latin – 'I swim back' is 'reno', 'I play' is 'ludo' and 'I learn' is 'disco'. The board game does indeed take its name from the Roman language, though the other two are coincidences. *Discothèque* was originally French for a library of phonograph records, while the city in Nevada was named after Jesse L. Reno, a soldier in the American Civil

War. Though he too had French roots: his ancestors had Anglicised their name from 'Renault' when they moved to America in 1770.

Paul has a team of three, and calls in specialist question-setters for the different programmes, but still contributes lots of questions himself. 'My wife always says that anyone who wants to do well in *Round Britain Quiz* should find out where I've been on holiday and which books I've been reading in the previous six months.' The influence of your own knowledge can be a hard thing to compensate for. 'If someone else's question happens to dovetail with my own references, it's quite difficult to assess how easy or hard it is. Obviously anyone's definition of whether a question is hard or not is "did I know it?" You have to ask around the office to check how commonly known it is.'

I test Paul with a question I've often used in my own quizzes: 'Which fictional nineteen-seventies TV character offered the advice "if you can't do the time, don't do the crime"?' He quickly gets to *Porridge*, and initially offers Mr Mackay, but my mouth has no sooner opened to correct him than he follows up with: 'No, it's probably Fletcher, isn't it?' Indeed it is, and Paul's speedy arrival at the answer is all the more impressive because so few people ever get it. This never fails to astonish me. The quote's obviously about being in prison – how many 1970s TV series *were* there about prison? As it happens, shortly after meeting Paul I happen across an old episode of the show. Warren, played by Sam Kelly, places a chamber pot on one side of the cell to symbolise the sun, and a satsuma on the other to symbolise Earth. On that scale, he asks, how far away would the nearest star other than the sun be? Godber guesses the recreation yard, Fletcher the married quarters. Warren gives them the correct answer: Johannesburg.

While Paul's in the chair, so to speak, and because it's cropped up that he's a massive Beatles fan, I also test him with a question I've devised recently about their single-word number ones. 'Help' was the only one in the UK – but which two other songs topped the charts in America? Paul quickly gets 'Yesterday', but then stumbles on the second. He says 'Michelle' – it was 'Something'.

'Incredible that for all its fame,' I say, ' "Yesterday" didn't get to number one over here.'

'It wasn't actually released as a single until early 1976,' replies Paul. 'EMI reissued all the band's previous singles, plus "Yesterday". I can't for the life of me remember why, but the singles chart was suddenly full of them.'

It's the 'early' that I like. Not just '1976', but '*early* 1976'. This sort of thing matters to Paul. One of the reasons he does the job he does, of course. I sense he's like me: aware of his nerdish instincts, but capable of channelling them. (At least I hope that makes him like me.) There's an irony that the word 'quiz' used to mean 'nerd'. As an article in the *Sporting Magazine* of December 1794 put it: 'To peruse any book of improvement is called Quizical; in short not to be extremely dissipated and extravagant is to be a Quiz.'[7]

Paul is aware that quizzes tend to attract a certain type of person. In short: men. 'I'd say our applications are biased five to one in favour of men. Obviously it's something you're aware of, and you do what you can to ensure there's a balance, not just in terms of gender but of where people are from, age and so on. I'd say that by the time we've whittled it down to the contestants [the process involves a combination of sample questions and phone interviews], the male bias is down to four to one.' Paul adds that the programme's presenter Paul Gambaccini has a theory about quizzers. 'He says that men's brains are just better at retaining trivia.' As someone who's previously written about the copious neurological evidence for this, I'm not going to argue. 'And that's the sort of knowledge that quizzes depend

---

7 The reason for the word's modern use isn't clear, though the *Oxford English Dictionary* thinks the obvious link with 'inquisitive' might be correct. There's also the story that Richard Daly, manager of Dublin's Theatre Royal, invented 'quiz' in 1791 as part of a bet that he could popularise a new, meaningless word within 48 hours. His employees were paid to chalk it all over the city's doors and walls, and 'quiz' soon passed into popular usage. Sadly there isn't any evidence for this.

on. That's how I always reassure people if they do badly. "Look, doing well in this is nothing to do with intelligence." '

Paul relates a story from Jeremy Vine about the erstwhile Egghead CJ de Mooi (it's pronounced 'Mooey' – he was born Joseph Connagh, but changed his surname to the Dutch phrase meaning 'the beautiful'). 'They were talking about a film Jeremy loved. A Howard Hawks film, I think it was, or an early Hitchcock one – something like that. They had a long conversation in which CJ listed the cast and the year it was made and the locations they filmed at and who wrote the music and all sorts of other details. At one point Jeremy said "do you remember the bit where..." and CJ replied "oh, I've never actually seen it." That's your professional quizzer to a T.'

We talk about our favourite media quizzes of the past. *A Question of Sport*, we agree, benefits from the same advantage as *Counterpoint*: although they're both single-topic programmes, those topics are big enough to make for a great programme. 'And constantly changing, too,' adds Paul. 'Sport is being played all the time, and new music is being written all the time, so there are always new questions you can ask about things that have happened since the last series.'

I confess to an admiration for Bamber Gascoigne, on the grounds that you have to trust someone who clearly has a brain the size of Cornwall. If a contestant got a question wrong he'd know *why* they'd got it wrong: 'Ah, no, see what you've done there – that's from Henry the Fourth Part *Two*.' Paul agrees, and also admires Gascoigne's successor. 'Paxman's "come *on*" is great – it's chucked in for drama, but it also reminds you that the reason he's getting impatient is the answer's so obvious to him.' A wide range of knowledge is an asset possessed by *Counterpoint*'s own presenter too. 'Every now and then Gambo will come up with a back reference – he'll always have an anecdote about the Temptations or Aretha Franklin, or being in the back of a cab with Art Garfunkel. But he also tries hard to pepper the programme with anecdotes about Leonard Bernstein and English National Opera as well. And to keep abreast of what's new – he makes it his business to go to stuff at the South Bank and wherever, to know what's going on.' Paul reminds me that Gambaccini is the only person ever to have had their own show on Radios 1, 2, 3 and 4.

A good quiz question in itself.

* * *

A couple of hours later, I'm sitting in row three of the Radio Theatre inside Broadcasting House. This art deco venue, intimate and stylish, takes you back to the days when the BBC held orchestral performances here. The days when they only had listeners, rather than viewers.[8] Only six other seats among the three hundred or so are occupied, all on the front row, all by the contestants for the two episodes that are going to be recorded this evening. Paul stands on the stage and runs them through the rules, how the rehearsals will work and so on. 'If we tell you an answer is wrong,' he says, 'and you're absolutely sure your answer was right, do let us know. We'd much rather sort it now, when we can re-record if necessary, than when we've all gone home and there's nothing we can do about it.' He and I talked about this earlier. It's impossible for the team's fact-checking to be absolutely definitive, especially on 'negative checks' – for instance, questions about the only artist to achieve such-and-such a feat. It's perfectly possible that the contestant will know something the question-setter didn't.

On the left of the stage is Gambaccini's table. He's flanked by Stephen Garner, a member of Paul's team who acts as scorer, and David Kenrick, one of the question-setters who's here as adjudicator. Opposite them is the contestants' table, on which stand three delightfully old-fashioned metal boxes whose fronts light up when the buzzers are pressed. The rehearsals are quick rounds of a few sample questions, and prove Peter Ustinov's

---

8 It wasn't until 1936 that the BBC settled on the word 'viewer'. Before that a consumer of its fledgling TV service had been a 'televiewer' or 'looker-in'.

point that you should always rehearse no matter how simple you think something will be. He was once in a play where two actors had the sole task of stretchering a body off, something so simple that they didn't bother rehearsing: on the first night they picked up the stretcher to find themselves facing each other, then quickly put it down – and turned round so they were facing away from each other. The difficulty tonight is for Tony Lazarus, who after several questions of his rehearsal says that he can't hear what's being said. A speaker is moved closer and the table repositioned to help him out. Understandable that he should have hearing difficulties: he's 69. We know this because he has pointed out that his surname is the title of the last album by David Bowie, who was born in the same month as him. At least I'm assuming we all know that Bowie appeared on 8 January 1947, which happened to be Elvis's 12th birthday. If I can't make that assumption in this company then where can I?

After the rehearsals Paul and I retire to the control room at the back of the auditorium. The audience file in: it's a full house tonight, so the BBC door staff are kept busy. Thankfully they're more friendly than the commissionaires of yesteryear. One legendarily unwelcoming car park attendant, who only had one arm, once asked Eric Morecambe for a ticket to a recording. 'We don't want you,' came the reply, 'you can't clap.' In the control room conversation turns to 'Dumb Britain', *Private Eye*'s regular collection of the incorrect answers given on various quiz shows. Jill, in charge of the Radio Theatre's huge mixing desk, remembers an episode of *Pointless* where someone thought the political figure who founded the Quit India movement was Nelson Mandela. The same programme offered us Alexander Armstrong asking for people with the first name William. 'I'll go for the playwright who wrote *Hamlet*,' came the reply, 'William Tell.' Elsewhere there was: 'Which film starring Bob Hoskins was also the name of a famous painting by Leonardo da Vinci?', to which someone said '*Who Framed Roger Rabbit*?' And 'How many kings of England have been called Henry?' was met with

'Er, well, I know there was a Henry the Eighth... er... three?'
But my favourite exchange was:

> Host: 'In which country would you spend shekels?'
> Contestant: 'Holland?'
> Host: 'Try the next letter of the alphabet.'
> Contestant: 'Iceland? Ireland?'
> Host: 'It's a bad line. Did you say Israel?'
> Contestant: 'No.'

The standard is a little higher on Radio 4, thankfully, so once the first episode gets under way we're treated to some impressive knowledge. The opening round asks the contestants one question each in rotation, with bonus points available to the others if they can't answer. There's an early hitch for music promoter Jane Wallace when she mishears a 'he' as 'she' and guesses Cilla Black: the correct answer is Burt Bacharach. A little younger than Tony, her auditory trouble is due to an infection, but as soon as Gambaccini points out the error she comes straight back with Bacharach.

'That's OK,' says Paul B. to Paul G. via talkback, 'it's not fair to penalise her for a mishearing. Let's record that again.' Gambaccini repeats the question, Wallace gives her correct answer, and the programme moves on. But Jane still looks tense, and indeed will remain so for the rest of the quiz. You're torn between wanting her to do well and knowing that human frailty is part of the mix.

Another, as Paul said this afternoon, is the supplementary information given by Gambaccini. When Alastair Smith (consultant haematologist, melodious Scottish burr) is asked for the name of the theme song from the Bond film *Skyfall*, the presenter follows up with the fact that 'The Writing's on the Wall' was the first Bond theme to reach number one.[9] When Jane is

---

9 The record-buying public are obviously as hard to please as Bond producer Cubby Broccoli. When Paul McCartney played him 'Live and Let Die' Broccoli replied: 'OK, that's the demo – when can you do the proper version?'

asked which of the Merry Men was played by Ronnie Corbett in the Lionel Bart musical *Twang!*, he lets us know that the show's early demise freed Corbett from his role as Will Scarlett, so allowing him to appear in *The Frost Report* and launching his TV career. But my favourite discovery in round one comes from the actual 'body' of a question itself: 'What useful, if not essential, accessory for a night at the opera was invented in the nineteenth century by Antoine Gibus?' It was the collapsible opera hat, a 'topper' that could be squashed down for easy storage under your seat.

Despite her nervousness, Jane finishes the round in first place, two points clear of Alastair Smith and one of John Grant, a voluntary worker from London whose flat cap stays fixedly in place for the whole quiz. The second round offers the contestants a choice of themes. Alastair goes for Tchaikovsky, Jane for Rod Stewart and John for the impish-sounding 'Musical Monopoly Board'. Alastair's decision is justified when he gets a question on the 1812 Overture, because 'I've sung it in the Albert Hall'. (Kudos, though the best-ever use of the hall remains a non-musical one – an indoor marathon in 1909. The two runners had to complete 524 clockwise laps of the arena.) One of John's Monopoly questions uses the 'income tax – pay £200' element to ask which Beatles album opens with 'Taxman'. It's *Revolver*, and gives Paul his statutory Fabs question for the episode. One of the other round choices was 'Music for More than One Piano'. I ask Paul if that would have included the never ending chord at the end of 'A Day in the Life'. As it happens it wouldn't, so Gambaccini would have been denied the chance to tell everyone that the E major was played on three pianos shared by John, Paul, Ringo and the band's roadie Mal Evans, plus George Martin on a harmonium. Everyone then had to sit as still as possible for as long as possible. Turn it up on headphones right at the end and you'll hear a squeak: rumour has it that this was Ringo shifting on his piano stool.

Alastair and John both score heavily, so the pressure is now on Jane to maintain her lead. Sadly her Rod Stewart knowledge proves lacking, and she drops into a distant last place. Meanwhile Jill and I are comparing notes on Rod, my 'he begged his mum to let him buy her a stupidly expensive present and she asked for a bread bin' is met by a picture of the star himself on Jill's phone (she worked on a Radio 2 programme with him). This in turn reminds me of the time I took my parents to Langan's restaurant in Mayfair, and discreetly alerted my mother to the fact Rod Stewart was standing right behind her. 'Don't worry, I won't make a scene,' she said. Then, slowly extending her elbow over the back of her chair until it reached Stewart's jacket, she yelled: 'I've touched him!'

Things get even worse for Jane in the final round. It's on the buzzer, incorrect answers losing you points, and her score actually goes down rather than up. The other two surge away, helped by their knowledge, among much else, that Deep Purple's 'Smoke on the Water' was inspired by a recording studio burning down on the shore of Lake Geneva and that Sergei Prokofiev died on the same day as Joseph Stalin.[10] John is the winner with 26 points, earning himself a place in the semi-final.

A quick changeover for the next episode brings Tony Lazarus to the stage. He's joined by Bunny Hambleton-Relf (as unlike his name as possible – retired social worker from Yorkshire whose braces have musical notes on them) and Nathan Hamer. Nathan has quizzing form: he once bagged six and a half grand on *The Chase*. 'Winnings on quiz shows are tax-free, aren't they?' I asked him earlier. 'Oh yes,' replied Nathan with a smile. 'At least I hope they are – I work in financial crime.'

Bunny and Nathan vie for the lead throughout the quiz, but Tony's also in with a shout. I experience a 'how can I have forgotten that?' moment when Gambaccini asks who sang the opening line of 'Do They Know It's Christmas?'. The name 'Paul Young' escapes me completely, though in fairness it does

---

10 Every musician in Moscow was required for the dictator's funeral and associated events, so at the composer's service his family could only play a recording of his *Romeo and Juliet* march. They were also forced into using paper flowers, as all the real ones were reserved for Stalin.

the same to Bunny, who goes for Bono. During a round titled '20th Century Blues' we learn that George Gershwin was 25 when he wrote *Rhapsody in Blue*, and during the 'Sorted for Es and Whizz' round that 'Vera' – as mentioned in The Shamen's 1992 hit 'Ebeneezer Goode' – is rhyming slang for Rizlas (Vera Lynn – skin). We do not engage, because no one chooses the topic 'United States of Music', with the question of which US state Ray Charles 'had on his mind', which is just as well, as the annoying pedant in me would have felt obliged to point out that the Georgia in question was the songwriter Hoagy Carmichael's sister rather than the place. Nor do we hear about Lynyrd Skynyrd writing 'Sweet Home Alabama' as a riposte to Neil Young's less than complimentary song 'Southern Man'. Or indeed about the band's name being a riposte to Leonard Skinner, the schoolteacher who suspended them for having long hair. He later became an estate agent, and the band put a photo of his board on one of their album covers. This prompted calls from fans in the middle of the night. 'They'd say "Who's speaking?" and I'd say "Leonard Skinner", and they'd say "Far out!", which it really wasn't at four in the morning.'

The final question of the programme reveals that Benjamin Britten occasionally played through all of Brahms's works 'to see if he's as bad as I thought – and I usually find him worse'. Nathan finishes a few points clear of Bunny, allowing him to join John in the semis. All that remains is for Gambaccini to do a few retakes and record a trail, as well as provide several 'clean' renditions of each of the contestants' names, should they need to be dropped into the programme at any point. He varies the emphasis each time: once you've heard 'Bunny Hambleton-Relf' pronounced in half a dozen different ways the whole world begins to feel vaguely surreal.

Gambaccini has to leave straight after the recording, but just about everyone else takes up Paul's invitation of a drink in the Green Room, where the conversation is soon buzzing with talk of questions and answers and cross-references from both. Nathan and John are obviously both happy to have won, but

the losers are just as happy about an enjoyable evening. Bunny
in particular wears a smile of delight at having tried something
new; and his fund of trivia, not just about music but everything
else (his beloved Sheffield Wednesday, for instance[11]), temporarily removes my suspicion of people in comedy braces. All in all
it's a delightful reminder, after Northampton, that the real joy of
quizzing is not in being first but in being there.

After a while talk turns to drummers, and I'm reminded of a
fact I recently discovered, so astonishing that I couldn't believe
I'd never discovered it before. This happens from time to time,
as with the revelation that the person who said 'you *know* when
you've been Tangoed' in the adverts was Gil Scott-Heron. How
had that escaped me? I mean, I knew that Gil Scott-Heron's
father was the first black footballer ever to play for Celtic – by
what subterfuge had the Tango thing got away? It was the same
with the drummer fact. This concerns the identity of the person
who wrote the opening drum riff for Stevie Wonder's 'Super-
stition'.

I ask if it was just me. Reassurance comes from Nathan: he
doesn't know it either. Nor John. Nor David, Stephen or Paul.
By now I'm feeling a bit better. During their thinking time – in
true quiz-purist style they resist asking for the answer straight
off – we talk about the drums on the final version being played
by Stevie Wonder himself (smart-arse), and thence the drums
as well as every other instrument on Paul McCartney's 'Coming
Up' being played by McCartney himself (ditto). But at no point
do they identify the actual writer of the riff. The answer is Jeff
Beck. We all agree how surprising it is that such a famous bit of
black American soul drumming was created by a white British
blues guitarist.

Stephen turns to Nathan and John. 'Pity you were in the room
at the time,' he says. 'We can't use that as a question in the semis
now.'

. . . .

SIX

Who is the only person ever to receive an Oscar
nomination for acting in a *Star Wars* film?

I suppose there's a certain irony in your car breaking down
on the way to the National Motor Museum, but as I ram the
accelerator into the floor in a fraught attempt to reach the top of
a hill in Essex it's an irony that's lost on me.

The Motor Museum, which hides among the trees of the
New Forest, is my destination this boiling hot Saturday in late
July because it's hosting a quiz. A charity quiz, to be precise, a
form of the beast I've been meaning to bag for some time. A
body called It's Your Choice provides advice and counselling to
young people in Hampshire, and needing new premises after
losing their current ones they've set themselves the task of raising £250,000 in 250 days. Part of the strategy is tonight's quiz,
where nigh on 200 people will form 33 teams. Their hunger
will be assuaged by fish and chips, their competitive instinct by
questions on everything from literature to sport. I shall observe,
and while I'm down there make my first-ever visit to nearby
Southampton, whose history ranges from Jane Austen to the fish
finger.

All of this, however, depends on me finding four wheels and
an engine prepared to get me there. Fortunately the Essex hill
has a garage at the top of it, into whose forecourt the car just
about manages to judder. A kindly mechanic advises that it'll

limp on for a while, but only at low speeds – nothing beyond about 40 mph. Thankfully I've allowed plenty of time for the trip to Hampshire, so can pootle back home to Suffolk and arrange to use another car. It's a far from youthful Renault Clio, whose air-conditioning produces a tepid waft rather than an ice-cold blast, so on the trip down the M3 I have to keep both front windows open to avoid roasting. Thankfully the car's radio is working fine, so the strains of *Test Match Special* fill the journey. They remind me of Keith Miller heading this way during the Second World War (though in those pre-motorway days he would have taken the A3). The cricketer was returning from a friendly match in London to the RAF base at Bournemouth where he was stationed. Reaching a roadblock he asked what had happened: the pub where he would have been eating lunch with his comrades had been bombed. Cricket had saved his life. His war service explained his carefree attitude to the game from then on. As he put it himself when asked about the pressures of the sport: 'Pressure is a Messerschmitt up your arse.'

Eventually the three lanes of motorway give way to the rudimentary single-track roads of the New Forest. Traffic calming here is provided by the famous ponies: when they decide they've finished grazing on one side of the carriageway and want to reach the other, they simply walk out in front of your car. So renowned are they for doing this that I'm quite annoyed none of them do it to me. Just the other side of the village of Beaulieu itself is the turning for the museum. Several large buildings squat amid the trees, a monorail snaking between them, all in tribute to the invention that might not have taken off if Henry Ford hadn't been so bolshie. The Steve Jobs of his day, Ford delighted in telling his customers what they needed rather than the other way round. 'If I had asked people what they wanted,' he explained, 'they would have said faster horses.'

The museum's cars span the Victorian era to the present, a collection so renowned that I feel rather guilty about parking the Clio anywhere near it. Not that the model is without interest. In Japan it has to be sold as the Lutecia because Honda own the rights to the name Clio. And like other Renault models (the Mégane, for instance) it's named after a girl, a policy that led to a court case in 2010 when the firm introduced the Zoe. Two sets of parents, each with daughters called Zoe Renault, argued that the new name would lead to their children being bullied. A French judge sided with the firm.

There were early plans for tonight's quiz to take place in the main building, but with numbers having grown it's being held in the Brabazon Restaurant, so I decide to get my fill of the wheels on show right now. First up is a car built for John Henry Knight of Surrey. Rather agricultural in appearance – no roof, a steering lever rather than a wheel, front wheels smaller than the back ones – it is still recognisably a car. Certainly the police recognised it as such when they stopped Knight and his assistant James Pullinger on Farnham's main street in October 1895, prosecuting him for not having a licence and not employing a man to walk in front of the vehicle waving a red flag. Knight was fined half a crown, thereby becoming the first person convicted of a motoring offence in Britain.

Next there's a De Dietrich from 1903, only eight years younger than Knight's vehicle but a quantum leap in design. This thing *really* looks like a car, its yellow body wrapping around the two front seats, its red leather upholstery luscious enough for the House of Lords. Let us skip past the fact that its current owner bears the name Count Luccio Labia, and instead record that it was originally purchased by Sir Joseph Robinson, a South African mining magnate who in 1922 used £30,000 of his immense fortune in an attempt to buy a British peerage from David Lloyd George. That's the equivalent of over £1 million in today's money. But the Prime Minister's trade in honours had reached such scandalous levels that the public demanded an end to it. Unfortunately for Robinson the stop button was pressed just as he holed up in the Savoy ready to receive his gong. A messenger sent to his room imparted the bad news. Sir Joseph, almost totally deaf, thought that the price was being raised and reached for his cheque book, grumbling: 'How much more?'

Nearby is the first Cadillac ever to reach Britain. The Model A – green leather seats, bright red wheels, polished gold plate at the front boasting its year (1903) – belonged to Frederick Stanley Bennett, the company's official UK importer. An early problem in convincing the public to take up motoring was their worry that the new technology would be difficult to repair. To prove them wrong, Bennett took three identical Cadillacs, dismantled them into one mixed-up pile of parts, then reassembled three cars. As well as many Rolls-Royces, the museum also has a collection of the famous radiator mascots – the Spirit of Ecstasy, or Flying Lady as she's more commonly known. There is even the original on which subsequent ones were based, titled 'the Whisper'. This was commissioned by the 2nd Baron Montagu of Beaulieu, an early motoring enthusiast (he was the first man to drive a car into New Palace Yard at the Houses of Parliament). It was for his own Roller, and the lady who modelled for it was his secretary Eleanor Thornton. The figurine was called the Whisper because Thornton was also his long-time mistress, hence the Spirit of Ecstasy's other nickname 'Ellie in her Nightie'. Henry Royce himself disliked the mascot, and rarely drove any of his cars fitted with one, but the public loved them. When Rolls-Royce introduced lower sports saloons in the 1930s a kneeling version of the mascot was commissioned so that drivers could still see the road. These days the Spirit is mounted on a special spring mechanism for safety reasons – it instantly retracts when touched.

I could easily spend the whole weekend in here, so to avoid missing the quiz I skip sections of the museum, pausing only for the choicest motoring morsels. In a way, it's the least grand specimens that really catch your eye, the humble family runarounds that take you back in time. The ultimate example of this is the Mini – the 1959 beauty here is tiny compared to the genetically modified monsters of today. Alec Issigonis designed the door compartment to hold several bottles of his beloved Gordon's gin, and saved space in the engine compartment by putting everything at right angles to the norm. As a result the distributor was at the front, which meant rain sometimes got into it. One man driving home in a downpour from the World Cup final in 1966 solved this problem by reversing along the A40 – fortunately it was two o'clock on the Sunday morning by then and there was no other traffic about.

You do wonder what the museum's insurance premiums must be like, with all the priceless vehicles on show.[1] These things are no longer the concern of the museum's founder, the 3rd Baron Montagu, who died in 2015 having spent 86 years as a member of the House of Lords, the third-longest period of service ever. (He inherited the title aged two on the death of his father.) The institution's future is now overseen by, among other trustees, Nick Mason, whose time behind the drums in Pink Floyd has produced a pretty fine car collection of his own. I know someone whose child went to the same school as one of Mason's offspring. Everyone else contributed to the summer fete by baking cakes and the like – Mason took people for spins round the field in one of his Ferraris. Another rock star petrolhead is AC/DC's Brian Johnson: his fleet includes a 1928 Bentley Vanden Plas with its accelerator in the middle, where modern brakes are. Johnson says this can lead to accidentally increasing rather than reducing speed as you take a corner: 'It makes your arsehole go like a rabbit's nose.'

Over in the Brabazon (more cafeteria than restaurant, but with balloons on the tables and a well-stocked bar in the corner it's looking good), preparations for the quiz are nearly complete. Alice Brown, the charity's press officer, introduces herself, and then Tara and Charlotte, the university students who are interning with It's Your Choice. They're in general meet-and-greet mode at the moment, but will soon be touring the room on raffle ticket duty. Alice also points out a man in his fifties, who's setting up a PA system and checking it can be heard in all three

---

[1] The record for the largest private claim in UK motoring goes to Rowan Atkinson, who lost control of his McLaren F1 near Peterborough in 2011, hit a tree and landed his insurers with a repair bill for £910,000.

wings of the restaurant (the fourth is the kitchen that will supply our fish and chips). This is Ian Woolley, who lives not far away and is managing director of Quiz Britain ('Promoting quizzing to the next level').

'Ian's our question-master this year,' says Alice.

'You haven't got CJ back, then?' I ask. Mr de Mooi, the Egghead. He was last year's host.

'No,' replies Alice, not without firmness. 'Hopefully the questions will be a bit easier this year. CJ's were unbelievably hard. Though at least that raised us a bit of extra money – he sold clues for fifty pence.'

Tonight will not, however, be an Egghead-free occasion. As well as writing and asking the questions, Ian has also arranged for a star of the show (also a Hampshire resident) to come along and offer his expertise. The star is none other than recently crowned World Quizzing Champion Kevin Ashman. I say hello, and, as he'd left Northampton before his victory was officially confirmed, offer my congratulations. I also ask how he's going to be helping out tonight.

'I'm playing on a different team in each round, I think. I'm going to be "drawn". Not hung or quartered, thankfully.' Kevin has the same relaxed air he displayed at the world championship. Unlike CJ, he doesn't have a clause in his contract stipulating that he has to be taken for afternoon tea at a nearby hotel.

Ian, after finishing his soundcheck and changing into his question master's suit (the black would be sober were it not for the faint sparkle to the jacket), tells me about Quiz Britain. They've developed an app that tells you where your nearest pub quizzes are. Low-tech versions of the same information lie around on the tables in the form of leaflets: 'Quizzing in Hampshire', 'Quizzing in York' and so on. (I check 'Quizzing in Edinburgh' and find Goose's events.)

'We're also organising a big event here next year,' adds Ian. 'It's going to be called QuizFest. We're having pro quizzes, amateur quizzes, you name it. I've got Tom O'Connor and Joe Pasquale coming along to host.'

Tonight's crowd is arriving by now, people greeting each other and finding their tables. Some team names are in the traditional quiz mould – Knowmads, Les Quizerables – while others display a marked lack of confidence: Last Place, Epic Fail. There are local references (Brainy Badgers, Badgers' Tadgers), and some in questionable taste (Big Hand for Jeremy Beadle). As everyone gets themselves seated, I examine a copy of the picture round. It's a mix of people, buildings and objects, including the Men's Singles trophy from Wimbledon. I only recognise it because this year's tournament has just been played, and I've read about the trophy having a pineapple on its top. It also (though the picture is too small to make this out) features the wording 'The All England Lawn Tennis Club Single Handed Championship of the World' – two-handed play used to be seen as unsporting.

Ian's first job is to get everyone's attention, and as so often at a charity quiz it's far from easy. The difference between this type of event and a normal quiz is that the latter attracts people – and only those people – who want to go to a quiz. A sizeable proportion of the crowd at a fundraiser, on the other hand, are only there because they've been persuaded to 'do their bit' for the cause. Their tenner entrance fee, they decide, has bought them the right to sit there and have a damn good natter about whatever they like. You can sympathise with them. Some people's idea of a good night out is catching up with Maureen on how her sister's divorce is going, or how their fortnight in Fuerteventura went, not having some bloke they don't know ask them for the capital of Ecuador. They've stumped up and turned up, haven't they? Now leave them alone. The issue arises every year at the fundraising quiz I host for my son's primary school. There's not much you can do, beyond forming the odd alliance with quieter members on a team and encouraging them to shush their colleagues. Or nicking Ronnie Scott's line from the days when he compèred at his own jazz club: 'Shut up, you're not here to enjoy yourselves.' Ian takes a different approach, pausing in the middle of a sentence and saying: 'No, I can still hear some people talking.' Each to his own.

Eventually quiet (or the closest we're going to get to it) descends, and Ian announces how we'll decide which team benefits from Kevin's expertise in the first round. This isn't, as Kevin thought, a simple draw, but a tiebreaker question. Ian wants a member from every team to come to the markers' table (three volunteers are fulfilling this role) with a piece of paper bearing their guess as to how many steps the Leaning Tower of Pisa has. This reminds me of my own question on the tower, namely how many degrees from the vertical does it lean? Always a bit of a wheat/chaff separator, this one – the highest answer I've encountered was 70 – though the correct answer is a surprisingly low 3.97. The tower doesn't even hold the world record any more: that belongs to a church steeple in the German village of Suurhusen, whose tilt measures 5.19 degrees.

I have plenty of time to recall all this, because processing a queue of 33 team representatives and establishing whose answer was nearest takes some doing. After some off-mike discussions between Ian and Alice it's agreed that from now on they'll stick to a draw.

Beyond the Pail's guess of 285 steps has bagged Kevin's services, as the correct answer was 294 steps. ('Or 296,' adds Ian.) The round is Geography, and starts with: 'The Spratly Islands have recently been ruled by the Permanent Court of Arbitration as belonging to which country?' Kevin leans quickly in to his temporary teammates at their table in the corner – obviously he has made an impressive start. But question two – 'Which country produces more pears than the rest of the world put together?' – results in prolonged discussion. The World Champ seems unsure. When Kevin returns to the centre of the room at the end of the round he tells me this was indeed the only question he wasn't confident on. The Spratly Islands belong to the Philippines, Britain's most southerly city is Truro, the modern-day country in which the Chernobyl disaster happened is Ukraine... but pears. Pears. In the end Beyond the Pail guessed China, helped by Kevin's knowledge that the fruit 'certainly originated in that part of the world'.

The correct answer? China.

Benefiting from Kevin's help in the second round are Six of One, Half a Dozen of the Other. The subject is 'Books and Literature'. We cover the English port in which Dracula comes ashore (Whitby), the Dickens novel featuring Wackford Squeers (*Nicholas Nickleby*), and the Christian name of Lady Chatterley (Constance). Question four plays on the fact that this is a spoken rather than written quiz – I assume Ian is asking 'Which chef's autobiography is called *Blood, Sweat and Tyres*?', though actually the apostrophe comes after the 's', because the answer is the Hairy Bikers. 'How are authors Gerald and Charles better known?' is intriguing, but not entirely fair, as Ian should have said 'publishers': they were Mills and Boon. 'Which famous author also wrote under the pseudonym Mary Pollock?' is on the mark, however, the answer being Enid Blyton. (Her secret was soon uncovered, though not before one reviewer had opined: 'Enid Blyton had better look to her laurels.') Also on the children's book front, Ian asks which character, created by Theodor Geisel, wears a red and white striped hat? It is of course The Cat in the Hat, Geisel being the real name of Dr. Seuss, which we all pronounce to rhyme with 'loose' but should actually be 'Zoice' (Geisel was German and Seuss was his middle name). The writer once included the word 'contraceptive' in one of his drafts to check that his publisher was paying attention, while his story *If I Ran the Zoo* contains the first mention of the word 'nerd'.

Last up in this round is the first of several 'Kevin-proof' questions Ian has written: he's confident that even the esteemed Egghead won't know the answer. As it happens he's right in this case. 'In 2014,' he asks, 'officials in the Polish town of Tuszyn banned which literary character on the grounds that he was of "dubious sexuality", "half-naked" and "inappropriately dressed"?' The answer is Winnie the Pooh.

Delicious smells are now wafting from the kitchen, but before they're allowed their fish and chips tonight's quizzers have an appointment with History. They encounter the war during which the Battle of Pork Chop Hill was fought (Korean), the first US President to live in the White House (John Adams) and: 'Who is the only British monarch from which DNA has been taken?' Most teams work out that it's Richard III. A sample was taken from the bones found underneath a Leicester car park in 2012, to confirm that the remains were indeed those of Richard. The first attempted comparison was with a preserved hair of Edward IV held by the Ashmolean in Oxford, but the DNA in that had degraded too much. Eventually a successful match was made with Michael Ibsen, a London cabinet maker who sits on a branch of the family tree 17 generations down from Richard.

During the meal Kevin and I continue chatting. Before becoming a professional quizzer he was a civil servant, at the Ministry of Defence as well as the Department of Culture, Media and Sport. He was once trodden on by John Prescott. It was by mistake in Trafalgar Square rather than as part of government policy, and considering what Prezza got up to with at least one of his other civil servants Kevin got away lightly. We compare notes about Wikipedia, and agree that it's almost always the best starting point for research. The site has become shorthand – though only with people who never use it – for inaccurate rumour-mongering. 'If anyone can post on it,' goes the thinking, 'it must be riddled with untruths.' Yet 'anyone', in my experience, tends to be the pedant who comes along and corrects everyone else. Wikipedia always gives you a source – in fact when (as so often) the truth is hazy and can't be determined, it gives you sources for all versions. The only time Wikipedia ever disappoints me is by disproving a 'fact' I've always cherished. To take a reference from that last round: the White House. For ages I loved the story about it only being white to cover up smoke damage after British troops burned it in 1814. But, Wikipedia reports, this is a myth: 'The earliest evidence of the public calling it the "White House" was recorded in 1811.'[2]

'Isn't "wiki" the name for the bus at Honolulu Airport?' I say.

---

2 The shade currently used is Whisper White by Duron. The house requires 570 gallons.

'I don't know,' replies Kevin. 'I know "wiki" is the Hawaiian for "quick".'

Hence the site's name, obviously – but this half-formed memory is annoying me. I solve the problem – how else? – by looking up Wikipedia on Wikipedia. And sure enough, the buses that transfer you between the airport's terminals are known as 'Wiki Wiki buses'. This leads to us mentioning that the Hawaiian language only has 13 letters, which is why words so often repeat them.

'Like "ukulele",' says Kevin. 'It means "jumping flea".'

I'm eating fish and chips and learning facts like this: can a Saturday night get any better?

A big difficulty in fact-checking is that the most unlikely-sounding stories can turn out to be true. Coincidences often play a part. 'We had a case of that in my own family,' says Kevin. 'The story that always got told was that my mother was born in Wandsworth Prison at the same moment two men were being hanged there. The first bit is definitely true – my grandfather was a warder there, and my grandmother gave birth in the married quarters.[3] But then a few years ago there was someone working on *Eggheads* who had a connection at the prison, had access to the records and so on. They looked up the dates for me, and it turned out the hangings were two days later.'

The tale of the tale doesn't end there, though. 'Much later in life, when my mother was in her fifties, she was working in a shop in Winchester [where Kevin was born and bred]. She got talking to one of the regular customers, and it turned out this woman had been one of the prosecution witnesses in the case of the hanged men. It was an armed robbery where they ended up killing someone. The woman had been there and seen it, then over half a century later she's talking to my mother in Winchester.'

Our food is followed by some questions on food, this being

---

3 This book's second mention of a prison's married quarters. Coincidences within coincidences.

the theme of round four. The shellfish frequently served with chips in Belgium can only be mussels (I once saw a pub menu offering 'moles mariner'). Question eight asks: 'Which type of coffee takes its name from the Italian word for "stained"?' People who know about the books I write sometimes say they want me on their quiz team, and I have to tell them that most of the time I don't know the answer – I know something *related* to the answer, but not the answer itself. And so it is here. I know how the cappuccino got its name. Capuchin monks wore brown robes so distinctive that the name of their order came to be used for the colour itself, and then (because coffee is brown) for the drink. But I don't know which Italian word means 'stained'. It's *macchiato* – the coffee is stained with a splash of milk.

Next up is sport. This includes another 'Kevin-proof' question: 'Which sport used to be scored on a clock dial?' My heart starts to beat a little faster – for once, I know the answer. And, it turns out, Kevin doesn't. As ever he's perfectly happy to admit this, and genuinely interested in learning that it was tennis – the hand would be advanced to 15 minutes, then 30, then 45. When the advantage point was introduced it was marked at 50 minutes, with the third point dropping back to 40. Hence the system used today. If I achieve nothing else for the rest of my life (form an orderly queue at the bookmakers, people), I'll be able to look back on this evening as the time I knew something an Egghead didn't. Indeed, the time I knew something the reigning World Quizzing Champion didn't. You might even say that this makes me the *new* World Champion. You'd be incorrect, though no more incorrect than those Scottish football fans who claimed that their 1967 victory over England entitled them to the World Cup.

As we know, Ian is no longer using his 'who gets Kevin?' tiebreakers, but the one for the TV and film round would have asked how many characters had died in *EastEnders* up to and including the recent demise of Peggy Mitchell. The answer is 111, meaning Barbara Windsor fell foul of cricket's unlucky number. Revelations from the round itself include the first name of Mrs

Brown in *Mrs Brown's Boys* (Agnes), the island on which *Captain Corelli's Mandolin* was filmed (Kefalonia), and the only person ever to be nominated for an acting Oscar in a *Star Wars* film (Alec Guinness, whose name went into the Best Supporting Actor envelope for the original movie, despite his opinion that his lines were 'bloody awful' and 'banal').

And that, it appears, is that. Time is against us, announces Ian (it's gone half-ten), so he'll be dropping the music round and moving straight on to the raffle. Alice has a quiet word to ask whether he might reconsider: several teams have been looking forward to this round. At first Ian relents, but then unrelents, so raffle time it is. Certainly there are lots of prizes to get through – many local businesses have made generous donations, from beer and wine through chocolates and flowers to any number of vouchers for various experiences. There are also a couple of books, the autobiographies of Jim Bowen (inscribed 'Look at what you've won!'), and CJ de Mooi (*CJ – My Journey from the Streets to the Screen*). It's understandable that faced with choices including 'Ringwood Brewery Tour for Two', 'UK Paintball for Five', 'Mango Thai Tapas £35 Meal', 'New Forest Ice Cream 4 Litre Tub' and so on, the books are initially overlooked. But eventually Bowen's memoirs find a home.

CJ, however, proves less alluring. I don't know how many of tonight's participants were here last year, and if so whether the memories are affecting their decisions, but *My Journey from the Streets to the Screen* remains stubbornly in place. The White Scents bath salts are chosen. The New Forest Show family ticket is chosen. The box of Thorntons Moments is chosen. CJ is not chosen. In the end it's down to the last two prizes – the book and a small bottle of Boost, a 'Daily Vitamin B12 Oral Spray' which promises to 'aid memory and concentration'. The holder of the penultimate ticket hums and hahs, weighing up the relative temptations of both prizes… then plumps for the spray. By now the resistibility of CJ's book has become a running joke, so there's a huge cheer when the holder of the final ticket turns out to be the wife of the charity's chief executive.

All that remains after this is the announcement of the actual result. Quidditch have scored an estimable 51 points to come third, Strangers on a Train are ahead of them with 54, but pipping them to the title by just a single point are Charlie's Angels. Despite the name this is a mixed-sex team. One of the female members stands out from her teammates with shrieks of delight that verge on hyperventilation. They all have their picture taken with Kevin and the huge box of goodies that is their prize (the airport-sized Toblerones would have been worth the effort on their own). And that's it – the charity's made a few quid, we've all had a laugh, it's time for bed.

For me this means a drive back through the New Forest and over the River Test to Southampton, ready to explore the city tomorrow morning. In daylight the forest was picturesque and inviting, but now that it's dark the trees seem to crowd round my car, and thoughts turn easily to more sinister episodes in the area's history. Brusher Mills, for instance, the 19th-century hermit who lived in the forest and earned his living catching snakes, some of which he sold to London Zoo as food for their birds of prey. There was also Beaulieu's role during the Second World War as the training camp for the Special Operations Executive, the 'dirty tricks' unit which Churchill christened his 'Ministry of Ungentlemanly Warfare'. Agents were sent here to prepare for their missions of subterfuge behind enemy lines in Europe. A Glaswegian bank robber taught them how to blow safes, while a burglar, released early from a prison sentence, tutored them in lock-picking. They were kitted out with all sorts of Bondesque gadgets, like the pipe whose tobacco bowl covered a space where messages could be hidden, and shoelaces containing razor wire that could be used to garotte. They were given false papers backing up fake identities that had been created in minute detail – even the agents' fillings were replaced with new ones that matched European dentistry. And they were taught the importance of avoiding tiny mistakes: one agent in France had ordered a café noir, not knowing that milk rationing meant this was the only type of coffee available. His cover was promptly blown.

The thought of what the Nazis would have done to him is distinctly unpleasant, so instead I think about Noreen. She was one of the attractive young women employed to train the agents in surveillance techniques. They would be sent to the seaside with a description of her, to see if they could track her down and then keep her under observation. To really test whether they could blend into the background Noreen would enter Bournemouth's largest department store and head for the lingerie department.

*   *   *

The first thing that greets me as I step out from my hotel to savour the delights of a Sunday morning in Southampton is a zebra. It is the first of many dotted around the city centre, all made of plastic and decorated in different styles to raise awareness of (and funds for) Hampshire's Marwell Zoo. The initiative is called 'Zany Zebras': 'we're certain that it will create a sense of fun'. This sort of wording normally fills you with foreboding, but actually the zebras are pretty good. One is painted with the famous *Abbey Road* cover (think about what the Beatles are walking across). I remember that the pinstripe suit Paul McCartney wears in the famous shot is the same one he wore a couple of years later to the High Court when he sued the other three band members. And while we're on zebra crossings (as it were), my Hampshire research has thrown up the story of the one that appeared overnight in 2000 across all three lanes of the M3. The police were never sure how the April Fool jokers managed to paint it without being caught, but a spokeswoman added that 'we do get a lot of ducks down there so perhaps they will appreciate it.'

In Guildhall Square there's a farmers' market, one stall offering kedgeree eggs, a smoked-fish twist on the traditional Scotch egg. There's also fruit and veg from Berry Hill Farm, the name tantalisingly close to Benny Hill, himself a son of Southampton.

Indeed he once had a milk round in nearby Eastleigh, the inspiration for his hit song 'Ernie (The Fastest Milkman in the West)'. In the 1950s Southampton was where Birds Eye tested their new product of fish fingers. The delicacy was nearly launched as 'Battered Cod Pieces' until someone came up with the snappier name.

I pass a pub called The Spitfire. The legendary plane was designed and developed in Southampton, though like fish fingers it had naming problems – an early suggestion was the Shrew. In the end the old English word for someone with a fiery temper prevailed, and Second World War history was ready to be made. One of the planes even performed heroics despite having run out of ammunition: pilot Raymond Holmes spotted a German bomber heading for central London, so simply flew into it, disabling it over Victoria station. The Spitfire's camouflage was so good that when several were used in the movie *Battle of Britain* they could hardly be seen, and had to be filmed against clouds. An unexpected bonus was that their under-wing mountings could be modified to carry beer barrels rather than bombs, allowing deliveries (donated free by the breweries) to be made to troops fighting in Normandy. Until HM Customs and Excise found out, that is, and warned the breweries that they were violating the law by exporting beer without paying tax.

Heading south towards the docks I reach Palmerston Park, named after the one-time MP for South Hampshire: the board that explains this says he is best remembered as a 'reforming Prime Minister and jingoistic Foreign Secretary'. On a bench sit two East European guys drinking cans of Stella, while the opposite bench is taken by a respectable middle-aged Sikh couple, the man's turban a resplendent shade of lemon. Getting a coffee from a nearby chain shop, I hear the white-haired German guy in front of me greet his cappuccino with a loud: '*Wunderbar!*'

It's 10.30 now, and the gates of the Marlands shopping centre are unlocked to admit the waiting punters. Most are dressed smartly, the women fully made up – Sunday best used to be for church, but these days retail is the religion. One group comprises three generations of females from the same family. They stop outside Savers, examining the window display. One points to the bottles of Foam Aroma ('fragranced powder for a sparkling loo'). 'Ooh,' says her sister, 'is that the new one?' At the nearby Disney unit a young girl points through the as yet unlocked shutters, repeatedly saying 'Elsa!' to her bored mother. The crowds put me in mind of Will Champion, a chap from Southampton who features in one of my favourite quiz questions: 'Jonny Buckland, Guy Berryman and Will Champion are often seen in public with a fourth man – who is he?' The answer is Chris Martin, the other three members of Coldplay having kept their anonymity so successfully they can enjoy their vast fortunes and still go shopping without being recognised. Not that I imagine Champion gets many of his purchases in the Marlands centre, but you take the point.

Further down the main street is the Bargate, a 12th-century gatehouse which used to protect the city but is itself now protected by hideous metal shutters while it undergoes restoration. Past the Dolphin Hotel, in whose bow window Thackeray sat and wrote his novel *Pendennis*, and where Jane Austen had her 18th birthday party. A pavement plaque (one of a series highlighting local history) quotes the *Whitehall Review* of 1878: 'The garb of the Southampton youth is fearfully and wonderfully made.' By now you can almost smell the sea air, and the nautical references have started, such as the flower bed centred on an anchor from the *QE2* (donated by Cunard after the ship's retirement in 2008). The ship's forerunner the *Queen Mary* was supposed to be the *Victoria* (it was a Cunard tradition to use names ending 'ia'), but when they asked George V for permission to name it after Britain's 'greatest queen' he replied that his wife would be delighted.

The first ship I see on reaching the water is a Red Funnel ferry bound for the Isle of Wight, but more momentous events soon make themselves felt with the large stone obelisk commemorating the sailing from Southampton in 1620 of the *Mayflower*. The ship then called in at Plymouth, along with a second ship called the *Speedwell*. A lesson in tempting fate, that name – the *Speed-well* sprang a leak and couldn't make it to America, leaving the *Mayflower* to take all the glory. Not that English people hadn't headed that way before. Marcus once won the £1000 at the Prince of Wales by knowing what was notable about the birth of Virginia Dare on 18 August 1587: she was the first baby born to English parents in the New World, her mother and father having journeyed from London to what is now North Carolina.

A little further along the docks, I see Southampton's present beautifully framed inside its past. A lovely old brick gateway spans the road, 'Associated British Ports' written across the top. The name and architectural style conjure up images of black-and-white Britain so convincing you expect Margaret Rutherford and Alastair Sim to come walking along at any moment. What you actually see through the gateway is the *Navigator of the Seas*, a vast modern cruise ship so expensive that just the artwork on board cost $8.5 million. Also based in Southampton is the Maritime and Coastguard Agency. As part of its watery remit it oversees the Shipping Forecast, that cultural institution which, even though it's forbidden to go over 370 words, forms a plank upon which the measured contentment of Middle Britain depends. Performers as disparate as Marti Caine and Radiohead have referenced it, the former choosing it as one of her records on *Desert Island Discs*, the latter mentioning Lundy, Fastnet and Irish Sea in the lyrics to their song 'In Limbo'. Bringing us back to those bound for America, Fastnet is named after the most southerly point of Eire, a rock known in the 19th century as Ireland's Teardrop because it was the last part of the home country seen by those sailing for the States.

Heading back into town I pass a young girl doing the zebra trail.

'Then we'll have a snack,' says her mother.

'And then we're back on track,' rhymes the girl, quick as you like.

My favourite zebra is the one painted simply as a normal

zebra and called Dave.[4] A path leads through a surviving section of Southampton Castle, the section which archaeologists
think was used for banquets because its garderobe (toilet) could
seat many people. Then it's Asda, where the sign for the staff
entrance labels the workers 'Colleagues': two of them sit outside
on an early lunch break, devouring a box of chocolate cereal
bites each.

And so my time in Hampshire draws to a close. On my way
home the M3 will carry me under Spitfire Bridge, so called
because in 1941 George Rogers of 400 Squadron flew his plane
(actually a Tomahawk rather than a Spitfire) underneath it. A
lorry coming the other way forced Rogers to swerve, so clipping
the bridge and losing three feet off one of his wings. This made
for a tricky landing, but he walked away unscathed. Thankfully
I see no such exploits this afternoon, though I do see more than
one example of perhaps the most famous piece of engineering
ever to come out of Southampton: the Ford Transit. Like the
Shipping Forecast the van is a British emblem, used by builders,
small-time rock bands and criminals alike. Scotland Yard once
called the Transit the 'perfect getaway vehicle', reporting that it
was used in 95 per cent of bank raids. It was in a Transit that
Margaret Thatcher's body left the Ritz hotel. And when a Czech
driver complained that the milometer on his Transit only ran to
six digits, and so had stopped at 999,999 kilometres, Ford fitted
a new one for him.

But my favourite fact ties the weekend back to its beginning,
to one of the vehicles I saw at the National Motor Museum.
It was built for a movie in 1968, its chassis taken from a Ford
Transit. You'd never guess it from the rest of the car, with its
curvaceous silver bonnet, its elegant running boards, its polished
wooden doors and its famous number plate 'GEN 11'. But yes –
the car that sits on that humble Transit base is none other than
Chitty Chitty Bang Bang.

---

4 You're reminded of the old joke about the young zebra asking its dad for an Arsenal kit
and being told no, it'll have to support Newcastle like the rest of the family.

SEVEN

·······

Who was the only female competitor at the
1976 Summer Olympics who didn't have
to undergo a gender test?

Late August now, the season when evening winds sigh through
the trees, the sound of another year contemplating the turn
for home. The month also sees my birthday, and as this one has
taken me closer to 50 than 40, autumnal thoughts seem particularly fitting. It's a good sport for the older chap, quizzing. An
outlet for your competitive instincts which doesn't involve torn
ligaments or broken bones.

I ponder the project's next trip. The world of Quiz has been
offering some choice nuggets. *The Times*'s daily run-out asks us
why there are 33 buttons on a Roman Catholic cassock.[1] The
Edinburgh Festival's annual search for the funniest one-liner
awards fifth place to Will Duggan's story of attending a pub
quiz in Liverpool: 'Had a few drinks so wasn't much use. Just
for a laugh I wrote "the Beatles" or "Steven Gerrard" for every
answer. Came second.' And my own file of questions continues
to expand with facts that cross my path. That at the height of
his success, for instance, the drugs baron Pablo Escobar was
spending $1000 a week on rubber bands for his cash. That
Barbra Streisand once complained to Tim Cook, the head of

---

1 One for every year of Christ's life.

Apple, about the company's digital assistant Siri pronouncing her surname 'Strei-zand' when it should be 'Strei-sand'. And that the first player to score 100 Premier League goals at the same ground was Thierry Henry at Highbury. Sometimes a question can take a while to come together. The V&A in London bans a certain activity in one of its exhibitions, but simply asking which activity wouldn't be fair – another clue is needed. Months later, reading an interview with David Hockney from the early 1980s, I find it. Back then the National Gallery had just introduced the same ban. 'How obnoxious!' said Hockney to an attendant. 'How do you think these things got on the walls if there was no ******ing?' The answer is 'sketching'.

I also make a visit to the Prince of Wales, finding that Marcus is in the chair. We learn that Napoleon and Dwight Eisenhower both had a morbid fear of cats (Eisenhower decreeing that any in the vicinity of the White House should be shot on sight), and that T. S. Eliot, while working at Faber and Faber, rejected George Orwell's *Down and Out in Paris and London*. I know what South Africa's Norman Gordon became the first former Test cricketer to do in 2011: celebrate his 100th birthday (at the time of writing he is still the only one). But I don't know which country had a town called Berlin that changed its name to Kitchener during the First World War (Canada). Marcus's love of silly questions shows through in: 'Trevor Ward-Davies, a member of the nineteen-sixties pop group Dave Dee, Dozy, Beaky, Mick and Tich, died in January 2015 aged seventy. Was he Dave Dee, Dozy, Beaky, Mick or Tich?' Apparently he was Dozy. The only Dozy – in the band's history there have been two Tiches, three Beakies and three Micks, only one of whom was called Mick.

Marcus also indulges his habit of what I sometimes call, with the greatest of respect, 'giving so much information that you might as well read out the bloody answer itself'. This is particularly frustrating when you work it out early on and other teams can't. Marcus once gave a list of people who had been called the fifth Beatle. I got it at George Best – of course Pete Best featured too, and by the time Marcus reached George Martin I had to be restrained from running across the pub and grabbing the mike from his hand. Tonight's 'clue too far' comes with the story of the Australian man who suggested the name 'Lanesra' for his daughter. His wife thought it sounded 'unique and romantic', and didn't realise for a full two years what her husband had done. By playing around with the letters you could probably work it out – but just in case, Marcus decides to give the game away by asking: 'Which football team did her husband support?'[2]

Let us not be grouchy, though. The quiz also contains the revelation that Shania Twain, Sharon Stone, Pink, Jay Leno and the founder of Amazon Jeff Bezos all worked, 'when less successful than they subsequently became', in McDonald's. There is, as so often at Marcus's quizzes, a question about James Bond: 'Pierce Brosnan kills forty-seven people in *GoldenEye*, the highest total of personal Bond killings in the series. In which film does Roger Moore kill only one person?' (*The Man with the Golden Gun*.) And tonight is also one of those quizzes in which Marcus gives away books he's reviewed in the course of his journalism, and which would otherwise clog up his flat. He does this by means of tiebreakers tacked on to the end of each round – nearest the correct answer wins the book. How many decibels, for instance, was Maria Sharapova's loudest-ever grunt, measured at Wimbledon in 2005? (101.2.) Even if you don't win the book you get the pleasure of Marcus's thoughts on it. Alastair Campbell's first volume of diaries, I remember, was 'a very long book, which seems even longer'.

At one point Marcus asks me how the project is going, and I mention that I've been thinking again about what makes the perfect question. We begin to discuss the issue, but don't get very far. That's the thing about a quiz – it makes prolonged conversation about anything impossible. You've just started to engage with a topic when some impertinent chap clutching a sheet of A4 is tapping his microphone and asking you which three of the

---

2 Should you still (God knows how) be struggling, read the name backwards.

clubs who founded the Premiership in 1992 were also founder members of the Football League in 1888. (Aston Villa, Blackburn Rovers, Everton.) Marcus and I agree to meet soon for a pint and a more relaxed analysis of the perfect question.

In the meantime, I have an appointment with a machine.

* * *

Some of the places to which this project has led me could have been predicted. The pub, obviously. The BBC, probably. The House of Commons, perhaps. But a small industrial estate at the junction of the A52 and the M1? Unlikely.

One of the companies occupying this collection of modern low-rise office buildings in the East Midlands is Gamestec. The largest gaming and amusement machine operator in the UK, they have over half a century's experience in inducing people to put a coin into a slot in search of fun. It was while waiting for a friend in a pub recently that I glanced over at the row of machines against the wall, the sort that used to be called 'one-armed bandits', and remembered just how much they've evolved since my childhood. As well as digitised versions of the old-fashioned fruit machines, there are now units on which you can play roulette or poker, versions of TV shows like *Deal or No Deal*, pure-chance lottery games . . . and also quizzes. This, then, had to be my next adventure: playing a pub quiz machine.

But first I want to learn more about the terrain. Gamestec's Stefan Podolanski has agreed to give up a section of his Friday afternoon to talk me through it. Stefan is a Mancunian, his surname deriving from a Polish grandfather who was stationed in the north-west during the Second World War. Podolanski Snr stayed put after falling for a local girl: it must be one of the very few marriages ever between a Ludwig and a Beryl. Stefan takes me through to the meeting room. I am willing to bet, without having seen any of the other meeting rooms on the Interchange 25 Business Park, that this one is the coolest. The size of a tennis court, it contains a pool table, sofas and chairs in plush black leather, artwork showing a close-up of the two cherries from a fruit machine game, and – lining the walls – lots of gaming machines. Some are state-of-the-art, some are retro originals (Space Invaders, Pac-Man[3]), some are genuine originals. The thing that strikes you about the early machines, as with old televisions, is how far they stick out from the wall. That and the clunky graphics, their pixels seemingly numbered in the dozens. I'm reminded of my first chat with Kevin Ashman, when we mentioned Steve Davis's dominance in the 1980s. Knowing that he would be at the world snooker championship for the full two weeks, Davis used to have Space Invaders machines installed in his hotel room. As is obligatory for two men of our age in this setting, Stefan and I reminisce about Pong, the early tennis game you could play on your television which involved nothing more than moving your 'bat' (a short straight line) up and down the screen to intercept the 'ball' (a dot). Now it seems like something from the Stone Age. In the 1970s it amounted to witchcraft.

Working our way round to the quiz machines we pass the pinball machines. These were always works of art, but what's astonishing nowadays is the variety. There are models themed around Spider-Man, *Game of Thrones*, *Transformers*, Wrestle-Mania, you name it. There are Metallica and Kiss pinballs, the latter featuring a 3D head of Gene Simmons in full make-up sticking his tongue out. Hard to believe he was born Chaim Witz in Israel. His band's distinctive double 'S' has to be redrawn in that country because it looks too similar to the banned Nazi version.

By comparison the GamesNet FiVE[4] to which Stefan leads me is a model of anonymity, its plain black exterior putting you in mind of a polite Darth Vader.

'Yes,' agrees Stefan. 'Very different from jukeboxes.' They were the product that gave the company its start all those years ago

---

3 Initially called Puck Man, because he looks like a hockey puck, but later changed to prevent vandals altering the first letter.
4 Modern 'upper versus lower case' usage is nothing less than a minefield.

(there's a freestanding one near the Pac-Man). It wasn't until about 25 years ago that the first quiz machine appeared. 'I think the first one – funny you should have mentioned Steve Davis – was called "Give Us A Break". I'm pretty sure it was based on a snooker quiz game Dave Lee Travis used to do on his Radio 1 show.'

Of course the technology back then was fairly rudimentary. Even as late as 1998, when *Who Wants to Be a Millionaire?* appeared on our TV screens, the quiz console it inspired was a 'single game cabinet' – that is, you could only play one quiz on it. But then multi-game terminals evolved, and the pub became Gametec's oyster. 'In the heyday – about ten years ago – we were operating eight thousand, maybe ten thousand of these terminals,' says Stefan. 'We would be going to Endemol, Celador and the others [the TV production companies responsible for the quiz shows] and working on branded games with them.' A single terminal might offer you *Deal or No Deal*, *The Weakest Link*, *Bullseye* and a host of other programmes. 'There were those, and the more generic games as well, the ones not linked to a specific show. We were adding new games every month.'

It wasn't just Gamestec and their competitors who were raking it in. Pub quiz machines attracted dedicated players who made serious pocket money, or in some cases even their living. Mark Bytheway, who won the World Quizzing Championship in 2008, didn't have to touch his salary for six months when he began playing at the Beehive pub in Swindon. In fact he only got into competition quizzing in the first place because one of the pub's regular teams noticed his initials on the machine and asked the landlord who it was. (Bytheway died of cancer in 2010, aged 46 – the trophy for the British Quizzing Championships is named after him.) I'd heard rumours of what you might call 'professional machinists', in particular one who used to stand helping people with answers until the very last minute, at which point he'd walk away and leave them floundering. Then when they got the next question wrong he'd return and win all the money they'd put in. But rumours can often be precisely that – it's only research for this project that brings final confirmation. There's Christian Drummond, for example, who as recently as 2012 told the *Daily Mail* about his £60,000 per year income from the machines. Tax-free to boot, because the money is classified as winnings from gambling. Drummond's university education, luxury holidays and wedding were all financed by his skill – and skill it was, because you need a lot of knowledge to keep on winning. Drummond can name all the characters in Dickens (500 or so), and the number of sets played in every Wimbledon final. That said, the games' patterns helped him out: he noticed that whenever the answer was numerical, the correct one was the middle of the three values. Likewise with dates: it was almost always the earliest.

But don't imagine that money like this comes easily. Drummond estimated he'd visited over 10,000 pubs, usually setting out on trips of a fortnight or so. A typical route was Sheffield to Glasgow, taking in Leeds, Manchester and Newcastle. He sometimes played for ten hours straight. His wife didn't mind his profession, though 'I'm not allowed to play the machines when we are out together.' Only once had he been thrown out of a pub (Harrow on the Hill). On two other occasions barmen turned machines off to stop him winning. (Another machinist was banned from a Bournemouth pub in 2006. 'It is not the first time people have reacted badly,' said Paul Johnson. 'I have been involved in car chases before.') However, Drummond was getting tired of a life that had become 'drudge work . . . I wanted to use my brain to earn money, and I am doing that, but it is not quite how I imagined I would do it . . . I want to get a normal job.'

You can see why quiz machines would do this to you over such a long period. But what I hadn't realised, until Stefan told me, is that Britain as a whole is falling out of love with the things. 'We're way down from the ten thousand peak now,' he says. 'It's about two and a half.'

'Really? I still see people playing them.'

'Yeah, there are some left. But it's a dying market.'

'Why?'

'Partly the decline in pubs generally – lots of them are clos-
ing. But even the ones that are left don't want the terminals.
They don't make enough money from them.' Modern technology marches at such a pace that the must-play device of a few
years ago now lies unwanted in the corner of the pub. People
are too busy playing on their smartphones, not just quiz apps
but a million other games as well, their graphics and all-round
cleverness consigning quiz machines the size of postboxes to
history. Stefan looks wistful as he remembers the good old days,
when the terminals were updated every month. 'Now we get
about four new games a year. If that.'

It would seem, therefore, that I had better get to a pub and
play one of these things while I've still got the chance. Fortunately, the city where I'm going to do it is one of my favourites in
Britain. Stefan looks up a venue, and off I go.

* * *

Surely we can forgive a place changing its name when the
original one began with the syllable 'snot'. In Saxon times that
word meant 'wise', so you can see why a chieftain would take it
as his name. Add on 'inga', meaning 'the people of', and 'ham',
meaning 'homestead', and Snot had his Snotingaham. Gradually
this became Snottingham. Then its residents got tired of the
inevitable jokes, and dropped the first letter.

The A52 that leads me from Gamestec to Nottingham would,
if I drove along it the other way (westwards), take me to Derby.
As a tribute to the man who managed both Nottingham Forest
and Derby County, the road is known as Brian Clough Way. One
of the first things I see after dropping my bag at my hotel (Jo will
join me later, so we can see her cousins who live in the city) is
the statue of Clough on King Street. An appropriate thorough-
fare: yes, I know it ended messily and he didn't get everything
right, but you have to love the man whose quotes, written into
the pavement surrounding the statue, include: 'I wouldn't say I
was the best manager in the business. But I was in the top one.'

And: 'We talk about it for twenty minutes and then we decide I was right.'

The pub I need for the quiz machine is The Roebuck on St James's Street, a cosy alley made all the more inviting because one of its other inhabitants is a chippy displaying one of those orange 'Pukka Pies' signs. These are to my eyes what bells were to the ears of Pavlov's dogs. But duty calls, so into the pub I march. Being a Wetherspoon it has some excellent displays of local history on the walls, including a section about Nottingham's famous Goose Fair. Originally held in the 1500s to trade the birds that came from as far away as Lincolnshire and Norfolk, the annual event morphed into one offering entertainment. Among the attractions in 1819 was a collection of waxworks owned by one Madame Tussaud. A few years later John Boot founded his business on Goose Gate, his son Jesse taking over and selling herbal remedies. These days the UK headquarters of Boots are outside the city centre: the purpose-built estate includes a garden growing some of the plants Jesse used in his original medicines. As a tribute to the street where it all began, the garden is in the shape of a goose's foot.

As if to confirm Stefan's words, there is no one playing the quiz terminal, so I don't have to wait my turn. Feeding 50p into the slot, I peruse the games on offer. 'Pub Quiz' seems the most basic title, so I tap the screen and prepare to do battle. To give everything an old-school feel the questions are displayed in a handwritten font on a blackboard. The first question reads: 'Which of the following is a famous film actress?' We're back to that problem again: computerised quizzes mean multi-choice. The options are 'Anjelica Huston', 'Anjelica Dallas' and 'Anjelica Fort Worth'. Clearly a deliberately easy opener. Next up is: 'Which of the following is NOT a genuine film star? Jude Law, Orloomdo Bland, Hugh Grant.' OK – two easy openers. Third question: 'Charles Dickens did NOT write ...? *Nicholas Nickleby, Oliver Twist, David Chopperfield?*' Right, that's your game, is it? Thankfully the final question in this first round is a proper one: 'To whom does the Mel refer in the TV programme *Today with*

Des and Mel?' I can discount Mel Smith (that would have been a very different show), but am unsure whether it's Melanie Sykes or Melanie Blatt.

Only now does the clock come in. The previous questions were so easy I'd barely registered the time ticking away in the corner of the screen: you're allowed 15 seconds per answer. And somehow the decreasing numbers – we're down to seven already – freeze my brain. I'm like a *Mastermind* contestant stuck in a 'pass' spiral, so fixated on the horror of the situation that I'm unable to think my way out of it. Eventually I stab my finger at the part of the screen saying 'Melanie Sykes'. It's a panic reaction, though I realise even before my flesh leaves the glass that I've panicked correctly: Blatt was the one in All Saints, Sykes was the one who presented with Des O'Connor, the one who came to fame in those Boddington ads. I feel like blurting all this out to the terminal, to try and save face even though I haven't lost any. This is, after all, a computer.

Round two is 'Pop Music'. We start in silly territory again, deciding whether the well-known Welsh band is the OK Furry Animals, the Super Furry Animals or the Crap Furry Animals. Then it's more serious: 'Which of the following were a well-known American recording act famous for their vow of celibacy?' Not being a watcher of the Disney Channel in the mid-Noughties (or indeed now) I have never heard of the Jonas Brothers, and only choose that option because the Bonas Brothers is probably a smutty pun and Zonas doesn't sound like a surname.[5] Then I have to decide whether the recording artist who in December 2006 became a proud father to twin girls was P Diddy, Badly Drawn Boy or Jarvis Cocker. It could have been any of them – my guess of P Diddy is just that, a guess. But it's a lucky one.

Round three is called 'World', and offers the first opportunity of reward: get through this and I'll win £1, putting me 50p to the good. The financial pressure brings the panic flooding back.

---

5 At least one of the brothers now admits to having broken the vow.

I'm asked: 'Which channel flows past the city of Cardiff?' The Discovery Channel can be dismissed, but for some reason, faced with the remaining choices of the Bristol Channel and the Irish Channel – and even though I know Cardiff faces south towards England rather than west towards Ireland – I find myself choosing 'Irish'. It feels foolish even writing that, but as generations of quiz show hosts have said to red-faced punters, it's amazing what pressure can do.

The game allows me to play on: it seems you get a couple of lives. 'Which city,' I'm asked, 'has over 2300 bridges?' The options are Hamburg, Amsterdam and Venice. Torn between the last two, and operating on the principle of 'it probably isn't the one you're immediately drawn to', I choose Venice. Game over. It's Hamburg. Though I don't discover this until later – the machine doesn't give you the right answer. This is always a failing in a quiz. *University Challenge* is the same: if the gong goes in the middle of a question, even when it's become obvious what the question is and your curiosity has been roused, Paxman simply draws proceedings to a close. Similarly, a quiz machine cannot be quizzed – that is, you can't wander up to it between rounds and ask for more information on a particular answer. Only in the later research do I discover that Hamburg's high number of rivers, canals and streams gives it more bridges than any other city in the world.

Time to deposit some more money. A pound this time, enough for two games: I'm showing intent, telling the machine I mean business. First I choose 'Pub Quiz Fortunes'. Again the early questions are farcical ('Anteaters prefer what to eat? Termites. Pizza. Curry.') Then there are some you could be forgiven for not knowing, like: 'Which liqueur was known in the nineteenth century as "the green one"?' I happen to know it's absinthe, but wouldn't have scoffed at anyone choosing the other options (curaçao and amaretto). Finally, in the second round – your progress is displayed by pictures of emptying pint glasses – I come up against: 'Which year of the 1980s did the TV series *Casualty* begin?' The choices are 1987, 1986 and 1988. I choose the last of these. Game over – it was (he writes, having had to look it up) 1986. You're left wondering if the clumsy phrasing of the question was meant to distract you from not caring about the answer.

My second go at 'Pub Quiz Fortunes' follows a similar trajectory. Nemesis finally arrives in the form of 'Who wrote the novel *Typee?*' (it was Herman Melville), though not before I have correctly worked out that the first singer to get five Top Ten hits from one album was neither Elton John nor Elvis Presley but Michael Jackson. I'm pretty sure the album was *Thriller*, but the game doesn't specify US or UK charts, so if it can't be bothered with the question I can't be bothered with the answer.

Despite a growing sense that this terminal's approach to quizzes doesn't fit with mine, the interests of proper research demand that I deposit another pound coin. Choosing 'Robin Hood Quiz Quest' – might as well go with a local connection – I answer the tea named after a British Prime Minister (if you need help choosing between Earl Grey, Darjeeling and Rooibos then perhaps quizzing isn't for you), and the first name of Miss Cartwright, the voice of Bart in *The Simpsons* (Nancy).[6] But I don't know which of Patsy Kensit and Gillian Taylforth was Reg Kray's goddaughter. I think the game thinks that it's Patsy Kensit, despite Kray's own autobiography confirming he was godfather to Kensit's brother rather than her.

Mind you, at least I could work out what was going on in that game: you had to trail around a forest collecting points. The next game, 'World of Sport', defeats me entirely. Admittedly this doesn't take much – ever since childhood, on the rare occasions I have found myself in front of a gaming screen, other people have stood at my shoulder saying 'no, you have to go there/ chase that/attack him'. In this game different-coloured squares containing different numbers and different categories light up in turn, my stabs at the button to try and choose the question

---

6 If parents recognise her and ask her to 'do Bart' for their children Cartwright refuses, as it tends to freak them out.

worth the most points having seemingly no effect whatsoever. Occasionally I get to provide an answer, and eventually come to grief, though not before learning that rugby players' slang for grabbing an opponent's testicles is 'bag snatching'.

'Pop Quiz' comes to a halt with my ignorance as to who released the album *Disintegration* (The Cure), and then 'Hangman Saloon' – which intersperses quiz questions with a game of Hangman – defeats me by asking which country hosted its first Grand Prix in 2011. I pick Qatar, and am left wondering – though not very hard – whether it was Saudi Arabia or India. There are one or two more games I could try, but by now the pattern has become depressingly clear. Quiz machine quizzes waste your time with 'reel the punter in' non-questions. They defeat you with arcane enquiries to which only the Eggheads of this world will know the answers. They incur your ennui with posers to which the only possible reply is 'who cares?' But they do not, at least in my book – and in fairness that might not be the book they want to inhabit – qualify as quizzes at all.

The disappointment doesn't last long, though. There is, after all, Nottingham itself to be explored. And before I leave the city it'll have presented me with another idea for a quiz, a proper one that will tick all the right boxes. None of them multi-choice.

* * *

'Dough Haus.'

I've been looking at the words for about a minute now, trying to deduce how they might correspond to what's going on inside. As the bar's window (in which the words are displayed) is quite high up, so restricting my view of its inside, this isn't easy. The other words are the bar's name – Das Kino – and 'Ping Pong'. Clearly this is one of Nottingham's more self-consciously stylish venues, of a piece with the other establishments in this part of the city centre. We're just round the corner from Paul Smith (of which more later), not to mention Baresca, whose pork bocatas come with guindilla mayonnaise. Even the bouncers are stylish

– all three are dressed head to foot (a distance of no less than six feet for any of them) in black, the only exception the luminous green ID badges strapped to their biceps, and even these are so bright they could be by Versace. Because it's still only seven o'clock, the bouncer nearest me has nothing better to do than answer my question. 'What does "Dough Haus" mean?'

He gives a shrug. 'They sell pizzas. I s'pose it just means that.' The verdict is delivered in a broad Nottingham accent, its tone and content instantly dispelling any fears you may have had that the city was getting above – or, even worse, up – itself. The legendary friendliness is still there, and unlike a lot of places' 'friendliness' it's genuine, a quality expressed for its own sake rather than to be admired, a simple assumption that they're going to like you unless you give them a reason not to. It was something I first noticed when I came to the city to watch cricket matches: unlike the stewards at other grounds, Trent Bridge's didn't make you feel they were doing you a favour by showing you to your seat. The impression only grew stronger after I started coming here with Jo to visit her cousins. It's more – or perhaps I mean less – than friendliness: it's simply a lack of side, a presentation of yourself that's the same to everyone, for the very good reason that there's no other version of yourself to present. Tonight, in fact, I realise that I could never live in Nottingham. I *need* side, deception, facets of personality, both in my behaviour to other people and theirs to me. And I feel guilty about this. I record the fact as a criticism not of Nottingham but of myself.

A tram trundles quietly past as, in Tesco, a young woman leans on the National Lottery ticket stand to write a birthday card, while her friend waits patiently with a bunch of flowers. Round the corner in Pelham Street is the Bodega, whose upcoming gig list includes Sorority Noise, Dilly Dally, Let's Eat Grandma and Tigercub. There are also individual posters for Oscar (colourful coat plus dog), Sunflower Bean (moody poses in front of world map) and Cigarettes After Sex (artful black-and-white shot of a feather). You always look at these posters, the effort and the dreams and the ambition they imply, and know that the bands will almost certainly remain obscure. But there is that 'almost'. Statistically it's highly likely that (depending on your vintage) you once saw a poster for a then unknown Amy Winehouse or Blur or Dire Straits. Just as you may well have been served by a waitress who went on to become a film star: as Marcus's 'they used to work for McDonald's' question shows, we all have to start somewhere. I always imagine a photo – which of course would never have been taken, because in the mid-1980s he was just a London waiter handing over a bill – of someone paying not the slightest bit of attention to Daniel Craig.

The odd person heads into the Bodega for a drink, but it's way too early for the music to start. Instead the bangin' toons come from Formula One, a gym across the street. Because it's on the first floor and Pelham Street is narrow I can't see the class being put through their paces: all that's visible is the instructor's blonde ponytail at the top of her occasional jumps. Heading downhill, I reach Clumber Street. These days it's home to Virgin Media and Santander, but in 1811 the area was full of slums. On 18 October, in one of them, William Abednego Thompson was born. His middle name came from the Book of Daniel, Abednego's colleagues Shadrach and Meshach giving their names to William's co-triplets. The three were the last of 21 children, but it was William who grew up to achieve fame, as one of England's foremost bare-knuckle boxers. His agility in the ring gave him the nickname 'Bendy', which then combined with Abednego to produce 'Bendigo'. Five-figure crowds attended the illegal fights where he taunted his opponents by pulling faces and reciting rhymes about them. Shades of Muhammad Ali, though unlike Bendigo, Ali stopped short of insulting their wives and mothers.

Cited as the first-ever southpaw – he once won a bet by throwing half a house brick over the River Trent with his left hand – Bendigo became All England champion at the age of 28. The bout was held on No Man's Heath in Leicestershire, his opponent James 'Deaf Un' Burke. With the title and £220 (£20,000 today) at stake Burke got hammered, becoming so frustrated at Bendigo's onslaught that in the tenth round he headbutted him, a foul move which meant disqualification. When Thompson got back to Nottingham to meet his fans he was so excited that he somersaulted into the crowd, broke his kneecap and put himself out of action for two years. Later in life he found God, and preached sermons in front of his boxing trophies. 'See them belts?' he would ask. 'See them cups? I used to fight for those, but now I fight for Christ.' Not that his old habits had completely died. When the crowd at one sermon got too noisy, Thompson closed his Bible, looked up and, reminding the Almighty that he had 'devoted my life to Thy service', went on: 'I'll take with Thy kind permission just five minutes off for me sen.' He then jumped over the pulpit and used more than words to establish good order. A Nottingham pub named Bendigo's in his honour survived until the 1990s, when it was forced to close. Due to fighting.

I head to Trinity Square, where four Asian teenagers play table tennis overlooked by the Curious Manor Food and Drink Emporium with its offer of 'Spiffing Cocktails'. I'm more in need of a pint myself, so nip into a pub called Langtry's, whose walls are adorned with not-bad drawings of modern folk heroes. There's one of 'Vivien Standshall': only in Britain could you pay tribute to someone while misspelling both their names. At least the quote that goes with the picture – 'if I had all the money I'd spent on drink, I'd spend it on drink' – is site-appropriate.

Up the road is the Theatre Royal, currently awaiting visits from Ronan Keating and Northern Ballet's *Beauty and the Beast*, but it was the venue on 6 October 1952 for the world premiere of a certain play. As we know from Southampton, George V wasn't averse to tributes to his wife, and nor was Queen Mary herself. So when the BBC offered her a special broadcast of her choice to mark her 80th birthday in 1947, she asked for a new play by Agatha Christie. The novelist duly supplied *Three Blind Mice*. Five years later it transferred to the stage, in an expanded form and under a new title: *The Mousetrap*. Two-thirds of a century later it's still going, complete with a couple of elements from that

first night in Nottingham: the clock above the fireplace in the
main hall, and the radio news bulletin, recorded by comedy actor
and king of the washboard Deryck Guyler. Agatha Christie's
grandson Mathew Prichard continues to enforce the secrecy surrounding the murderer's identity, even forcing Wikipedia to list
the plot spoiler in a separate, clearly headlined section. Cabbies
who drop you off at St Martin's Theatre in London are said to tell
you the ending if you don't give them a tip.[7]

Friday night is beginning to kick off now. A newly qualified
teenage driver in a funky blue VW Polo drops off her parents:
will she return to collect them at eleven, and will they try and
hide how drunk they are? Just north of the city centre, on the
way to Sherwood (the suburb where I'm meeting Jo and the
others), is an Indian restaurant with one dish where 'yoghurt
is added to flavoursome the original rich taste'. Then there's
the Dice Cup, a café where geeky teenagers gather to sip high-
energy drinks and play board games. The shelves offer Warcraft,
Dead of Winter and Beowulf, though Friday nights seem to be
reserved for Magic. A notice explains that Standard entry is £1,
Draft entry £12. On Wednesdays, meanwhile, there is Modern
entry for £5 and Value Draft entry for £9 ('Re-draft rares in prize
phase'). As usual I find a strange delight in *not* understanding
something. Further along there's gaming of a more traditional
sort: Nottingham Bridge Club in their large Victorian house,
its stained-glass windows showing the symbols of the four card
suits.

Finally, occupying a few of the tables outside a large pub, are
Jo, her cousins and their gang. Some of them are quite a bit
older than her, and as grandchildren have begun to feature the
full count is now about 917. Andrew and Chris and I are soon

---

7 Another artistic first for Nottingham was the debut gig by Wings. On 9 February 1972 they
   headed north from London, saw a sign for Ashby-de-la-Zouch and liked the sound of it.
   Finding that the town had no suitable venue, they asked where the nearest university was.
   Elaine Woodhams, the social secretary behind the student union bar, was understand-
   ably sceptical when told Paul McCartney was in the car park asking if he could do a gig
   (especially as it was lunchtime). But venturing outside she found the ex-Beatle 'waving
   out of an old van'.

swapping notes on the Nottingham trivia I've uncovered. The reason Forest wear red, for instance. At their founding meeting in a pub called the Clinton Arms, the committee decided that Forest should honour the Italian nationalist Garibaldi by wearing his traditional colour. Back then (1865) clubs displayed their colours on caps rather than shirts, so a dozen red ones were bought, complete with tassels. By 1886, when Arsenal was founded, shirts had become the thing, and Forest generously donated a set to the London club. Arsenal play in the colour to this day: in the late 1990s, after their French manager Arsène Wenger had signed several of his compatriots, the scoreboard flashed up the message '*Allez les rouges*'.

More ground-breaking redness at Nottingham's university, where the geneticist Don Grierson helped to create tomatoes that would ripen more slowly than usual – purée made from them was the first genetically modified food sold in the UK. Back in 1930 the university (or rather a building that's now part of it) hosted a lecture by Albert Einstein. As soon as he'd finished they painted varnish over the blackboard to preserve his notes – you can see them there to this day. (No such posterity for Einstein's last words: he said them in German, the nurse who was with him was American, so we'll never know what they were.) Finally, on a lower intellectual level, the city gave us Zippy and George from the kids' TV show *Rainbow*. Or rather it gave us their voices, in the form of Nottingham-born actor Roy Skelton. He could even do the pair having an argument. The presenter Geoffrey Hayes remembered: 'It sounded like he'd double-tracked it, as they seemed to be talking over each other. It was a wonderful technique and I don't know how he did it.'

The conversation turns to the subject of quizzes, and Chris asks the question that, in a frankly disgraceful oversight, I haven't yet asked myself: who organised the first-ever pub quiz? Sadly the tradition's precise origins are now lost, though it seems to have started in the north. The first formalised version came in 1976, when Sharon Burns and Tom Porter realised quizzes could help pubs get custom on nights that would otherwise be quiet. They formed a company to cash in on this by organising a quiz league, initially on Sunday nights in Hampshire and Dorset, but eventually growing to incorporate over 10,000 teams. Burns and Porter would post the questions out to the pubs each week, then collate the results into a league table. Such was the venture's popularity that they published books of their quizzes. Needless to say Messrs Amazon were soon commissioned by me to track one of these down.

Chris remembers a quiz he used to attend at the Sherwood Inn in Nottingham. 'One week this bloke came in, with his face buried in a plastic bag. He was breathing in heavily, like he was sniffing glue. We told the landlord, and he threw the guy out, and confiscated the bag as well. When we looked inside it there was a jar of cockles. The lid was still in place, but it was chewed all round the edges.'

All of a sudden Tuesday nights at the Prince of Wales seem rather dull.

* * *

The next morning, before heading back down the motorway to collect our son from my parents, Jo and I savour a couple more heir-free hours. Without meaning to, I stumble across the idea for my next quiz.

We're swanning around Nottingham, ticking off some of the things I didn't have time for last night. The city's arboretum, for instance, which contains a small bell tower commemorating the 59th (2nd Notts) Regiment's role in the Opium Wars of 1857–61. The bell hanging there now is a replica of the one captured by the regiment from a temple in China, though until the 1950s the tower housed the original. In 1863 a local councillor was fined £5 for entering the arboretum carrying a plank with which he wanted to 'try out' the bell. Today's naughtiness is less ambitious – into the concrete of a pathway someone has scratched the phrase 'Fuck Pokemon Go'.

I also visit the first-ever Paul Smith shop, a tiny unit on tiny

Byard Lane. For just £125 you can get a belt in the famous stripes,
the ones which have graced everything from a scarf worn by the
Dalai Lama to a specially commissioned Land Rover Defender.[8]
An assistant asks another customer if he needs any help.

'Just looking,' replies the man.

'It's all the new season stuff now,' continues the assistant.

At which point the man falls victim to Awkwardness in an
Expensive Clothes Shop syndrome. 'Absolutely,' he says. 'It's my
first time in ... So ... Good to know.' After this he knows there's
nothing for it but a speedy exit.

Over at the Council House – a huge, full-on dome-and-pillars
job overlooking the main square – I admire the board giving
the building's history, so old it is itself now part of the history.
(Rather like Isaac Newton's blue plaque on Jermyn Street in
London, which has a panel underneath giving the dates of its
installation and repositioning – a blue plaque with its own blue
plaque.) The Council House was built in the 1920s, its Portland
stone mined from the same quarry that brought you St Paul's
Cathedral. Its bell weighs 10 tons and its E$\flat$ – audible from seven
miles away – is the lowest tone of any bell in Britain. Adminis-
trative staff have now moved to a modern building (though full
council meetings are still held in the chamber here), so much
of the building has been given over to retail units. Jaeger, Patis-
serie Valerie, Oasis and Castle Fine Art occupy the spaces under
the four murals on the inside of the dome. These show scenes
from the city's history. When he painted them, local artist Noel
Denholm Davis used Nottingham people as models. The Robin
Hood scene, for example, includes Notts County goalkeeper
Albert Iremonger as Little John. Iremonger was, at six foot five,
the tallest player in the league.

The Council House is guarded by two stone lions, which have
become famous as meeting places. There's now a Nottingham
magazine called *LeftLion*, and behind the animal in question
lies the building's foundation stone. It was laid, apparently, by

8 Not the one used by Gordon Goody in the Great Train Robbery.

Alderman Herbert Bowles 'on Thursday 17th March 1927'. I like the inclusion of the day. It should happen more often: we always get dates, but rarely days. A quiz question I've used several times is: 'Which day of the week was September 11 2001?' It's not meant to be morbid – instead people seem to enjoy the challenge, piecing together that it was the day they did pilates and that was a Tuesday ... or was it a Wednesday?[9] Yet plaques shun days, even though the fact that something happened on a Thursday is far more important than the fact it happened on 17 March. I even want to know the time of day: you are a very different person at 6 p.m. on Friday from the one you are at 10.30 a.m. on Monday, and this affects the way you do things. It also affects the people watching you. Was Alderman Bowles's audience a late-afternoon one (willing him to get on with the stone-laying so they could get back home for dinner), or a mid-morning one (wanting him to stretch it out so they wouldn't have to go back to the office)?

It's during a mosey round John Lewis that I find my next quiz. Literally: it's in the board games section. Sitting with the Scrabbles and the Monopolies and the Cluedoes is a box whose sides have a brick-wall effect, and whose cover looks like a blackboard chalked with the game's title: 'Pub Quiz'. It contains 1000 questions, with rounds including History, Science, Quotations, Film and so on. The box is sealed, but the cover shows a sample General Knowledge round. 'Prior to the Chelsea Flower Show in 2013,' you read, 'the Royal Horticultural Society lifted its century-old ban on which garden accessory?' A news story stirs from the depths of my memory, but won't quite break the surface, so I have to Google it. As I do the answer to another question: 'How old must an object be for it to be considered an antique by HM Revenue and Customs?' Respectively: gnomes (though one veteran says she regularly broke the ban by hiding her lucky gnome Borage behind the leaves) and 100 years.

I am, as the phrase goes, having this.

---

9 The old 'do you stick with your first answer?' conundrum. In this case you should: it was Tuesday.

* * *

Bethany is the problem.

The two teams have fallen into place: down the left side of the table are Chris, Catherine and Richard, down the right are Jo, Molly and Will. So Bethany, at the far end, facing me (the quizmaster, unable to play), is messing up the numbers. We should have thought of this when we invited them round for slow-cooked lamb followed by *quiz à la pub*. Options include someone sitting out the quiz (never going to happen) and uneven teams based on an assessment of everyone's relative intelligence (a bad idea at the best of times, and certainly after gin, prosecco and red wine). In the end it's Bethany herself who has the bright idea: she'll switch teams halfway through.

Answer sheets are distributed, and we begin with a round of Arts and Culture. An easy starter ('who painted the ceiling of the Sistine Chapel?') yields to a 'sounds difficult until you give it five seconds' thought' question: 'Which sculpture can be found at the top of Corcovado Mountain?' It's Christ the Redeemer (only now do I realise I thought it was at the top of Sugarloaf Mountain). Question six – 'Denise Van Outen, Claire Sweeney and Ashlee Simpson have all played which character from *Chicago*?' – shows this could be a close quiz, as Will and Catherine, on opposing teams, have both seen the musical. This is because they're husband and wife. As are Richard and Molly, and Chris and Bethany. There could be plenty of shared knowledge – and indeed shared gaps in knowledge – spanning the table.

Question seven is: 'In 1979, which art historian and Surveyor of the King's Pictures was exposed as the "fourth man" and a Soviet spy?' While the teams discuss it and scribble their answers, the pedant in me wonders why the question said 'King's' rather than 'Queen's'. But as Blunt – appointed in 1945 under George VI – served as both, and by 1979 was neither (he'd left the position six years earlier), the phrasing seems fair. A related question is whether barristers appointed as QCs under Elizabeth II will become KCs on her death (assuming we get

Charles or William). Sad enough to be fascinated by this, I have for years been asking legal experts about it. None of them seem to know for sure, as it's been so long since the issue arose.[10]

'Do you want me to mark your sheets?' I ask, when the round's over. 'Or are you happy to swap papers?'

Everyone's relaxed about swapping papers: perhaps competitiveness won't be getting out of hand. Will and Catherine both managed to remember that the *Chicago* character was Roxy, so there are no crowing rights there. LHS ('Left Hand Side') score eight, but SS Massive (nothing sinister – most of the members live on Swan Street) bag a perfect ten. The box contains a rather fetching chalkable-and-wipeable scoresheet the size of a blackboard, but to save pinning it to the wall I'm noting the scores on a piece of paper.

We move on to round two. You can pick whichever subject cards you want whenever you want – everyone says they feel like a bit of Film and TV, so off we go. 'Which relatively unknown actress,' I read, 'shot to fame playing scavenger Rey in the 2015 blockbuster *Star Wars: The Force Awakens?*'

Chris, on LHS, clutches his head. 'Argh – I can picture him.'

Bethany, playing for now on SS Massive, laughs at her husband. I repeat the question, and Chris realises his mistake. No one knows the answer, though. There's more joy with subsequent questions. I see them noting down 'Holly Golightly' (Audrey Hepburn's character in *Breakfast at Tiffany's*), 'Stephen Hawking' (portrayal for which Eddie Redmayne won his 2015 Oscar) and 'Shelby' (Cillian Murphy's character in *Peaky Blinders*). Question seven is tricky: 'As of 2016, which actor has played James Bond the most times?' You could query the definitions here: including Sean Connery's unofficial *Never Say Never Again* makes it a tie, but the answer on the other side of the card is 'Roger Moore (seven times)', so the manufacturers of the quiz clearly haven't.

---

10 Enquiries to the Bar Council reveal that even they're not *absolutely* certain, though are pretty sure QCs will become KCs.

Question eight is: 'Brandon Lee, the son of Bruce Lee, was killed during the filming of which 1994 movie?' There's silence on both sides of the table, before Molly gathers in her SS Massive teammates, muttering: 'I know it, I know it.' Despite the good-natured atmosphere so far, Richard now gives his wife a peeved look. 'She knows a lot,' he says to his teammates through gritted teeth. 'It's *really* annoying.' Then, as Molly writes down an answer for her colleagues to consider, he adds: 'We can't lose this quiz. We just *can't*. I'm not putting up with her crowing all weekend.'

The increase in feeling seems to spread. Bethany notices Chris asking me to repeat the question about the TV series *The Man in the High Castle* ('what alternate reality is its central premise?'), then realises from his excitement at remembering the answer that she knows it too. (The premise is that Hitler won the war.) When it comes to the answers, Will and Molly try to hide their disappointment that Jo talked them out of Moore in favour of Connery, but the 'never mind's' don't entirely convince. That said, they soon give way to Molly's shouts of jubilation at hearing her Brandon Lee answer (*The Crow*) was correct. Richard watches her, saying nothing, grinding his teeth again.

This is the halfway point (we've agreed to play four rounds), so Bethany makes to move her chair round to LHS. But Chris, Catherine and Richard reject her, saying they've come this far on their own so they'd rather stick with the teams as they are. 'Fine,' says Bethany, putting her chair back, flicking the Vs at her husband. All of a sudden, one senses, things are mattering rather more than they did.

Both teams scored five on that round, so as we head into Food and Drink SS Massive retain their two-point lead. They're also playing their joker now, edging up the tension another notch. Everyone looks confident about the main flavour of Ouzo (aniseed) and the city which hosts the Oktoberfest beer festival (Munich), but there are puzzled faces at: 'Available in Salzburg, Austria, what are "Mozart Balls"?' And at: 'In 1776, Bekir Effendi invented which popular sweet that is known locally as *lokum*?'

When it comes to marking we'll discover that neither team got the first question – they guessed 'profiteroles' and 'doughnuts', but the answer is 'chocolate sweets'. And while LHS thought Bekir Effendi came up with the humbug, *SS* Massive worked out that his name sounded Turkish, put 'delight' after it and so produced the right answer. That point is the difference between their scores, 8 playing 7. Or rather, because of their joker, 16 playing 7. The overall lead is now 11 points, and Molly is very happy. Richard is not. 'I have to live with this,' he says to his teammates. 'She is going to be a nightmare tomorrow. A *nightmare.*'

All he can do, this being the final round, is hope that LHS's joker works some magic. It might: the round is Sport, on which he and Chris are both strong. Chris is so strong, in fact, that within seconds of me asking the first question – 'What does it signify if a football club has triangular corner flags?' – he and I are agreeing (without mentioning the answer, of course) that we're sure it's a myth.[11] Both teams manage to work out the only female competitor at the 1976 Summer Olympics who didn't have to undergo a gender test (Princess Anne), and both know the youngest footballer to score for England in the 20th century (Michael Owen – Wayne Rooney took his record, but not until 2003). LHS, unlike *SS* Massive, know the first cricketer to score 10,000 Test runs (Sunil Gavaskar), and this together with the corner flags question gives them a two-point advantage in the round. Their 8 gets doubled to 16, giving them an overall score of 36. With 37, therefore, *SS* Massive claim the game's cardboard gold trophy... but no, hang on, both teams are saying they want one more round. Who am I to argue?

We choose History, and cover the first country to give women the vote (New Zealand), the object discovered in Egypt in 1799 which made possible the deciphering of hieroglyphics (the Rosetta Stone) and the London bridge known as the 'Ladies'

---

11 We're right – some clubs have triangles simply because they like them, not because they've won the FA Cup. Though that would be a better reason than *SS* Massive's guess: 'Because they're Muslim.'

Bridge' because it was built largely by women during the Second World War (Waterloo). One question asks: 'In which month in 1969 did man first walk on the moon?' Jo knows the answer, though only because she has the misfortune to live with an Apollo obsessive. As she takes the pen and writes 'in July' I silently wonder if, just for once, she's feeling grateful rather than annoyed about sharing her life with someone who knows that Buzz Aldrin was the first man to have a wee on the moon.

The marking is completed, and the round totals are checked. Advisable, because both markers have been drinking quite heavily, though tricky, because so has everyone else. Eventually we're satisfied that LHS have scored seven, as have SS Massive. This means SS Massive retain their one-point lead, and are tonight's winners. There is much celebration. Molly emits several whooping sounds, then starts chanting 'go Massive, go Massive' while doing that 'stirring a giant Christmas pudding with both hands' dance.

Richard sits opposite, contemplating his wife. Finally he says: 'I hate her.'

And I'm thinking: '*This* is what quizzes are all about. You can keep your inanimate screens on emotionless terminals in the corners of pubs. What machine can interact with its quizzers, engage in banter about their previous answers, tease them that they've seen what another team have put for question six and it's different from their answer, though you're not saying which is right and which is wrong, or indeed whether both are wrong? What machine can deliberately leave a pause before reading out an answer, allowing a bum-clenching silence to descend over the room? What machine, even if it isn't loaded with ridiculously easy questions then ridiculously hard ones, has the slightest feeling for the joy, the despair, the sheer raw emotion that a good quiz can generate?'

We have, then, reached another element of the perfect question: it has to be asked by a human being.

EIGHT

....

Which is the only English city whose official name begins with H?

The year's drawing to a close now, and the project's final quiz is looming. It's a type I haven't been to yet, one I've been meaning to tick off. In the meantime, however, questions for my own quizzes continue to appear. The news is as fertile a source as ever. 'Who, in October 2016, told the US talk show host Stephen Colbert that he was looking forward to working in an office that had corners?' It sounds cryptic but isn't – you'll soon work out that Barack Obama was nearing the end of his eight years in the Oval Office. Then there are the chance references. Someone tells me that the baggy trousers worn by Madness's saxophone player in the video for the song of that name (the one where he's hoisted up by a crane) belonged to Peter Ustinov. Susie read the fact in an interview with Ustinov himself – digging around I find that they weren't his personal trousers, but a pair hired from a theatrical costume suppliers. Exactly what question I will sculpt from this raw material remains to be seen, but simply receiving an email from the sax player in Madness is a joy in itself. Apparently the trousers had a 42-inch waist.

More ammo is unearthed in a charity shop, in the form of 500 Amazing True Facts. These are issued as a pack of cards, but instead of suits and values each card bears ten pieces of trivia. As usual with these things you have to be careful. The 'True' rings warning bells, for a start – if it isn't true it isn't a fact. And indeed there are errors, like the old chestnut about the lowest number to contain an 'a'. I'd used this in several quizzes myself, giving marks for the answer 'one thousand'. Then someone submitted 'one hundred and one', and I realised my fact-checking had gone astray. Even so, the cards yield some delights. For instance, 52 of your 206 bones are in your feet. Vodka is Russian for 'little water'. Liechtenstein didn't give the vote to women until 1984. There are reminders of things I once knew but had forgotten, like LL Cool J standing for 'Ladies Love Cool James', and 111,111,111 times 111,111,111 equalling 12,345,678,987,654,321. There is also that rarest of things, an interesting Apollo fact I hadn't encountered before: Neil Armstrong placed his left foot onto the Moon first. But the best thing to come out of the pack isn't actually in it – it's a reminder of something else. The Eiffel Tower fact isn't that good in itself (the tower took the title of world's tallest building from the Washington Monument): rather, it brings back a curiosity I've been meaning to use as a tiebreaker. 'If all the metal in the tower was melted down and poured into a mould the size of the tower's base, how high would it reach?'[1]

Barney, meanwhile, provides some evidence that quizmastering is hereditary. Once in a while I badger Jo into acting as host of the 'Birthday Game', in which you guess the ages of the celebrities blowing out the candles on a particular day. Jo sits there with the newspaper, calling out the names, and I have to say how old they are. Before you accuse me of being sad, I would say (a) try it yourself and see how much fun it is, (b) I once saw a couple in Caffè Nero doing exactly the same thing and (c) even Jo has been known to get drawn in when I reverse the process and test her. A recent run-out saw me open horribly on Monica Ali and Danny Boyle – I said 42 and 54, they were 49 and 60. I hit a bit of form with Allan Donald and Mark King, my guesses of 49 and 57 each being just a year too low. But the dream of a bullseye proved elusive, even though I thought I had inside

---

1   2.46 inches.

info on the jazz guitarist Martin Taylor. He'd been on a radio programme five days before, and mentioned that he was 60. So I said 61. But he'd obviously meant his 60th was imminent, because that was the answer. As a boy Taylor yearned for the guitar Val Doonican was playing on a particular album cover. One Christmas his mother said: 'You know that album you're always looking at?' Taylor's pulse quickened, only for his mother to present him with an exact copy of Doonican's jumper. She'd knitted it specially.

Now that Barney is seven his reading and maths are good enough for him to host the game, leaving Jo and me free to compete against each other. One Saturday towards the end of October we find ourselves in a Suffolk pub with a newspaper, and Barn in the mood to play Jeremy Paxman. First up is Saffron Burrows, an actress I'm only hazily aware of, so I let Jo go first: in this way you can (to quote golfers who watch their opponent's putt) 'go to school' on the other person's answer. She says 48, I go 51, it's 44 and first blood to Jo. Next up is George Cohen, an England 1966 World Cup winner, so the roles are reversed. My 77 inspires an 80 from Jo – the answer is 77. (Cue the sort of '*yes!*' that only a direct hit produces.) Jo re-establishes her lead through Catherine Deneuve (71 to my 79 – it's 73), but I level again on Plan B (29 to Jo's 26 – it's 33). An unlikely trinity of Jeff Goldblum, Mike Hendrick and Derek Jacobi gives me a clear lead (they're 64, 68 and 78 respectively). The final name is Arsène Wenger. I happen to have read an article about his recent 20th anniversary as Arsenal manager, which included the fact that he was 46 when he took over. So I add the 20 years, and one for today's birthday, producing 67. Barn gives an involuntary smile, which Jo spots. 'Ah, I bet that means Daddy's spot on, doesn't it?'

'Maybe I'm doing it to trick you,' says a quick-thinking Barn. Jo gives him the benefit of the doubt and says 64. The correct answer is 67.

Our son is clearly relishing the sense of power the role gives him, because he also turns quizmaster using an iPad game. Little

Alchemy is designed to teach kids basic scientific principles: by dragging different things on top of each other you see what they produce. Fire and water, for example, produce steam. You can then drag steam over earth and produce 'geyser'. Some of them verge on the historical – ship and iceberg produce *Titanic*. Barn likes testing me by reading out an answer then asking which two elements produced it.

'Honey,' he says.

'Bee,' I reply.

'Yes. And?'

'Flower?'

'Nope.'

'Pollen?'

'No. Think of where bees live.' The game can get slightly quirky like this.

'Oh, OK – hive.'

But Barn's giving another smile. (The answer on the screen, it will transpire, is 'beehive'.) 'Sorry,' he announces. 'I'm going to need you to be *more* precise than that.'

* * *

Pubs were made for October afternoons like this. The clouds are so dark it might as well be night, the rain can't make up its mind whether or not to stop. Dodging into a tiny side street not far from Savile Row, and then into the Windmill, which like a lot of Young's pubs displays pictures of Prince Charles and the Queen Mother pulling pints (the company have close links to 'the Firm'), I shake the raindrops from my coat, arm myself with some bitter and wait for Marcus. We have chosen this venue because it's just round the corner from Buck's, the gentlemen's club whose annual quiz Marcus is hosting tonight. He is not a member, but they like the cut of his quiz, so he keeps getting the gig. Their claret is very good, he reports, and of course being a trivialist he knows that in 1921 the club's barman invented Buck's Fizz.

As it happens I too am quizzing tonight, albeit as a team member rather than a host, so when Marcus arrives we are both in the perfect frame of mind to discuss the perfect question. I kick off by listing the qualities identified by my travels so far – it has to involve teamwork, it has to teach you something and it has to be asked by a human being. Then as fodder for our discussion Marcus tests me on some of the questions he's using tonight.

'Only three English mammals hibernate,' he reads. 'Bats, dormice and what?'

'Hedgehogs?'

'Correct.'

'You should be able to work that out.' I hunch my shoulders. 'You mentally do that, then it sort of comes to you.'

Marcus nods. 'The extraordinary thing is that there are only three. And I've left out the easy one – bats and dormice are harder than hedgehogs.'

Hmm. We're back to the 'Marcus likes an easy question' problem I've noted before. 'You can't have every team getting every question right, can you?'

'No, of course not. But there is a real satisfaction in a question which lots of teams get, yet when you read out the answer they all cheer. That means although they've got it right, they had to work it out and think about it. As a quizmaster you've done your job – you've made them happy.'

On to the next question. 'Cadbury's Heroes may or may not have been named after the David Bowie song. But which chocolate and sweet assortment was definitely named after a play by J. M. Barrie?'

'Quality Street. I only know that because it was in my last book.'

'Mmm. That might have been where I got it from. I can't remember now.' No shame in this. I once failed to get one of Marcus's questions at Highgate even though I knew he'd read the information in one of my books. You can imagine how happy my teammates were at that. Sometimes the traffic has been the other way – I've taken questions from Marcus's books. For instance: 'What does the "T" in Captain James T. Kirk stand for?' (Tiberius.) In the same book (*Set Phasers to Stun*, Marcus's book about *Star Trek*) we learn that the sound of the *Starship Enterprise*'s sliding doors was a recording of an airgun played backwards.

'I didn't know the Bowie thing about Heroes,' I say. 'Is that true? True that it's a possibility, I mean?'

'No. I just made it up.'

'*What?*'

'It's fun, it adds value. It makes you wonder if they *were* named after the song.'

'But you know they weren't.'

'Yes, but...'

'Marcus, you – like I – make a living from writing about this stuff. The urban myth is our enemy. You can't go around putting more of them out there.'

He seems more relaxed about this than I am, but eventually admits that he's annoyed whenever a question he's written turns out to be based on a myth. 'Like that thing about Mel Blanc [the voice of Bugs Bunny] being allergic to carrots. He wasn't allergic to them, he just didn't like them. Also I had a question about South Korea having a foreign secretary called Lee Bum Suck. It wasn't quite right – it turned out to be Be-yom-sock or something. So I've had to stop using it.'

We return to the issue of how difficult a question should be. 'My favourite questions are very easy,' says Marcus, 'but they don't necessarily *sound* that easy. They don't test anything you know – they test what you might know if you knew it, which you don't.' Despite this sounding rather Alice in Wonderland, I know what Marcus means. He illustrates it with a question. 'Which three-word phrase, which could be said to define a certain phlegmatic variety of Britishness, wasn't actually British at all, but was recorded first in the Boston newspaper *The Massachusetts Spy* in 1815?'

You're very unlikely to know that, but most people could, I

think, work their way towards 'stiff upper lip'. 'And even if you didn't get it,' I say, 'you'd still kick yourself when you heard the answer.' Marcus and I agree that this is the corollary of his 'cheer when you've got it right' point.

We talk about themed rounds. I once set one where the answers were the numbers from one to ten, or words that sounded like them. 'What is the sixth word,' ran one question, 'of the second sentence of the twentieth paragraph of the first chapter in the German language version of *Mein Kampf*?' Of course the answer is '*nein*'. But despite repeated reminders, one old couple simply couldn't get it into their heads that there was a hidden connection that would help them spot the answers. They sat there muttering and grumbling about how ridiculous it was, expecting them to know every word in *Mein Kampf*.

'Another aspect,' says Marcus, 'is how well written a question is. How much care has gone into crafting it.' This could sound pretentious, but you know what he means. There's the basic issue of clarity – how many hastily assembled quizzes have you been to where the host has to rephrase a question three times before you can even understand it? There's also the more subtle point, continues Marcus, that some questions just need very precise wording before they'll work. 'I once had one that ran: " 'Never, never criticise Muslims! Only Christians. And Jews, a little bit.' Wise words, from which local radio presenter and former chat show host?" No one got it, or maybe one team. Then the next time I added the word "fictional", and everyone got it: Alan Partridge. That extra word made it work.'

Another one was: 'Torpedo, Pyramid, Perfecto, Presidente, Lonsdale, Robusto and Churchill are all types of what?' I guess cigar, and I'm right. 'But the first time I used that,' says Marcus, 'I didn't include "Churchill" – and hardly anyone got it. Put Churchill in, everyone gets it.'

I report the latest 'word' question I've encountered – 'Aibohphobia is a fear of what?'[2] – and then we move on to the

---

2 Palindromes. Take a closer look at the word.

topic of the 50-50 question, a creature for which both Marcus and I have great fondness. 'Tonight,' he says, 'I'm using an old favourite: "Barry Manilow had a huge hit all over the world with 'I Write the Songs'. Did he write that song?" ' I guess 'yes'. It's 'no'.

We also discuss tiebreakers. Marcus occasionally uses a whole load of them in what he calls an 'eliminator round': 'All ten questions have numerical answers, and I let everyone know that the numbers get bigger as we go on. The answer to question two is higher than the answer to question one, and so on. For instance, early on we'll have: "What is the minimum number of raisins that Elizabeth Hurley deems to constitute a snack?" I read that in an interview with her once. It's six.' When it comes to marking, on each question Marcus eliminates the team furthest from the correct answer. The last team standing at the end is the winner. Obviously this has to be used as a stand-alone round that's separate from the main quiz, rather like the beer round at Highgate. 'I did an eliminator round at a quiz last week, and the team that won it was the team that came last in the quiz itself. That was really satisfying.'

I test Marcus on my '*Titanic* rivets' tiebreaker. He guesses 30 tons: his face when I tell him it's 1200 is a picture. There's also: 'Beethoven made every cup of coffee with exactly the same number of beans – how many?' Marcus guesses 13 – it's 60. The same answer, coincidentally, as one of Marcus's favourite tiebreakers: 'In 1841, Queen Victoria survived an assassination attempt when she was shot by a hunchback. By nightfall of the same day, how many hunchbacks had the Metropolitan Police arrested?'

'Which is better,' I ask, 'a tiebreaker question like that, or a nice, silly "fifty-fifty", or a longer crafted question like the Alan Partridge one?' Even as the words leave my mouth, it's obvious what the answer is: none of them are better than the others. They all, and several other types of question besides, have their place. 'We're really looking for the perfect quiz rather than the perfect question, aren't we?'

Marcus nods. 'Or perhaps the perfect round. I always think

the perfect round is three easy questions, four middling ones and three difficult ones.'

'The crafting applies to the whole round, the whole quiz, as well as to individual questions.'

'Yes. For a start you need a spread of subjects. I have a tendency towards questions about people, where the answer is someone's name, so I have to guard against including too many of those. The same with film questions. And I have to work hard to get some science and nature questions in there, because I don't automatically favour them.'

'It's almost showbusiness, isn't it? Think of your audience, make 'em laugh make 'em cry and all that.'

Marcus nods. 'What is a quiz if it isn't an entertainment? It's nothing. You're not there for any other reason.'

Indeed you are not. But as Marcus and I take our leave of each other, and I head off through the streets of Mayfair, reflecting on our conversation, I think of the reason everyone else is there, the audience rather than the question master himself. I see it now, in a way I hadn't before. It's control. Marcus and I and all the other people who love quizzes, who turn up week after week, are relishing the chance to exercise a bit of control. You can do that with quiz questions. You can't with the big questions: the meaning of life, where am I going, all that sort of stuff. Indeed, as Douglas Adams pointed out in *The Hitchhiker's Guide to the Galaxy*, you can't even know what those questions are – the computer Deep Thought gives the answer to 'Life, the Universe and Everything' as 42, but then reveals that it doesn't know what the question was.

So for most of your life you stumble along, hoping you're getting things vaguely right but never really knowing what the score is. At a quiz, though, you know exactly what the score is. You can identify your triumphs and celebrate them. You can remember your mistakes and learn from them.

At a quiz, just for a few glorious, fleeting moments, it's You 1, Life 0.

* * *

If there was any doubt as to what this place is famous for, it would be removed by the topiary golfer.

He stands in the middle of a mini-roundabout, the latest in a long line of mini-roundabouts whose signs have guided me through the darkness of an early November evening, the road curving through the grounds of the Belfry. I have driven past the turning for the hotel, past the various conference suites, past the headquarters of the Professional Golfers' Association, and now I'm at the mini-roundabout outside the golf shop. Clubs and equipment and golf wear are visible through the shop's doors (now closed for the night), but it's the life-sized golfer that's really got my attention. Standing tall above the other greenery, he's at the top of his swing, a real club threaded through the leaves to complete the picture.

A couple of quizzical references have pointed towards this part of the Midlands earlier in the project, both of them questions I haven't yet had the opportunity to use. 'Adolf Hitler chose the codename "Operation Regenschirm" for the bombing of Birmingham because *Regenschirm* is the German for which item? It was an item Neville Chamberlain – whose home city was Birmingham – carried to his negotations with Hitler.' (Umbrella.) And: 'On the evening of Thursday 4 August 2016, after a day spent commentating on the Edgbaston Test match, Shane Warne persuaded Henry Blofeld to try something for the first time. It caused Blofeld to utter the sentence: "There is a glass inside my glass." What was Blofeld trying?' (A Jägerbomb.) But what has finally brought me here, to the countryside at the fringes of Birmingham, is the one breed of quiz I haven't yet sampled: a corporate quiz.

Returning past the PGA offices (their parking spaces labelled 'Chairman', 'Group Finance Director' and so on, all the way down to 'Executive Assistant to the Chief Executive'), I find the Woodlands Suite. This is the venue for today's national conference of CliniSys, a company who specialise in software that helps the NHS tell what's wrong with you. Bloodhound, for instance, which according to one of the promotional boards lining the foyer area is 'the leading blood-tracking system'. There's also Picsara, which 'supports any medical image from any device from any location'. Various computer screens show 'diagnostic intelligence' information that's way above my pay grade, so instead I head through to the main room. It is huge, 23 tables each awaiting ten people for dinner. At the far end is a screen – too big to stand on a central tripod, it's attached to two vertical towers. To the left of the screen is a lectern, behind which stands a man working on a laptop. His spotlight hasn't yet been turned on so I can't make him out, but as I weave between the tables and get closer I see that it is indeed Jack Waley-Cohen.

Jack's in his late thirties, but his spectacles and five o'clock shadow give him the air of a university student working his way through an essay crisis. How prompt he was with his course work I don't know, but the student bit is definitely true. During his time at Oxford, Jack was President of the Quiz Society. Shortly after leaving, he founded QuizQuizQuiz, the company which has gone on to host over 3000 events, distributing 300,000 answer sheets, 120,000 picture rounds and 75,000 branded pens. The teams tested by Jack and his colleagues have adopted many different names. Old favourites like 'Quizteam Aguilera' keep resurfacing, as do tongue-twisters such as 'Ken Dodd's Dad's Dog's Dead'. Some teams are self-deprecating ('And In Last Place'), while others – this being the corporate world – opt for self-promotion: a team from Deutsche Bank used 'Deutsche Wish Your Girlfriend Was Hot Like Me?' If you're looking for an all-purpose team name to use yourself, one of the best audience reactions Jack ever encountered was to a misheard song lyric: 'Israeli Men, Hallelujah, Israeli Men'.

After finishing his soundcheck and technical run-through, Jack leaves the room so the CliniSys staff can tackle their braised blade of beef and passion fruit cheesecake. We find a quiet spot in a far corner of the building, where we're joined by Benjamin, tonight's scorer. In his early forties, Benjamin spends his days as a composer for musical theatre. 'After hours at the piano, I need to get out and do something different,' he tells me. 'I need some words.'

Sitting down we notice a CliniSys sign, and I mention that QuizQuizQuiz went for the same 'no spaces' approach.

'Yes,' says Jack. 'It's called "Camel Case".' Being slow I take a second to get the reference. (And presumably I should have written it 'CamelCase'.) But Jack knew his name worked in principle when it came to opening the company's bank account. 'The woman said "Name?", I said "QuizQuizQuiz". She said "And what do you do?" I said "Want to take a guess?" She said "Quizzes?"'

Having played to people from virtually every profession under the sun, can Jack sum up how they differ at quizzes? 'Overall I'd say people are people. But there are one or two things we've noticed. Lawyers really do keep a tally of the score all the way through – not just their own but every other team's score as well. And traders are very noisy and competitive. But also they do listen and pay attention, even when it seems like they're not.'

Jack knows what to expect from tonight's crowd because the company is a regular client (twice a year for several years). But new clients are asked to fill out a questionnaire in advance, so QuizQuizQuiz can tailor the evening to their exact requirements. Not that questionnaires are foolproof. 'People often underestimate the number of women for some reason,' says Benjamin. 'They'll put "fifty-fifty", then when you get there it's ninety per cent women.'

'But we've got enough questions in the database that we can change things around at the last minute,' adds Jack. 'You arrive and find that, say, everyone's a lot older than you were expecting – we can cater for that. Our picture rounds, for instance. We've got different ones aimed at different crowds, based on who you could expect them to have heard of.' I'll see these listed on Jack's computer later, with titles like 'International, Young' and 'UK, Mixed-older'. Tonight's picture round, which the teams are already working on over dinner, includes Justin Welby, Otis Redding and Denise Van Outen. The results, as so often, will confound expectations. Most teams will correctly identify Rory Kinnear, but many will think that Christopher Hitchens is the actor Roger Allam. Also on the sheet are some 'what comes next in this sequence' posers. 'Charles III, William V, George VII...' is easy enough (line of succession – it's Charlotte I), but '3128, 3130, 3130, 3131' is more difficult. Until Jack tells you that the commas are there to distract you – it's the number of days in each month, so the answer is '3031'.

This could be seen as tricky, but it certainly doesn't count as a trick question. Like all right-thinking quizmasters, Jack dislikes trick questions. 'There's one on our database [the firm has two full-time writers regularly supplying the hosts with new questions] that goes: "Which 1972 Olympic gold medallist's wedding was watched on TV the next year by a global audience of a hundred million people?" Most teams are very pleased with themselves and put "Princess Anne".' This reminds me of the 'gender test' question in our quiz at home the other week – but unlike then, Princess Anne is the wrong answer. It's actually the man she was marrying, Mark Phillips. 'Most teams let out a groan of disappointment,' says Jack, 'but they enjoy the question. It's not a trick – all the facts are there, and Anne wasn't the gold medallist. He was.'

Similar issues could arise with: 'Which is the only English city whose name begins with the letter H?' If you phrased it like that, it might be seen as unfair. Lots of people put 'Hull', but that city's official name is Kingston upon Hull. The answer is in fact Hereford. 'If you left out the word "official",' says Jack, 'people might say "everyone calls it Hull, that's not fair". I'd rather not have that confusion as a possibility, so I'd make sure I said "official name". Once I've done that, I don't think teams have got any grounds for complaint.'

Reading QuizQuizQuiz's website, I was struck by a reference to jokers. It came in the section on how the firm are happy to adapt at the last minute. 'You need two extra rounds? Fine.

Dinner's early? No problem. You've just told us that there's a whole team of Slovenian tailors? OK, we can make that work... but our quizmasters know that there is a point where it is better to, as politely as possible, say no [because] it's not going to help the quiz run well.' One of the examples they give is someone saying there must be jokers. Does Jack agree that they make a mockery of scoring?

'They just don't tend to fit with the quizzes I like to run,' he replies. 'I do rounds of different lengths, of different paces, where there are different numbers of points on offer. If one team played their joker on a round which scored ten points and another did it on a round of twenty points, it wouldn't be fair. Plus jokers mean you have to tell people what the subject of each round is at the beginning of the evening, and we're often editing the quiz as we go along – dropping a round for time, or because the pace needs picking up or whatever. So they just wouldn't work.' He pauses and smiles at a memory. 'But then sometimes you do a quiz at an expensive prep school where the mothers have spent all week hand-embroidering jokers. Then you make sure you find a way of using them.'

Jack's comments about pacing have reminded me of an interview I once heard with Bob Geldof. As evidence of how useless the Boomtown Rats were in their early gigs he said they started with several fast songs in a row. It's a thought that stays with me as Jack, Benjamin and I move through to the main room, and the evening's entertainment gets under way. Seeing a quiz take place in a setting like this is (to continue the music analogy) like seeing your local pub band playing at the O2. There isn't quite dry ice, but Jack starts by playing some music (a generic, theme-tunish piece), and then, having got everyone's attention, introduces himself. 'It's good to see so many familiar faces from our previous quizzes.' Indicating Benjamin, seated at a table to one side, he adds: 'Those of you who remember our scorer Rosie will notice that she's grown a moustache and put on some weight.'

Within seconds Jack has established just the right mood. The crowd's eyes and ears are telling them this is a big production number – and so it should be, that's what they've paid for – but it's still going to have the familiar, down-to-earth qualities that they love in a quiz. Content that they're in safe hands, they settle down for Round 1. This is titled 'Culture Clash'. The gentle opener asks which piece of modern sculpture, completed in 1998, is sometimes known as 'the Gateshead Flasher'. As 23 teams write down 'the Angel of the North', Jack fades up the music again, much as Goose did in Edinburgh. Only now do I notice that his laptop has a small external unit plugged into one of its ports: it's a round volume control, giving precise and instantaneous control over the level, avoiding the lag that can sometimes occur with keyboards. Jack starts the music before he needs it, fading it up below his words – a radio-presenter trick the listener takes for granted. Only when you hear someone getting it wrong (starting the music clean, at full volume) do you appreciate the skill. Similarly Jack holds the microphone underneath his chin to prevent consonants popping.

'Culture Clash', it becomes clear, is more a general know-ledge round than specifically about the arts. 'Which former MP,' runs one question, 'represented Great Britain in the two hundred metres at the 1964 Olympics?' (Many teams guess Jeffrey Archer – it's actually Menzies Campbell.) 'What is the most visited English-language newspaper website in the world, with over eleven million daily visitors?' (Mail Online.) Even when the question does relate to culture, things can get cryptic. Jack displays an image on the screen, asking which pop band it represents. From left to right we see a rowing oar, a bird, a male figure and several vacuum cleaners underneath a light bulb. The answer, which several teams get but I can't, is 'Oar-kestrel-man-hoovers-in-the-dark'.

Tonight's age mix is everything from twenties to sixties, so it's no surprise that some references escape the younger particip-ants. 'Choppers, who died in 2016 at the age of forty-eight,' for example, 'was the last survivor of the original cast in adverts for which brand?' The legendary PG Tips campaign will only be legendary to those of us who were around to see it. And when the answer to one question is '*Auf Wiedersehen Pet*', it's quicker for a forty-something at one table to take the pen and paper from his younger colleague than to whisper the strange phrase to her.

After the round is finished I tell her (mid-twenties, I'd guess) that she's just made me and her colleague feel old. He agrees, she apologises, and we get into a conversation about how YouTube, Netflix and the like have deprived today's viewers – even the intelligent, culturally aware ones (which this woman clearly is) – of just about everything from before they were born. It's a topic the project has touched on before: the woman in Edinburgh who'd never heard of Kate Bush, for instance. Marcus and I regularly engage in old-man grumbles about how difficult it is to set questions these days, because no one under 30 has heard of anything or anyone.

'When we were young,' says the man, 'there were only three TV channels. So you watched what everyone else was watching.'

'And there were so many repeats from yesteryear,' I add, 'that you also knew what your parents had been watching when *they* were kids.'

The woman is nodding – whenever you have this conversation with youngsters (a word that itself makes me sound like a High Court judge), you realise they're aware of the issue.

'You'll be telling us next,' I continue, 'that you haven't heard of Morecambe and W—' Even as the words leave my mouth I can see the blankness in her eyes, the apologetic look starting to form. 'Morecambe and Wise? *Please* tell me you've heard of Morecambe and Wise?'

She laughs nervously. 'Sorry.'

And although I Google a picture of them on my phone and show it to her, and she says yes, she's seen them before, it's just their names she didn't know, it doesn't matter: a small part of me has died tonight.

At the front Benjamin is marking the first round. He is astonishingly good, ticks appearing down the right-hand side of each

sheet like bullets from a machine gun. (I'm terrible at marking
– a busy night at Highgate freezes my brain to a standstill.) As
Benjamin works his way through the pile he places the highest-
scoring teams to one side.

'That's for me,' explains Jack, 'so I can name-check some of
them. We deliberately don't give a full rundown of the scores
after each round – once a team knows they're lagging behind
they can give up, and sometimes get rowdy. But if you read out
the teams who have done well on a particular round, it makes
them feel good about themselves, helps keep the mood upbeat.
Something simple like that can make a real difference to how
the evening goes.'

Once Benjamin has finished, I compliment him on his speed.
'You're assuming I wasn't just putting down ticks at random,' he
replies. 'Like those people who pretend to do the *Times* crossword on a train, writing in any old words.'

'OK, straight on to round two,' announces Jack. 'And it's what
we call a Five-Four-Three-Two-One round.' Music plays, as does
a quick graphic of each of those numbers appearing and getting
larger until it fills the screen. 'There are just five questions here
– the first one is worth five points, the second one four points
and so on.'

It's a great concept, and works well in keeping the pace up.
The first question is: 'Alongside the UK and the US, which
five other countries are in the G Seven?' (Canada, Germany,
France, Italy and Japan.) For the second question the teams
have to identify four logos. That of Dulux paint, for example,
a figure waving a multicoloured banner (it's surprisingly hard
with the name removed). Question three is a beauty. Jack calls
it 'Crossed Names'. 'For instance, if I asked "which member of
the Beatles starred in *Star Wars*?", you would answer "George
Harrison Ford".' The teams have to identify the singer who met
his wife on a TV reality show and won the first of his eight
Grand Slam singles titles at Wimbledon in 1992... the founder
and lead singer of the band Jesus Loves You who was one of the
founding fathers of the United States... and the film in which

a sexually frustrated suburban father has a midlife crisis and is kept imprisoned in an enchanted palace by a grotesquely cursed prince. The answers are Peter Andre Agassi, Boy George Washington and *American Beauty and the Beast*. Though my mind is still wandering back to George Harrison Ford, and the holiday on which I heard a tennis coach call out to two of the kids he was teaching: 'George! Harrison!' Everyone chuckled, except for a woman who looked confused. 'Oh, I get it,' she said, after a moment. 'It's *Star Wars*, yeah? George Lucas and Harrison Ford?' How can you have heard of George Lucas but not the third most famous Beatle?

Next up is what Jack calls a 'Blitz' round – 25 questions in three minutes, with a further three minutes to hand in your answers. Each question is read out just the once, simultaneously displayed on the screen before making way for the next. Many are simple in themselves, but the relentless pace creates real pressure. Barely have you had time to register which sport Sir Francis Drake was playing when he heard news of the Spanish Armada than you're being asked the colour of the number plates on the back of UK cars. 'Who did David Tennant succeed in the role of Dr Who?' is swiftly followed by 'along with English, what is the other official language of Kenya?' No sooner have you decided on the colour of British passports between 1920 and 1988 than you're being asked for the two cities linked by the M8 motorway. And before you know it Jack is reading the final question – 'Which metal is the only chemical element with a three-letter name in English?' – and that's it. No repeats, just 180 seconds to decipher your scrawled handwriting and work out the answers you're missing.

Incredibly, one team are walking their answer sheet to the front almost before Jack has finished speaking. Even more astonishing, they're sure about 24 of their answers, and know that their guess of French for the Kenyan language is wrong. (They're right – it's Swahili. The other answers, in order, were bowls, yellow, Christopher Eccleston, blue, Glasgow and Edinburgh, tin.) Lots of other teams are almost as quick, and most score almost as highly. Truly the ability of the human brain – or rather ten human brains (gotta love that teamwork) – is astounding. The Blitz format has shown me a new facet of quizzing, a way to reinvigorate it, shake up the genre, challenge the neurons in a different style. It's wonderful to behold. Benjamin, meanwhile, is giving a rueful shake of the head. '*Why* do teams insist on changing names mid-quiz? You have to go back and try to match up the handwriting.' But he gets on with the task. And succeeds.

We're now heading towards the end of the quiz itself, and into the final. This will be contested by five teams. Four of the places have gone to the highest-scoring teams in the rounds so far, but the last place is a wildcard, awarded to the winner of a 'True or False' round. This works by everyone standing up. Jack will then read out a statement – if you think it's true you put your thumb up, if you think it's false you put your thumb down. Only those who get it right can proceed to the next statement: everyone else has to sit down. The last person standing wins the wildcard place for their team.

'David Beckham,' goes the first statement, 'was born in a hospital appropriately named Whipps Cross.' My instant reaction is 'true', but as always with a 50-50 the doubts are there quicker than you can say 'indecision'. Beckham was born in Essex – we all know that – and 99 per cent of me is sure there's a place in Essex called Whipps Cross, and 99 per cent of that 99 per cent is sure that it's famous for a hospital ... but perhaps Jack is toying with us? Perhaps Beckham was born in a different hospital? Thankfully I don't have to put my thumb on the line, but of those who do, the up-thumbers are the winners: Beckham was indeed born in Whipps Cross hospital.[3] Next, Jack states: 'When Robinsons Barley Water was first provided to players at Wimbledon in 1922, it contained one per cent alcohol.' You desperately want this to be true, and it certainly could be. Competitors in the 1908 London Olympic marathon were given champagne,

---

3 As were Graham Gooch, Jonathan Ross and David Bailey.

brandy and beef broth to drink along the way (the last because the games were sponsored by Oxo), though not water, as this was considered unhealthy. And during a 1930s MCC tour of Germany one player got so drunk he tried to start a fight with his own reflection. Sadly, however, the barley water was non-alcoholic.

The room's thinning out now, and to mow down even more people Jack asks whether Chancellor of the Exchequer Philip Hammond is or is not first cousin to the TV presenter Richard Hammond. I'm sure that if this was true I'd have heard about it: my certainty is justified, as it's untrue. Equally I happen to know that the next statement *is* true – novelist Kurt Vonnegut ran the first Saab dealership in the USA. But the next question is more tricky: 'In 1941 the senior German officer serving at Colditz castle was Major English. At the same time the highest-ranking prisoner was Colonel German.' Is Jack messing with us, doing a twist on the old thing about one of Britain's top officers during the *First* World War being French (Sir John French)? No, he isn't – the Colditz thing is entirely true.

There are still some tables with more than one person standing, so Jack reminds them of the simple tactic of showing different answers, unless they're absolutely sure they know it. Then he reads the next statement: 'In France, *beyoncé* (spelled the same way as the name of the singer) is a word to describe the state of griminess around the grouting in bathrooms, as in "damn, the shower is a bit beyoncé", or "*Zut alors! La douche est un peu beyoncée!*" ' Every fibre of my being wants this to be true, but sadly it's false. (Still a great question, though.) There are now only three people standing, all at different tables. And only one of them, asked whether Pope Francis I, the current Pope, used to work as a bouncer at a bar in Buenos Aires, points his thumb upwards. Which, since the statement is true, earns his team a place in the final.

The five contenders take their places at the front of the room. The team names have all been taken from their table number – Five Live, Legs Eleven and so on. (Table 14 have

called themselves 'Cat Horse'.) Sensing that a long day is
drawing to a close and the mood in the room is for a quick
finish, Jack chooses a format that allows just that. He reads out
a series of questions, the first person to shout out the answer
going through to the next round. The last person standing is
eliminated each time. It makes for speedy and exciting quizzing,
especially towards the end when he uses numerical tiebreaker
questions. Each person is allowed to guess in turn, Jack saying
'higher' or 'lower' to guide the next guesser. The total number
of letters in the names of all 51 English cities combined, for
instance. And the percentage of the UK's land area that is taken
up by England.[4] Eventually Five Live come out as winners. Jack
also announces that last place overall went to the hubristically
named Perfect Ten. CliniSys's Matthew Fouracre, who's in
charge of the conference, presents each member of the team
with a wooden spoon.

A short while later, as the Woodlands Suite echoes to the
sounds that follow any good quiz – congratulations, com-
miserations, resentful cries of 'I *told* you it was "Billy Elliot" '
– Matthew tells me that Jack has become a feature of the firm's
conferences. 'We've tried other things,' he says. 'Bands and what
have you. But they've never been as good.'

He looks around the room. 'Everyone loves a good quiz, don't
they?'

* * *

The Christmas lights are twinkling in the shops of Highgate,
and with just a couple of weeks to go until the big day I know
this will be my last Prince of Wales quiz of the year. Oscar, Nick
and Sue are in the chair, a triple act whose questions range from
maths to horse racing via the Bible: 12 per cent of Americans,
apparently, think that Noah's wife was Joan of Arc. Toby and
Martin have to explain the 'ark/Arc' error to me – clearly I'm

---

4 425 and 53 per cent respectively.

having another off-night. After a good start we plummet down the table, and as usual it's someone else's Snowball ticket that gets drawn rather than mine. But there's a brief moment of glory halfway through, when I win us the beer round by being nearest with the tiebreaker. Rather pleasingly it closes a circle from the beginning of all this: we started with Marcus's Tiger Woods question, and tonight's tiebreaker asks for the golfer's current world ranking. As usual with sport, Martin and Toby simply hand the pen and paper to me. Woods has been injured for ages, and even when he has played he's been embarrassingly bad. Remembering something about him possibly slipping out of the top 500 I put 471. Turns out he *has* slipped out – the answer is 652, but our guess is still good enough to bag the £20 bar tab. And with only three of us on the team there's money left over for pork scratchings. Who could ask for more?

At the end of the evening Marcus and I discuss our latest questions. Only two of the teams at his Buck's Club event knew the answer to: 'Jeremy Corbyn once owned a cat named after which Labour Prime Minister?' (Harold Wilson.) I've come up with: 'Which confectionery company was founded by Hans Riegel in Bonn?' (Haribo – the first two letters from each name.) I also pass around the Burns and Porter book, the firm that first organised quiz leagues in the 1970s. A consensus soon develops that the questions have dated badly, concerned as they are with TV programmes and news events of the time. But I don't really mind. As with all books of that era there's a page at the back offering other titles from the same publisher. There are boxes you can tick, and the phrase 'postal order' is used. Still produces a tingle after all these years.

And that's it. The evening's over, and so is the project. I walk round the corner and wait for the bus. All alone in the frosty stillness of a London night, I think about Chris, how the pubs of this area will never again echo to his laughter, his questions, his opinions on Pink Floyd. And then, in almost the same instant, I have another thought, one about life's beginning rather than its end. When Jo was pregnant with Barney she had to have an amniocentesis, the procedure in which fluid is extracted from the womb for testing. It's done with a syringe whose very thin needle is inserted through the abdomen. The doctor monitored Barney's movements on the ultrasound scanner: seeing he'd gone over to one side of the womb, she quickly inserted the needle into the other side. It was all over in a couple of seconds.

'Do you think the foetus is aware of the needle going in?' I asked.

'Oh yes,' said the doctor cheerfully. 'Sometimes they try and grab it.'

'*What*?! That must be horrific.'

'Oh no, it's fine, as long as they grab the shaft rather than the point. It just slips out of their hand.'

I've never forgotten that. From the very moment we become conscious, we want answers. Even before we leave the womb, if something new appears in front of us we want to know all about it. 'What's that?' 'Why does this happen?' 'How does that work?' And the trait never leaves us. Forty-odd years after I was in the womb myself, here I am, just finished a quiz, looking forward to the next one. Each question is a mini-dose of curiosity, the cure applied a few minutes later when the answers are read out. All over Britain I've seen that same itch being scratched, from Edinburgh to Oxford, Nottingham to London. By people seeking glory on the radio, raising money for charity or simply wanting a good night out down the pub. Quizzes are an expression of a fundamental truth about the human condition: we love learning. In all of us there burns the desire for a challenge, the simple joy of discovery. It's the buzz you get from looking at a blank answer sheet and hearing someone say 'round one, question one'. It's the excitement of knowing an answer. The excitement of not knowing an answer.

And you know the *real* joy? This thing called the quiz is going to see me out. It'll be there until the end, as long as I have the strength to order a pint and lift a pen. Because its raw material – the events that form the questions – will carry on happening. Sports stars will have affairs, actors will be nominated for Oscars, company names will be formed from the initials of their founders. As long as human beings do interesting and memorable things, other human beings will incorporate them into quizzes.

About that, as they say, there can be no question.

ACKNOWLEDGEMENTS

· · · · · · ·

Thanks...

...for allowing me to lurk at their quizzes: Patrick Kidd, Matt Chorley, Rob Hutton, Chris Hope, Andrew Wildgoose, Oli Parker, Callum Manson, Jane Allen, Chris Jones, Kevin Ashman, Paul Bajoria, Ian Woolley, Alice Brown, Stefan Podolanski, Jack Waley-Cohen, Benjamin Till, Lesley-Anne Brewis and Matthew Fouracre.

...for peerless education in the art of the quiz: everyone at the Prince of Wales, everyone at the Ram, everyone at QI and everyone at Blackwell's in Holborn.

...for expert help on specific queries: Emily Brand, Susie Dent, Susie Dowdall, Mark Ellen, Chris Fickling, Joe Mckay, Harry Mount, Jenny Parkerson, Simon Roberts, Lee Thompson and James Walton.

...for generous help with logistics: Damien Henderson at Virgin Trains, Anwen Dobson at the Caledonian Hotel in Edinburgh and Talking Tables.

...for academic rigour: Will and Catherine Bishop, Chris and Bethany Philbedge and Richard and Molly Plant.

... for publishing expertise delivered with wit and style: Alan Samson, Lucinda McNeile, Simon Wright, Kate Wright-Morris and Steve Marking.

... for superlative agenting: Charlie Viney.

... for everything: Jo and Barney.

INDEX

· · · · · · ·